The Muslim Creed

THE MUSLIM CREED

A Contemporary Theological Study

Amjad M. Hussain

THE ISLAMIC TEXTS SOCIETY

This first edition published 2016 by
THE ISLAMIC TEXTS SOCIETY
MILLER'S HOUSE
KINGS MILL LANE
GREAT SHELFORD
CAMBRIDGE CB22 5EN, UK.

British Library Cataloguing-in-Publication Data.
A catalogue record for this book is
available from the British Library.

ISBN: 978 1903682 94 4 cloth
ISBN: 978 1903682 95 1 paper

Front cover image: A *shamsa*, or 'little sun', from a Persian translation of *Annals of the Apostles and Kings* by Tabari (c. 839–923), Persian School (15th century),
© The Trustees of the Chester Beatty Library, Dublin / Bridgeman Images.

CONTENTS

DEDICATION

Bism Allāh al-Raḥmān al-Raḥīm

I dedicate this book to my late mother, Abidah Hussain, and my late sister, Shabnum Maryam Bi Hussain (may God Most High have mercy upon them both).

ACKNOWLEDGEMENTS

First and foremost, *al-ḥamd li-Llāh*, all praise and gratitude belong to God Most High, Who alone made it possible for me to complete this book. The Prophet Muḥammad (may God bless him and grant him peace) is reported to have said: 'Whoever does not thank people has not thanked God, Mighty and Glorious is He!' (*Musnad Aḥmad*, *Sunan al-Tirmidhī*).

I would like to express my gratitude to the many people who saw me through the writing of this book; especially my dear friend, Dr Mosa al-Blezi, who discussed and offered many invaluable insights on the topics found in this work. I also wish to thank my students at the Muslim College in London, who were very generous with their feedback. While I was teaching them about theology, they also helped me to learn in so many ways. I would like to express my thanks to my dear friend, Greg Barker, for reading through the draft of my first chapter and to Phoebe Luckyn-Malone for editing the manuscript. In addition, I am also indebted to my colleagues at the Marmara University Faculty of Theology for opening my eyes to new avenues of research. Furthermore, I would like to thank my brother Khalid M. Hussain and express my great appreciation to my wife, Shaheen Kausar, for her continued support and inspiration. Finally, my thanks go to the Islamic Texts Society for enabling me to publish this book. And last but not least, I beg the forgiveness of all those who have been with me over the course of the years and whose names I have failed to mention.

PART I
INTRODUCTION

Chapter One

ISLAMIC CREED AND THEOLOGY

What Is This Book About?

Currently, there are many fine volumes that introduce the reader to the ritual and legal aspects of Islam.[1] However, it is difficult to find any introductory book on the Islamic concepts of belief and faith. This may be due to fact that most Muslim scholars agree that Islam is predominantly a practical religion whose goal is to respond to God's call through correct conduct and good deeds. Historically, the religious law of Islam (the *Sharīʿa*),[2] or, more accurately, Islamic jurisprudence (*fiqh*),[3] has been the focus of Muslim scholarship rather than theology (*kalām*). This is because the need for Islamic legal opinions to guide

1 See, for example, William Shepard's *Introducing Islam*, 2nd ed., London and New York: Routledge, 2014 and Ruqaiyyah Waris Maqsood's *Teach Yourself Islam*, 3rd ed., Chicago: McGraw-Hill, 2006.

2 *Sharīʿa* is a far broader concept than law as it is generally perceived in the English language, since it includes not only penal, state, inheritance, commercial and family law, but also covers doctrines, manners and ethics, rituals and worship; each of these aspects has an impact in this world as well in the next world. Thus, *Sharīʿa* is of paramount importance for both the physical and the metaphysical worlds.

3 The term *fiqh* literally means 'understanding', and in the early period of Islam meant understanding or knowledge of all aspects of Islam. As late as the period of Abū Ḥanīfa (d. 150/767), the great jurist used the term *fiqh* to designate the tenets of faith in his book *al-Fiqh al-akbar* (The Greater Understanding). As Imran Nyazee has suggested, this implies that the term *al-fiqh al-aṣghar* was used to signify the jurisprudential aspect of the *Sharīʿa*, such as the rights and obligatory acts pertaining to purity, worship and ritual, family, inheritance, commercial and penal laws. Later on in Muslim history, the term *fiqh* was restricted to only the corpus of law; in other words, jurisprudence. For further details, please see Imran Nyazee, *Theories of Islamic Law*, Islamabad: Islamic Research Institute, 1991, pp. 20–26.

Muslim behaviour in all aspects of a person's life has largely superseded the need for a theoretical study of the Muslim belief system. However, although belief may appear peripheral in Muslim intellectual history in comparison to Islamic jurisprudence, it nevertheless constitutes the essential basis of all Islamic thought.

What then are the central beliefs that underpin all of the different dimensions of Islam? As this book will explain, the Muslim creed (*ʿaqīda*) consists of six articles of faith. They are the belief in God, His angels, His scriptures, His messengers, the Hereafter and the divine decree. This book is intended to introduce Muslim and non-Muslim readers alike to the articles of faith, and to survey the most important debates concerning them in Islamic theology, past and present. These key debates exemplify the range of opinions held by theologians over the centuries and demonstrate the unity as well as the diversity found within Islamic theology. Moreover, the present study is not only a concise introduction to what Muslims believe and practise, it also identifies the challenges facing Muslim beliefs today and explains why Islamic theology is so well placed to answer them.

Islam has two major denominations today and their adherents are referred to as Sunnis and Shiʿis, respectively. According to the Pew Research Center estimates in 2012, Sunnis represent 87–90% of the 1.6 billion Muslims living worldwide, whereas Shiʿis make up 10–13% of that total number.[1] The focus of this book is the creed and theology of Sunni Islam; however, it is safe to say that many Shiʿis share the same basic creed with Sunni Muslims (with the exception of some important differences which will be discussed later on in more detail). It should also be said that, although this book has been written in line with the standards of academic scholarship, it is sympathetic towards Muslim belief in the twenty-first century and is intended to be a response to inaccurate assumptions about Islam in the western Judeo-Christian milieu.

1 See the Pew Research Center's report, 'The World's Muslims: Unity and Diversity', August 9, 2012, http://www.pewforum.org/2012/08/09/the-worlds-muslims-unity-and-diversity/executive-summary/, accessed 17 May 2014.

Islam and the Six Articles of Faith

While Islam may be considered by many non-Muslims to be a young religion originating in seventh-century Mecca in the Arabian Peninsula, Muslims themselves believe it to be the continuation of a universal primordial religion. In other words, for them, Islam is seen not as a religion that began with the revelation of the Qur'ān to the Prophet Muḥammad (may God bless him and grant him peace),[1] but rather as the last in a series of revealed forms of faith that began with the very first human beings (Adam and Eve) and has continued over time under various names.

In Arabic, the word *islām* derives from the consonantal root that consists of the three letters *s-l-m* and means both 'peace' and 'submission to the One God'. Muslim theologians have long noted the significance of this double meaning: specifically, when one submits to God, one finds peace. The term *muslim* is also derived from the same root as *islām* and signifies 'the person who submits to the One God'. There are two primary sources in Islam that guide Muslims in their quest for peace through submission. The first is the Qur'ān, which is recognised by Muslims to be the literal word of God. The second is the *Sunna* ('way of acting' or 'custom') of the Prophet Muḥammad, which is preserved in the *Ḥadīth* literature that records reports of the Prophet's words and deeds.

The religion of Islam may broadly be divided into three aspects: belief, practice and spirituality. This is the division between *īmān* (faith), *islām* (submission through actions)[2] and *iḥsān* (good conduct). In a very basic way it may be said that *īmān* deals with what Muslims believe, *islām* with what Muslims do and *iḥsān* with spiritual awareness of the Divine or excellence of conduct. These three terms are

1 The Arabic phrase is *ṣallā Allāh ʿalayhi wa-sallam*. In the Qur'ān, Muslims are asked to confer peace and blessings upon the Prophet whenever his name is mentioned (see Q.XXXIII.56).

2 It is important to note here that the word *Islam* is used to describe the individual Muslim's response to God, as well as being the name of the religion itself.

never seen as entirely distinct from each other and their interrelationship is indicated in the Qur'ānic phrase, 'those who believe and do good deeds', which is often used to refer to believers. Muslim theologians have also continuously highlighted how the three terms are interrelated.

It is argued that the three terms are lexically different, but in legalistic terms *īmān* cannot be distinct from *islām* because they are inseparable; just like the inside and outside of a single object. One *ḥadīth* that is often quoted to explain this example is, 'Beware! There is a piece of flesh in the body; if it becomes good (reformed), the whole body becomes good but if it gets spoilt, the whole body gets spoilt and that is the heart.'[1] This has been interpreted to mean that the body is the *islām* aspect and the heart represents the *īmān* aspect. The third aspect, *iḥsān* is also closely connected to the other two parts as the spiritual feature: it brings the additional element of continuous awareness of God's presence to the Muslim's faith and practice.

A constructive way to elucidate the relationship between the practices required of all Muslims (*islām*), the six articles of faith (*īmān*) and spiritual awareness of the Divine (*iḥsān*) is to turn to the famous *Ḥadīth Jibrīl*, the Tradition of Gabriel. It is narrated that one day the Angel Gabriel appeared at a gathering attended by the Prophet Muḥammad disguised as a man with a handsome face and black hair, who wore a white robe. This visitor asked the Prophet to inform him about *islām*. The Prophet replied that *islām* is the declaration of faith (*shahāda*), meaning, bearing witness that there is no deity but God and that Muḥammad is his Messenger; performing the five daily prayers (*ṣalāt*); paying charity (*zakāt*); observing the Ramaḍān fast (*ṣawm*) and making the pilgrimage to Mecca (*ḥajj*). These five deeds are known as the five pillars of Islam.[2] Gabriel affirmed that his answer was correct. Gabriel then asked the Prophet to tell him about faith (*īmān*).

1 Bukhārī, *Ṣaḥīḥ*, II.45, http://sunnah.com/bukhari/2/45, accessed 22 February 2016. 'Allāh' has been changed to 'God' in all *ḥadīth* quotations for the sake of consistency.

2 The five pillars of Islam are religious deeds that are obligatory for all Muslims.

The Prophet answered that faith is to believe in God, His angels, His Books, His prophets, the Day of Judgement[1] and the divine decree, both the good of it and the evil of it. Once again, Gabriel affirmed that the Prophet's answer was correct. Then followed the third question, in which Gabriel asked the Prophet about *iḥsān*. The Prophet replied, 'That you worship God as if you are seeing Him, for though you do not see Him, He, verily, sees you.'[2] After that, the Angel Gabriel departed, and the Prophet informed his Companions that Gabriel had come to teach them their religion.

Muslims are expected to know that the three 'I's of *islām*, *īmān* and *iḥsān* are the three core aspects of their religion that work together virtually as one, and they are also expected to know the articles of faith, or 'creed' (*ʿaqīda*, pl. *ʿaqā'id*). Although the articles of faith were not set down in any authoritative document during the Prophet's lifetime, they were all encapsulated in the Qur'ān and the *Ḥadīth*. For instance, as mentioned already, the *ḥadīth* of Gabriel reports Muḥammad as saying, 'That you affirm your faith in God, in His angels, in His Books, in His Apostles, in the Day of Judgment, and you affirm your faith in the Divine Decree [both the good of it and the evil of it].'[3] In the Qur'ān, the first five articles of faith are mentioned explicitly: '[I]t is righteousness—to believe in God and the Last Day, and the Angels, and the Book, and the Messengers.'[4] In

1 Different names are given to this article of faith. In addition to the Day of Judgement, another version of the same *ḥadīth* refers to the Resurrection; see, for example, Bukhārī, *Ṣaḥīḥ*, LXV.4777, http://sunnah.com/urn/44550 and Muslim, *Ṣaḥīḥ*, I.1, http://sunnah.com/muslim/1/1. Two alternatives are found in the Creed of Imam al-Ṭaḥāwī: the Last Day and the resurrection after death. See Abū Jaʿfar al-Ṭaḥāwī, *The Creed of Imam al-Ṭaḥāwī*, New York: Zaytuna Institute, 2007, pp. 66–67 (article 84). In the present book, all of these terms are utilised to refer to this article of faith.

2 Muslim, *Ṣaḥīḥ*, I.1, http://sunnah.com/muslim/1/1.

3 Ibid.

4 Q.II.177. All English translations of the Qur'ān are from Yusuf Ali, *The Translation of the Holy Qur'an*, USA: Amanah Publishers, 2005. This translation's archaic capitalization and punctuation have been modified to match modern conventions. 'Allah' has also been changed to 'God' in all quotations.

another verse of the Qur'ān, four articles are mentioned sequentially: 'The Messenger believeth in what hath been revealed to him from his Lord, as do the men of faith. Each one (of them) believeth in God, His angels, His books, and His messengers.'[1] As for the last article of faith, the divine decree is described in the Qur'ān as follows: 'Say: "Nothing will happen to us except what God has decreed for us: He is our protector," and on God let the believers put their trust.'[2]

In time, scholarship on the articles of faith proliferated and became traditionally divided into three categories in Islamic theology. The first, *tawḥīd* (meaning the oneness and uniqueness of God), concerns the first article of faith—belief in God—and the last—the divine decree. The second category, *risāla* or *nubuwwa* (meaning the message or prophecy), consists of three articles of faith: believing in the angels, believing in the prophets (also called messengers) and believing in the revealed scriptures of God. The third and last category—variously referred to as *Ākhira* (the Hereafter), *Qiyāma* (the Resurrection) or *Maʿād* (the Return)—includes the belief in Paradise, Hell and Judgement Day.

As this brief overview of the articles of faith has indicated, there are substantial differences between the concept of faith in Islam and other Abrahamic religions.[3] For instance in the Christian scriptures, faith is described as the assurance of things hoped for and the conviction of things not seen.[4] According to the modern theologian Alister McGrath, faith in Christianity highlights the idea of trusting in God.[5] In the past, Martin Luther (d. 1546) described faith as trust-

1 Q.II.285.

2 Q.IX.51.

3 As the present work is published in English and many of its readers will reside in the UK and North America, Christianity will be the frame of reference for its discussion.

4 See Jaroslav Pelikan, 'Faith', in Lindsay Jones, ed., *Encyclopedia of Religion*, 2nd edition, Detroit: Macmillan Reference, 2005, vol. v, pp. 2954–59.

5 Alister E. McGrath, *Theology: The Basics*, Oxford: Wiley-Blackwell, 2012, pp. 1–17.

ing God, who makes promises and can be relied upon; while John Calvin (d. 1564) described it as a steady and certain knowledge of divine benevolence towards creation. This differs from the Islamic understanding of faith, which deems it to be a positive response to what God has clearly manifested to humanity. Yet much of the original Christian understanding of faith was the same: a response to revelation by trusting in God; it has only been more recently that it has become popular for Christians to interpret faith as being something outside of knowledge.[1]

For Muslim theologians, the concept of faith is inextricably linked to knowledge, which itself is specifically linked to revelation. They argue that God's revelation—both in the form of revealed scripture and His creation—contains clear signs that immediately lead to unambiguous knowledge of His existence. Therefore, in the Islamic world view there is no 'leap of faith' as there is in Christianity. Instead, the Muslim believer is a witness of facts as told by the One who knows what is true and false. As Wilfred Cantwell Smith eloquently pointed out three decades ago, 'For many Westerners, including Christians, faith has come to be thought of as having to do with something less than knowing, so that that to which it is oriented is 'taken of faith' or is 'believed' (and will be *known*, perhaps, only beyond the grave); hence also, 'the leap of faith'. To have faith is to believe, not yet to know. For Muslims, on the other hand, faith is on the other side of knowledge; not on this side of it.'[2] Thus, faith in Islam does not mean that Muslims are affirming their beliefs but rather they are bearing witness, or even recognising facts, after having received knowledge (*maʿrifa*). According to Smith, a Muslim regards the contents of his creed as 'facts, not theories, as realities in the universe not beliefs in his mind.'[3]

1 Ibid.

2 Wilfred Cantwell Smith, *On Understanding Islam: Selected Studies*, Berlin: Walter de Gruyter, 1983, p. 153.

3 Ibid., p. 126.

Because of this, Muslim theologians have defined faith as assent or acceptance (*īmān al-taṣdīq*). As a term, *taṣdīq* was widely used by Muslim logicians to describe an assent based on intellectual judgement.[1] The theologians in turn transformed this idea into *īmān al-taṣdīq*, which was not seen merely as an acknowledgement of the truth but also its pronouncement by the heart, and, finally, its actualisation in one's own life.[2] Faith in Islam is therefore an unshakeable conviction based upon divine revealed knowledge, and faith is the means by which the believer ascends to actualisation. Faith is the recognition of divine truth at a personal level, it is 'an inner appropriation and an outward implementation of the truth', writes Wilfred Cantwell Smith. 'Faith is the ability to trust and to act in terms of what one knows to be true.'[3] Therefore, faith is seen as more than knowledge. For example, the scholar Saʿd al-Dīn Masʿūd b.ʿ Umar al-Taftāzānī (d. 792/1390)[4] recognised it as positive knowledge acquired by free will.[5] Likewise, Muṣliḥ al-Dīn Muṣṭafā al-Kastalī (d. 900/1495) argued that faith is 'a yielding to what is known and a letting oneself be led by it, and the soul's being quiet and at peace with it and its accepting it, setting aside recalcitrance and stubbornness, and constructing one's actions in accordance with it.'[6]

Perhaps as a consequence, there is overwhelming agreement amongst Muslims regarding their belief and conviction in the One God, and with regards to their belief in the other core tenets. This is demonstrated by a recent survey conducted by the Pew Research

1 Cafer S. Yaran, *Understanding Islam*, Edinburgh: Dunedin Academic Press, 2007, p. 22.

2 Abū Ḥāmid al-Ghazālī, *A Return to Purity in Creed*, Philadelphia: Lamp Post Productions, 2008, pp. 30–33.

3 Smith, *On Understanding Islam*, p. 151.

4 Pre-modern dates in this book are presented according to the Islamic calendar (AH) and the Common Era (CE).

5 See Toshihiko Izutsu, *The Concept of Belief in Islamic Theology*, New York: Arno Press, 1980, p. 172.

6 Quoted by Wilfred Cantwell Smith, 'Faith as Tasdiq', in Parwiz Morewedge, ed., *Islamic Philosophical Theology*, Albany: State University of New York Press, 1979, p. 112.

Center's Forum on Religion and Public Life. This survey involved more than 38,000 face-to-face interviews with Muslims in over eighty languages across six regions of the world: the Middle East and North Africa, sub-Saharan Africa, South Asia, Southeast Asia, Central Asia and Southern and Eastern Europe. Interviewees were asked if they believed in the one God, in His Prophet Muḥammad, in Heaven, in angels and in predestination or fate. The survey found that there was nearly unanimous belief in the one God and in Muḥammad's prophecy in most of the thirty-nine countries surveyed. Nine in ten of the Muslims interviewed affirmed the existence of angels and broadly embraced all of the other main articles of faith that they were asked about.[1] Similar questions posed to American Muslims also reveal a universal belief in the core tenets of Islam.[2] Muslim theologians have argued that the reason for Muslims holding on to these core tenets so firmly is because they are all mentioned in abundance in the Qur'ān and *Ḥadīth*, and because they are so intricately and finely correlated.

What Is Islamic Theology?

So, is there an Islamic theology or do Muslims simply adhere to a creed (*ʿaqīda*) in a manner that precludes discussion? The simple answer is that the situation changed over time. At its inception, there was no place for theology in Islam; the Prophet Muḥammad was a messenger, not a theologian. As Hamza Yusuf explains, 'The first generation of Muslims, who took directly from the Prophet (may God bless him and grant him peace), did not engage in debates about Islam's essential creedal formula. It was uttered in their language, and its inherent theology was grasped more intuitively than discursively.'[3] Nonetheless, the precedent of speaking about God and His relation to creation had been set down in the Islamic scriptures: the Qur'ān and *Ḥadīth*.

1 Pew Research Center report, 'The World's Muslims.'

2 See ibid., 'Appendix A: U.S. Muslims: Beliefs and Practices in a Global Context.'

3 Hamza Yusuf, introduction to *The Creed of Imam al-Ṭaḥāwī*, p. 15.

Over time, the need arose to explain the articles of faith and God's relationship to creation. This need became especially acute in the years following the Prophet's death, when a series of leadership disputes raised fundamental questions about faith, fate and the value of good works. Another factor that contributed to the rise of theology was the increased contact between Muslims and the adherents of other faiths, including Jews, Christians, Buddhists, Hindus and Zoroastrians, due to the rapidly expanding Islamic conquests in the first century of Islam. Many of these non-Muslims converted to Islam and asked questions from the perspective of their former faiths, such as the status of prior scriptures and prophets.

In response to these questions concerning the core beliefs of Islam, a rudimentary network of scholars devoted themselves to answering them. This marked the beginning of a systematic study of faith that eventually gave rise to the highly sophisticated discipline of theology:

> In the same way that jurisprudence (*fiqh*), Qur'ānic exegesis (*tafsīr*), prophetic traditions (*ḥadīth*), history (*sīra*), grammar and the study of language (*ʿarabiyya*) emerged as autonomous disciplines within the classical Islamic tradition, *ʿilm al-kalām* (the science of dialectics) carved out its own smaller niche among the Islamic traditional sciences. *Kalām* had acquired two interrelated senses: first, in its wider generic sense *kalām* provided a platform for the rational synthesis of the panoply of religious dogmas and was viewed as being a form of scholastic theology, which was also defined under the rubric *uṣūl al-dīn* (the roots of faith); while, in a more confined sense, it was used to connote a sophisticated dialectical technique based on a form of dialogue that was

> employed by scholars engaged in theological discussions. Despite the early historical roots of this technique within the Islamic tradition, the broader meaning of the term prevailed with *kalām* becoming synonymous with the discipline of theology.[1]

By the seventh century of Islam, the scholar ʿUbayd Allāh b. Masʿūd al-Maḥbūbī Ṣadr al-Sharīʿa (d. 747/1346) defined knowledge within Islam as being made up of three things: knowledge of the tenets of faith (*īmān*), knowledge of ethics and mysticism (*taṣawwuf*, 'Sufism') and knowledge pertaining to acts (*fiqh*, 'jurisprudence').[2] What this suggests is that by that point in time, knowledge of the tenets of faith (and by implication, theology) had become central to Islamic scholarship and society.

It is important to appreciate that when approaching Islamic intellectual history from a Christian perspective, it is possible that *ʿilm al-kalām* (dogmatic or scholastic theology), *falsafa* (philosophy) and *taṣawwuf* (Sufism) could be confused with one another. This is because the subject matter covered by Christian theology is scattered across all three of these sciences in Islam. For instance, Sufis sought 'access to the highest realms of the life of the spirit' and wrote about their mystical experiences, philosophers speculated about metaphysical reality and theologians defined and defended the faith.[3] It is also true that the three disciplines of theology, law and Sufism 'were regularly reintegrated and seldom dangerously divorced', as Tim Winter points out.[4] And occasionally, there were great Muslim thinkers who

1 Mustafa Shah, 'Trajectories in the Development of Islamic Theological Thought: the Synthesis of Kalam', *Religion Compass*, vol. 1, no. 4, 2007, pp. 430–454.

2 Cited by Imran Nyazee, *Theories of Islamic Law*, Islamabad: Islamic Research Institute, 1991, p. 21.

3 S. H. Nasr, *Islamic Spirituality: Manifestations*, New York: SCM Press, 1991, p. 395.

4 T. J. Winter, ed., *The Cambridge Companion to Classical Islamic Theology*, Cambridge: Cambridge Press, 2008, p. 10.

succeeded in combining these sciences, such as Abū Ḥāmid al-Ghazālī (d. 504/1111) and Fakhr al-Dīn al-Rāzī (d. 605/1209).

Yet despite the considerable overlap in the questions asked by these disciplines, their methods and core interests remained very distinct.[1] For instance, Sufis, philosophers and theologians all proposed arguments for the existence of God, but they did so in different ways: theologians like Abū al-Ḥasan al-Ashᶜarī formulated the teleological argument for the existence of God and took the Qur'ān and *Ḥadīth* as its starting point; philosophers such as Ibn Sīnā developed a cosmological argument using the reasoning of the Greek philosophers, while the Sufi and scholar Abū Ḥāmid al-Ghazālī was famous for adding proofs derived from religious experience to prove the existence of God.

Theology also had an uneasy relationship with some of its neighbouring disciplines. At various points in history, theology was suspected of moving dangerously close to denying or complicating the revealed truth of God's message. It was also repeatedly claimed by some traditionalist scholars that there was no need for theology at all because the Qur'ān and the *Sunna* were sufficient to explain religion. Such was the argument, for example, from the traditionalist scholar Ibn Qudāma (d. 619/1223) in his book, *Taḥrīm al-naẓar fī kutub Ahl al-Kalām* (The Censure of Speculative Theology). It was also claimed that human reason was an unreliable and an unnecessary tool with regards to understanding faith. At the other end of the spectrum, Sufis such as ᶜAbd Allāh Anṣārī al-Harawī (d. 481/1089) also opposed theology, pointing out that it was a pitiable substitute for the true gift of mystical illumination.[2] However, the majority of scholars in Islamic intellectual history saw the need for a religious science of theology in order to preserve the principles of beliefs within Islam, especially on those occasions when they were faced with rational

1 Parviz Morewedge, 'Kalam', in Richard C. Martin, ed., *Encyclopedia of Islam and the Muslim World*, New York: Macmillan Reference USA, 2004, vol. 1, p. 385.

2 Shah, 'Trajectories in the Development of Islamic Theological Thought', p. 10.

arguments from other religions and philosophies (which was something that occurred throughout most of Islamic history).[1]

To return to the discipline of theology itself, one of the most succinct definitions of it may be found in the famous work *al-Muqaddima* (The Introduction) by Ibn Khaldūn (d. 808/1404). He described *ʿilm al-kalām* as the discussion and definition of the articles of faith, including the nature of God and His relationship with creation. He wrote that *ʿilm al-kalām* 'is a science that involves arguing with logical proofs in defence of the articles of faith and refuting innovators who deviate in their dogmas from the early Muslims and Muslim orthodoxy.'[2]

Understanding the nature of God means to recognise the concept of the oneness of God in relation to creation. True theology is perhaps, as Hamza Yusuf argues, 'the squaring of a circle within an enlightened mind.'[3] He continues by describing theology as 'a reaction, a creative response to tension in the mind of the believer who is confronted with propositions that challenge not his experiential faith but his intellectual understanding of it. Experience of faith and expression of faith are distinct yet bound in a way that is often lost in discursive theology. Language cannot express the reality of faith, but it can explain what one believes and why. This is of course, the central purpose of theology.'[4] Therefore, theology is perhaps best understood as overcoming paradoxes and seemingly insoluble problems by reconciling them through reference to the scriptures and the use of the intellect.

In fact, always taking the Qur'ān as its starting point was—and continues to be—a key characteristic of Islamic theology.[5] Another is its deference to the Prophet Muḥammad. Indeed, as T. J. Winter

1 Morewedge, 'Kalam', p. 385.

2 Ibn Khaldūn, *The Muqaddimah: An Introduction to History*, ed. and trans. Franz Rosenthal, Princeton, NJ: Princeton University Press, 1967, p. 34.

3 Yusuf, introduction to *Creed of Imam al-Ṭaḥāwī*, p. 13.

4 Ibid., p. 13.

5 Ibid.

states in answer to the question, what is Islamic about Islamic theology, all Islamic theology, in whatever form, can be traced back to the Prophet Muḥammad and the message that he conveyed about God.[1] As a consequence, God's oneness and Muḥammad's prophethood were never contested within Islamic theology despite other issues being debated extensively, such as God's attributes and essence, the tension between divine omnipotence and human free will, and the question of evil.

But what about theology in more recent times? In modern times, not all Muslims agree that theology exists as a distinct religious science within Islam, and it can even be a challenge for many to name which 'brand' of theology they follow.[2] Part of this, at least within a western context, appears to be due to the Christian definition of theology and what it is understood to cover. In western usage, the term commonly refers to discourse or speech regarding God. Originally, Plato used the word *theology* to describe the subject matter of the poets, such as their writings about the gods and their genealogies, whereas Aristotle applied the term to the work of scholars who dealt with mythology, or even metaphysics, as distinct from philosophical enquiry about the divine. During the first centuries of Christianity, Origen (d. 254) used the word *theology* primarily to designate the knowledge of God. But gradually, the application of the term shifted from Hellenic discourses to become exclusively applied to the study of the Christian God.[3] Throughout its history, much of Christian theology has been occupied with speculation about the nature of the Trinitarian Godhead. As a consequence of the association between this uniquely Christian subject matter and the word *theology*, there has been great resistance to using the term in contemporary Islam.

1 Winter, ed., *Cambridge Companion to Classical Islamic Theology*, p. 5.

2 Louis Jacobs and Ellen Umansky, 'Theology', in Michael Berenbaum and Fred Skolnik, eds., *Encyclopaedia Judaica*, 2nd ed., Detroit: Macmillan Reference USA, 2007, vol. XIX., pp. 694–99.

3 Yves Congar, 'Christian Theology', s.v. 'Theology', in Jones, ed., *Encyclopedia of Religion*, vol. XIII, pp. 9134–42.

But another reason why there is some reluctance to recognise theology as an integral part of Islamic scholarship relates to the nature of Islamic belief itself. This is illustrated by the views of contemporary Muslim scholar Tariq Ramadan, who writes in his book, *Western Muslims and the Future of Islam*, that 'there is no Islamic theology.'[1] His reasoning relates to the fact that, historically, Muslims have never questioned the absolute oneness of God. They have entirely agreed, based upon the scriptures, that God cannot be physically represented and that the Qur'ān is literally the revealed word of God. Ramadan further argues that to have an authentic 'theology' one has to speculate about God, which Islam has never done. It has also been argued that the creeds in Islam are straightforward and that the discipline of *ʿilm al-kalām*, which is often translated as 'theology', is simply dogmatic, and that the discipline deals only with the articles of faith and their defence against heresy. Is there really a need for Muslims to discuss the concept of God? After all, it could be argued that the insistence on the oneness of God is clearly established in Muslim religious tradition. While Christians have had much to discuss regarding the nature of God and the Trinity, Muslims simply do not need to engage in such speculation.

However, as already mentioned, although scholars of Islam have not questioned the existence of God (since it was already agreed that God existed due to the revelation of the Qur'ān), theology has certainly taken place in Islam but in a very different way than in Christianity. Hence, Ramadan has some justification in saying that it is wrong 'to compare the often peripheral discussions that took place among Muslim scholars (particularly from the tenth century) with the radical reflections that gave birth to "Christian theology".'[2] Despite there being some merit to Ramadan's remarks, the present

1 Tariq Ramadan, *Western Muslims and the Future of Islam*, Oxford: Oxford University Press, 2005, p. 11.

2 Ibid., p. 12.

book will show that characterising the debates of Muslim theologians as 'peripheral discussions' is much mistaken.

Moreover, it is not only a mistake to ignore the pivotal role of theology within past Muslim history, it is also a mistake to ignore the obvious need for this religious science today. For instance, contemporary theologian Muhammad b. Yahya al-Ninowy argues that there is an urgent need for theology (which he refers to as *ʿilm al-tawḥīd*, a more modern Arabic term for *ʿilm al-kalām*) in modern times to help Muslims defend their faith intellectually. He states, 'The articles of *ʿaqida* are the articles of faith [...] when you talk to a Muslim, textual proofs are enough [...] but when you talk to others [...] they want you to give them an intellectual proof. As a rule, the textual proof will never contradict the intellect [...] "*ilm al-tawhid*" (i.e. Theology) is obligatory upon every Muslim; upon every person accountable.'[1]

A Brief History of Islamic Theology

In the early history of Islam, there were a series of key socio-political developments that shaped the course of all later Islamic theology. Ultimately, these events led to the establishment of the main Sunni theological schools of thought, three of which have endured until modern times. After the death of the Prophet Muḥammad in 11/632, he was succeeded by four 'rightly-guided caliphs' (*khulafāʾ rāshidūn*), who took over as leaders of the Muslim community. The reign of the first two caliphs, Abū Bakr al-Ṣiddīq (r. 11–13/632–634) and ʿUmar Ibn al-Khaṭṭāb (r. 13–23/634–644), was relatively uncontroversial, but the assassination of the third caliph ʿUthmān b. ʿAffān in the year 35/656 changed all that; it led to civil war and triggered a wave of separatist movements.

After his murder, ʿUthmān was succeeded by ʿAlī b. Abī Ṭālib as caliph (r. 35–40/656–661). However, ʿAlī's leadership was not

1 Quoted in Jeffry R. Halverson, *Theology and Creed in Sunni Islam: The Muslim Brotherhood, Ashʿarism and Political Sunnism*, New York: Palgrave Macmillan, 2010, p. 153.

accepted by everyone in the Muslim community due to a perception that he was unable, or unwilling, to bring ʿUthmān's killers to justice. The first major uprising against Caliph ʿAlī was led by the Prophetic Companions al-Zubayr b. al-ʿAwwām and Ṭalḥa b. ʿUbayd Allāh. The ensuing battle became known as the Battle of the Camel because the Prophet's wife, ʿĀ'isha bint Abī Bakr (d. 58/678), participated in it mounted on a camel. ʿAlī b. Abī Ṭālib easily defeated them and ʿĀ'isha was respectfully escorted back to Medina where she retired from active involvement in the leadership disputes.[1] This battle was the beginning of what would later be known as the first *fitna* (time of trial), or the First Civil War.

THE KHĀRIJIYYA.[2] The greatest challenge to ʿAlī's caliphate came from Muʿāwiya b. Abī Sufyān, who was the governor of Damascus and a relative of Caliph ʿUthmān. In the year 37/657, the two sides fought the main battle of the civil war in a place called Ṣiffīn; the battle continued until arbitration was suggested. The caliph agreed to this, but then a group of his own soldiers rebelled against him. Their rebellion arose in large part from the group's doctrinal differences with the caliph. These men, known as the Khārijīs (those who secede), were thus one of the very earliest groups to hold a distinct theological position within the Muslim community. It was during this crisis that the first theological discussion arose in Islamic intellectual history, and it was focused on the relationship between faith and practice. The civil war between Muʿāwiya and ʿAlī led the Khārijīs to denounce their enemies as apostates, and they justified this theologically by claiming that committing a great sin was tantamount to unbelief. In other words, for the Khārijīs, the question of whether someone was a Muslim was not determined by the person's belief in Islam—that is, by his faith (*īmān*)—but by his deeds.

This group rebelled against ʿAlī when he accepted the offer of

1 H. U. Rahman, *A Chronology of Islamic History*, London: Mansell Publishing, 1989, p. 37.

2 More commonly known as the *Khawārij*.

arbitration between himself and Muʿāwiya, arguing that because God would have given victory to the man who was in the right, ʿAlī had forfeited his position as caliph by agreeing to arbitration. Accordingly, the Khārijīs' main slogan became *lā ḥukma illā li-Llāh* (no judgement but God's). Their slogan was based on the Qur'ānic verse, 'No decision but God's',[1] which the Khārijīs interpreted as meaning that if one did not abide by the decision of God, then one was not a Muslim, because *muslim* literally means 'one in submission to God' and consequently also to His decisions. They went as far as calling any Muslim who committed any major sin (known as a *kabīra*) as a renegade.

The Khārijīs were the first radical extremists in Islamic history; however, the group was not monolithic. Over time, they became divided into several subgroups whose theological views differed slightly from one another. The main Khārijī subgroup was the Azraqīs, who were named after their leader Nāfiʿ Ibn al-Azraq (d. 65/685). This group adopted a distinction found in the Qur'ān between people who 'sit still' and do not 'go out' to fight for the sake of God (and who are therefore unbelievers) and those who do.[2] On the basis of their interpretation of this distinction, the Azraqīs dissociated themselves from anyone who did not join the Khārijīs and declared such people to be non-believers.

Another major subgroup of the Khārijīs was the Najdīs; their name derives from that of their leader Najda b. ʿĀmir (d. 73/693). Unlike the Azraqīs, the Najdīs were able to hold real political power in certain areas and, because of this, in practice they found it necessary to modify the strict Khārijī teaching that any Muslim who commits a serious sin be deemed an apostate and killed. The Najdīs therefore distinguished between fundamentals and non-fundamentals in religion. They held that people who sinned out of ignorance could be excused, but when it came to fundamental matters of faith

1 Q.XII.67.
2 Q.IX.81.

and respect for the life and property of other Muslims, no excuse could be accepted.

Besides the Azraqīs and Najdīs, there were other Khārijī sub-groups who held more moderate positions. Due to the fact that these groups lived as minorities amongst mainstream Muslims, they pragmatically adapted to co-existence with non-Khārijīs by modifying their doctrinal position on a key issue. These groups defended the decision to abstain from revolution, or 'sitting still', arguing that this did not make anyone an unbeliever, just as committing major sins such as theft or adultery did not either.[1]

A Khārijī was responsible for the murder of Caliph ʿAlī in the year 40/661 and for a long time afterwards, the Khārijīs posed a continuing military problem for the succeeding Umayyad caliphate, which faced numerous Khārijī uprisings. Gradually, they disappeared from the heartlands of the caliphate, although some moderate Khārijīs continued to govern in some outlying states such as Oman, North Africa and Zanzibar. During the later Umayyad and early Abbasid period, a revolutionary form of Khārijism took root amongst some Berbers in what is now central Algeria, which gave them doctrinal justification for rebelling against the central government. However, by the eleventh century, the Khārijīs had died out as an extreme group and what was left of them had been transformed into more tolerant factions. One such moderate group is the Ibāḍīs, whose followers are today found in large numbers in Oman. Some scholars argue that the Khārijīs were a radical tendency rather than a single movement as such, whose supporters were inclined to interpret religion in a literal, authoritarian way. In modern times, this style of interpretation has re-emerged amongst extremist groups.

THE PROTO-SHIʿA. A proto-Shiʿi group emerged during the same period as the rise of the Khārijiyya. The name of the group originally held a purely political connotation, and at the Battle of the Camel indicated that its supporters were the *Shīʿat ʿAlī* (the party or faction

1 Yusuf, introduction to *Creed of Imam al-Ṭaḥāwī*, pp. 17–19.

of ʿAlī) as opposed to the *Shīʿat ʿUthmān*, who were the partisans of the assassinated Caliph ʿUthmān. This early period witnessed a difficult relationship between the Shiʿis and the Sunni caliphate at times, which sometimes resulted in open revolt. However, over the course of the first two centuries of Islam, the Shīʿa developed into a distinctive theological denomination with three main branches: the Ithnā ʿasharī, Ismāʿīlīs and Zaydīs.

The Ithnā ʿasharī (literally, 'Twelver') Shiʿis are those who followed Imam Mūsā al- Kāẓim (d. 183/799), the son of Jaʿfar al-Ṣādiq (d. 148/765), and they believe that the twelfth Imam, Imam Mahdī, went into hiding in the year 256/874 and will reappear at the end of time as the 'Lord of the Age'. Today, the Ithnā ʿasharīs are the largest Shiʿi group in the world and have majority populations in Iraq and Iran.

The Ismāʿīlīs share their first six Imams with the Ithnā ʿasharīs but then followed Imam Ismāʿīl (d. 138/719), the more militant son of Jaʿfar al-Ṣādiq. The Ismāʿīlīs came to power with the establishment of the Fatimid Caliphate in the fourth/tenth century, and were rivals of the Sunni Abbasids in Baghdad. Today, the largest group amongst them are the followers of the Aga Khan.

The Zaydīs share the first four Imams with the other two branches of Shiʿism, but followed a different line with the fifth Imam, Imam Zayd (d. 122/740). They do not believe that their Imams were infallible. Today, most of them are found in north Yemen.

THE MURJI'A. Another theological group that arose out of the civil war was the Murji'a. They were strong opponents of the Khārijīs, especially on the topics of what is required to be a true believer and on the place of sin. Their name Murji'a appears to originate from the concept of *irjā'* (postponement of judgement on those who commit serious sins). They believed that only God could decide whether a Muslim had lost his or her faith. Hence, they held that no one who had once professed Islam could subsequently be declared a *kāfir* (infidel)—mortal or major sins notwithstanding. During the Umayyad caliphate, the Murji'a remained neutral in the disputes that divided the Muslims and called for passive resistance rather than armed revolt against unjust rulers. Indeed, they believed that rebelling against a Muslim ruler could not be justified under any circumstances. Their views seem to have inadvertently encouraged the Umayyad dynasty's unfair policies, whose leadership more than likely saw the Murji'ī politically quietist attitude and tolerance as actual support for their own regime. The Murji'īs were known to have pragmatically accepted the rule of the Umayyads, agreed to the rights of the Hashemites (the family of the Prophet Muḥammad descended from ʿAlī and Fāṭima), opposed the Khārijīs in Basra and opposed the Shiʿi attempts at revolt in Kufa.

It should be appreciated that the Murji'a were more a group holding opinions on and engaged in scholastic discussion about postponement rather than a well-defined faction. It remained a very diverse and broad group of people with occasionally opposing views. They believed that Muslims who committed grave sins but still remained faithful to Islam were eligible for admittance to Paradise, and this was accepted with some modifications by later Sunni theological schools. But their more extreme doctrines—such as the belief that no Muslim would enter Hellfire no matter what his sins be—were rejected by the other theological schools. These extreme Murji'īs advocated that salvation was achieved by the sincerity of one's faith and love of God alone, regardless of one's deeds (even ritual duties, such as prayers and fasting). Jeffry Halverson, rightly points out that this idea very much resonates with aspects of the Christian theology of the German reformer Martin Luther (d. 1546) some eight hundred years later.[1]

It is important to note that Abū Ḥanīfa's (d. 149/767) name does come up in connection with *irjā'* with regard to faith and practice. W. Montgomery Watt's historical study names him as the chief theologian of Murji'ism.[2] However, Abū Ḥanīfa did not per se postpone

1 Halverson, *Theology and Creed*, p. 163.

2 William Montgomery Watt, *Islamic Philosophy and Theology*, London: Aldine, 1962, p. 34.

an opinion, but rather found an intermediate position between rigidity and laxity. His solution was to define faith (*īmān*) as confession (*iqrār*) with the tongue and assent (*taṣdīq*) with the heart. For him, this was what made one a part of the Muslim community. Later on, this definition was further developed by the Sunni Māturīdī school of theology, whose members stated that faith does not increase or decrease in degree.

THE PROTO-SUNNIS. The socio-political events described above, and the different groupings that resulted from them, also created a response that could loosely be called the proto-Sunni faction. This faction was made up of the majority of Muslims, including those who primarily supported the Caliph ʿAlī, along with those who remained neutral and refused to judge between ʿAlī, ʿĀ'isha and Muʿāwiya. A majority of these Muslims accepted Muʿāwiya as de facto caliph in 41/661. Hamza Yusuf describes its historical development as follows: 'This group would eventually be called the People of the Prophetic way and the majority of Scholars [*Ahl al-Sunna wa'l-Jamāʿa*], i.e. Sunnis, the overwhelming majority of the Muslim world. This title Sunni historically emerged as a response to the sectarianism of the first and second centuries of Muslim history but the title is based upon a *ḥadīth*.'[1]

THE QADARIYYA AND THE JABARIYYA. During the first century of Islam, the city of Basra in Iraq became a centre for philosophical and theological debate, and it was during the lifetime of al-Ḥasan al-Baṣrī (d. 109/728), who was known as a Companion of ʿAlī and who played a central role in the founding of a number of schools of theology,[2] that two theological sects called the Qadariyya and the Jabariyya arose. The focus of their arguments was free will:

1 Ṭaḥāwī, *Creed of Imam al-Ṭaḥāwī*, p. 112.

2 It was mentioned by Māwardī in his book, *The Ordinances of Government*, that once when al-Ḥasan al-Baṣrī was addressing the people, ʿAlī b. Abī Ṭālib decided to test his knowledge and found him fully qualified. See ʿAlī b. Muḥammad b. Ḥabīb al-Māwardī, *al-Aḥkām al-sulṭāniyya wa'l-wilāyāt al-dīniyya*, trans. Wafaa H. Wahba as *The Ordinances of Government*, London: Garnet Publishing, 1996, p. 269.

the Qadarīs argued that in Islam there was only free will and no divine decree, whereas the Jabarīs were determinists who did not accept any free will whatsoever.[1] The Qadarī Maʿbad b. ʿAbd Allāh al-Juhanī (d. 79/699), in his attempt to refute the determinist or fatalist doctrine of the Jabarīs, negated the whole concept of divine decree altogether. This negation of the divine decree (*qadar* in Arabic) earned his group their name, the Qadariyya.

Some of the members of the Qadarīs later split from the group to form the Thanawiyya (dualists). The Thanawīs associated light with the Creator and darkness to creation. Known for their rejection of the divine decree, they believed that God has no volition concerning human action once free will has been granted; that is, they believed that God created human beings and then humans created their own actions. The Thanawīs also believed that while good was from God, evil was not.

In response to the Qadariyya, the founder of the Jabariyya, Jahm Ibn Ṣafwān (d. 127/745), composed a refutation to their free will argument by defending fatalism. Thus, the Jabariyya earned their name due to their belief in fatalism (*jabr* in Arabic). They were known as the Jahmiyya due to their association with Jahm Ibn Ṣafwān. Some of the members of this group later came to believe in pantheism and became known for their negation of divine attributes.

In connection with this wider debate on free will and the divine decree, the scholar al-Ḥasan al-Baṣrī is sometimes described as a Qadarī in western literature.[2] This view—which is strongly contested by Sunni theologians—seems to have arisen from Orientalist research that focused on al-Ḥasan al-Baṣrī's letters to the Umayyad rulers. However, this is a misunderstanding. Although he disagreed with the caliph at times by refusing to praise what he considered to be the caliph's unjust actions (which later scholars interpreted as

1 Majid Fakhry, *A History of Islamic Philosophy*, New York: Columbia University Press, 2004, p. 46.

2 For instance, see Watt, *Islamic Philosophy and Theology*, p. 32.

evidence of al-Ḥasan's direct opposition to the Jabariyya), he was not a Qadarī. His actual position on free will and the divine decree was the same as that of the majority of scholars at the time, which was that the divine decree and human agency both existed side by side.[1]

THE MUʿTAZILA. Al-Ḥasan al-Baṣrī who, as mentioned above was central to the origins of other schools of theology, also contributed to a school founded by his student, Wāṣil b. ʿAṭā' (d. 130/748). They were known as the Muʿtazila. The origins of this group were described by the historian of religion Muḥammad b. ʿAbd al-Karīm al-Shahrastānī, who stated that al-Ḥasan al-Baṣrī was asked one day:

> 'Now, in our own times a sect of people has made its appearance, the members of which regard the perpetrator of a grave sin as an unbeliever and consider him outside the fold of Islam. Yet another group of people (Murji'a) have appeared who give hope of salvation to the perpetrator of a grave sin. They lay down that such a sin can do no harm to a true believer. They do not in the least regard action as a part of faith and hold that as worship is of no use to one who is an unbeliever, so also sin can do no harm to one who is a believer in God. What, in your opinion, is the truth and what creed should we adopt?'
>
> It is told that Imam al-Ḥasan al-Baṣrī was on the point of giving a reply to this query when a student of his, Wāṣil b. ʿAṭā', got up and said: 'The perpetrator of grave sins is neither a complete unbeliever nor a perfect believer; he is placed mid-way between unbelief and faith—an intermediate state (*manzilah*

1 The issue of free will and the divine decree will be examined in detail in Chapter Seven.

> *bain al-manzilatain*).' The teacher did not agree and is reported to have said, '*iʿtazala ʿanna*,' i. e., 'He has withdrawn from us,' which is where the term *al-Muʿtazila* (the Withdrawers or Secessionists) originated. Another report seems to point towards the name of *al-Muʿtazila* coming about after the death of al-Ḥasan al-Baṣrī. According to his statement, when al-Ḥasan passed away, Qatadah succeeded him and continued his work. ʿAmr b. ʿUbaid and his followers avoided the company of Qatadah; therefore, they were given the name of *al-Muʿtazila*.[1]

This school became known for the five principles followed by its adherents: divine unity or oneness of God, divine justice, reward and retribution, the principle of intermediate position[2] and the obligation to command good and forbid evil.[3] However, the Muʿtazila was also known for the use of excessive reasoning in their interpretations of scripture and their emphasis on just free will.[4] They argued that any contradiction between revelation and reason meant that the revelation in question needed to be reinterpreted by reason.

Their own name for themselves was the People of Unity and Justice (*Ahl al-Tawḥīd wa'l-ʿAdl*). By the term unity they argued for the denial of the divine attributes since their argument was that if the attributes of God are not considered to be identical with the essence of God, then 'plurality of eternals' would necessarily result and the

1 Al-Shahrastānī, *Kitab al-milal wa'l-niḥal*, quoted by A. J. Wensinck in *The Muslim Creed*, Cambridge: Cambridge University Press, 1932, p. 62.

2 This indicates that a Muslim who commits a great sin is regarded as neither a believer (*mu'min*) nor an unbeliever (*kāfir*).

3 Seyyed Hossein Nasr, *A Young Muslim's Guide to the Modern World*, Cambridge: Islamic Texts Society, 1993, p. 71.

4 Ibid.

belief in unity would have to be given up. By justice they implied that it is incumbent on God to requite the obedient for their good deeds and punish the sinners for their misdeeds. They argued further that God's justice necessitates that man should be the author of his own acts; only then can he be said to be free and responsible for his deeds. In this they were the successors of the Qadariyya. It is important to note that the Muʿtazila were not all of one single view and that major differences of opinions existed between their earliest scholars, such as Wāṣil b. ʿAṭāʾ, and later figures like Abū ʿAlī al-Jubbāʾī (d. 303/915).

The rise of the Muʿtazilī school of theology during the last quarter of the second/eighth century made the intellectual inflexibility of both the Qadariyya and the Jabariyya unviable.[1] In their turn, the Muʿtazilīs—whose excessive rationalism was shunned by the majority of Muslim scholars—were to be challenged by the Atharī (sometimes known as the Ḥanbalī), Ashʿarī and Māturīdī schools of theology.[2]

It is interesting to note that Muʿtazilī thought did not die out, and instead became reconciled with the Zaydī and Ithnā ʿasharī (Twelver) branches of Shiʿism. Zaydī theologians adopted Muʿtazilī doctrine wholesale and may be regarded as the main representatives of the school today. The Ithnā ʿasharī theologians, on the other hand, established clear boundaries between their notion of an infallible Imam and the tenets of the Muʿtazila. As a consequence of this, Ithnā ʿasharī theologians abandoned the Muʿtazilī tenets of the promise and the threat (*al-waʿd wa'l waʿīd*) and the intermediary position between the believer and the unbeliever (*al-manzila bayn al-manzilatayn*) of the grave sinner (*fāsiq*) because they conflicted with their ideas about the imamate and the resulting doctrine of belief that excludes works.[3] Hence, it was not a wholesale adaptation of the Muʿtazila

1 Neil Robinson, *Islam: A Concise Introduction,* Richmond, Surrey: Curzon Press, 1999, p. 77.

2 See Fakhry, *History of Islamic Philosophy*, pp. 43–66 and 210–15.

3 Sabine Schmidtke, 'Theological Rationalism in the Medieval World of Islam', *al-ʿUṣūr al-Wusṭā*, vol. xx, no. 1, April 2008, pp. 17–31.

thought since many doctrines particular to Twelver Shiʿism remained unchanged. However, the concept of divine justice was something that both the Zaydīs and Twelver Shiʿis heavily stressed and it became the main focus of their theology in the following centuries.[1]

THE ATHARIYYA. The earliest theological approach within Sunni thought to have survived till today is the school of the traditionalist or Athariyya.[2] Aḥmad Ibn Ḥanbal (d. 240/855) a traditionalist jurist found himself in the middle of the theological discussion that was taking place in Baghdad. During this time, the caliph had made the Muʿtazila school of thought the state orthodoxy. Ibn Ḥanbal strongly argued against the inquisition (*miḥna*) set up by the state to promulgate Muʿtazilī doctrines and what he saw as the excessively rationalist views of the Muʿtazila, since they were willing to re-interpret scripture on the basis of reason.[3] His opposition to the Muʿtazila and the inquisition led to his imprisonment by Caliph al-Ma'mūn (r. 198–218/833–848). Ibn Ḥanbal was seen as the principal advocates of this school of theology and, following him, the majority of Atharīs have continued to argue for a literalist understanding of the Qur'ān and *Ḥadīth* on matters of law[4] and theology.[5]

Some academics have gone as far as arguing that the Ḥanbalī, or Atharī, school was actually an anti-theological school because they argued strongly against the use of human reason in comprehending the creeds and because they saw theology as a dangerous exercise in

1 Sajjad Rizvi, 'The Developed Kalam Tradition: Part II', in *Cambridge Companion to Classical Islamic Theology*, p. 92.

2 Some argue that the term *Atharī* as a school of theology did not exist, but that its identity was superimposed later on in history. These proponents argue that the more accurate term is *Ḥanbalī* or *Ahl al-Ḥadīth*.

3 Susan A. Spectorsky, 'Ibn Hanbal (780–855)', in Martin, ed., *Encyclopedia of Islam and the Muslim World*, vol. 1, pp. 334–35.

4 The Ḥanbalī school of law is one of four Sunni legal schools and the smallest of them. The followers of this school have largely maintained the traditionalist or Atharī position.

5 W. Madelung, *Religious Schools and Sects within Mediaeval Islam*, London: Variorum Reprints, 1985, p. 110.

human arrogance. For this reason, some have labelled it as a creedal school rather than a theological school.[1] Whatever the label, for most of their history the Atharīs have argued against the two other Sunni schools of theology because they used reason to defend the faith. During the early period, there were some major clashes between the schools of theology due to such differences. In the early years of it inception, the Atharī school was a majority voice in Baghdad and formed a vocal and respected voice in Damascus; with the rise of the other theological approaches it continued to be a valid expression but only as a minority voice.

For many Muslims, the treatise *al-ʿAqīda al-Ṭaḥāwīyya* (The Creed of Ṭaḥāwī) is the main classical text expressing the early Muslims' creed.[2] Ṭaḥāwī had no school formed after him despite his influence, perhaps because he refrained from using any theological arguments when composing this treatise. Interestingly, many of the early followers of this creed were Ḥanafīs. This may be explained by the fact that Ṭaḥāwī explicitly stated in his book that he had followed the creed of Abū Ḥanīfa. That earlier creed seems to have originated with Abū Ḥanīfa and was transmitted through his two disciples, Abū Yūsuf and Muḥammad.[3] Nevertheless, all schools of law accepted Ṭaḥāwī's *Creed* according to Tāj al-Dīn al-Subkī (d.771/1369).[4]

THE ASHʿARIYYA. The second school of Sunni theology that has survived till today is that of the Ashʿariyya. Abū al-Ḥasan al-Ashʿarī, a former student of the Muʿtazila, insisted on adhering to the traditional principles of Ibn Ḥanbal, but at the same time refused to be a literalist and defended the necessity of using rational argumentation. According to Abū al-Ḥasan al-Ashʿarī, 'The Qur'ān and the teaching of the Prophet presented a reasoned exposition of the contingency of

1 Halverson, *Theology and Creed*, p. 2.

2 Madelung, *Religious Schools and Sects*, p. 10.

3 See Ayedh Saad Aldosari, 'A Critical Edition of al-Hādī in Māturīdī Doctrine of the Ḥanifite-Māturīdī Imām ʿUmar al-Khabbāzī', Ph.D. thesis, University of Wales Trinity Saint David, 2012.

4 Yusuf, introduction to *Creed of Imam al-Ṭaḥāwī*, pp. 34–35.

the world and its dependence upon the deliberate action of a transcendent creator, which, though not expressed in formal language, is complete and rationally probative.'[1] For this school of thought, revelation was the source of all fundamental truth, and rationality was used to understand revelation within the general framework set out by revelation. Thus, there could be no actual contradiction between revelation and reason.

The Ashᶜarī school of theology dealt with the main theological issues of Islamic faith, including arguments for the existence of God, divine unity, revelation, prophecy and eschatology.[2] By the late fourth/tenth century, the success of the Ashᶜarī theological approach overshadowed that of the Atharīs, and they had intellectually defeated the Muᶜtazilīs within the Sunni realm. At that point, their main adversaries became the Muslim philosophers, the *falāsifa*.

The Umayyad and Abbasid eras featured a wide range of theological challenges and debates that led to some groups accusing others of unbelief. In turn, this led to a wider debate amongst theologians about what faith (*īmān*) and unbelief (*kufr*) meant. Fakhr al-Dīn al-Rāzī (d. 606/1210) was an Ashᶜarī scholar who saw contradictions and conflicting evidence in the charges of unbelief made by various groups. In response, Rāzī tried to narrow the definition of unbelief as follows:

> One should know that theologians have had considerable difficulty defining *kufr* (unbelief) ...[it] consists in denying the truth of anything the Prophet (God bless him and give him peace) is necessarily known to have said. Examples include denying the Creator's existence, His knowledge, power, choice, oneness, or perfection above all deficiencies

1 R. Frank, 'Ashᶜari, Al-', in Jones, ed., *Encyclopedia of Religion*, vol. I, , p. 530.

2 M. Sait Özervarlı, 'Ashᶜarites, Ashᶜāira', in Martin, *Encyclopedia of Islam and the Muslim World*, vol. II, pp. 82–84.

> and infirmities. Or denying the prophethood of Muḥammad (God bless him and give him peace), the truth of the Qur'ān, or denying any law necessarily known to be of the religion of Muḥammad (God bless him and give him peace), such as the obligations of prayer, of *zakat*, fasting, or pilgrimage, or the unlawfulness of usury or wine. Whoever does so is an unbeliever because he has disbelieved the Prophet (God bless him and give him peace) about something necessarily known to be of his religion.[1]

Fakhr al-Dīn al-Rāzī further drew the attention of his readers to issues of belief, the affirmation nor denial of which would not lead to unbelief:

> As for what is only known by inference from proof to be his religion, such as whether God knows by virtue of His attribute of knowledge or rather by virtue of His entity, or whether or not He may be seen [in the next life], or whether or not He creates the actions of His servants; we do not know by incontestably numerous chains of transmission (*tawatur*) that any of these alternatives has been affirmed by the Prophet (God bless him and give him peace) instead of the other. For each, the truth of one and falsity of the other is known only through inference, so neither denial nor affir-

1 Fakhr al-Dīn al-Rāzī, *Tafsīr mafātiḥ al-ghayb*; translation from Nuh Ha Mim Keller, 'Kalam and Islam: Traditional Theology and the Future of Islam', lecture, Aal al-Bayt Institute of Islamic Thought, Amman, Jordan, January 4, 2005; text archived at http://masud.co.uk/kalam-and-islam/, accessed 5 January 2016.

> mation of it can enter into actual faith, and hence cannot entail unbelief. The proof of this is that if such points were part of faith, the Prophet (God bless him and give him peace) would not have judged anyone a believer until he was sure that the person knew the question. Had he done such a thing, his position on the question would have been known to everyone in Islam and conveyed by many chains of transmission. Because it has not it is clear that he did not make it a condition of faith, so knowing it is not a point of belief, nor denying it unbelief. In light of which no one of this *Umma* is an unbeliever, and we do not consider anyone an unbeliever whose words are interpretable as meaning anything besides. As for beliefs not known except through *ḥadīth*s related by a single narrator, it seems plain that they cannot be a decisive criterion for belief or unbelief. That is our view about the reality of unbelief.[1]

Most followers of the Ashᶜariyya were from the Shāfiᶜī and Mālikī schools of law, which slowly became the dominant legal schools in the Arab world, Indonesia and Malaysia. It is important to note that the Ashᶜarīs were not all of a single view on every doctrine and minor differences are apparent between well-known Ashᶜarī scholars, such as Abū Bakr Muḥammad b. al-Ṭayyib al-Bāqillānī (d. 402/1013) and Imām al-Ḥaramayn ᶜAbd al-Malik al-Juwaynī (d. 478/1085).[2]

THE MĀTURĪDIYYA. This leads us to the Māturīdī school of theology, the third and last Sunni theological school to survive into the modern world. This approach was founded by Abū Manṣūr Muḥammad b.

1 Ibid.

2 Halverson, *Theology and Creed*, p. 16.

Muḥammad al-Māturīdī, who was based in modern-day Uzbekistan, in contrast to Ibn Ḥanbal and Abū al-Ḥasan al-Ashʿarī who both lived in Baghdad. Māturīdī became popular in Central Asia for his intermediary position between the Muʿtazilīs and the Ashʿarī on controversial subjects like free will and the attributes of God. Many have argued that this was due to the stable intellectual climate in Central Asia, which was far removed from the Ashʿarī–Muʿtazilī ideological struggle in Iraq. Just as Abū al-Ḥasan al-Ashʿarī had done, Māturīdī recognised the traditional principles of Ibn Ḥanbal but he created a much stronger synthesis between tradition and reason than Ashʿari. He avoided subjugating tradition to reason (and vice versa) and instead struck a balance between the two.[1]

For Māturīdī, revelation and reason were in complete harmony and any perceived contradictions were illusory. His intellectual attitude is traditionally portrayed as a development of the thought of Abū Ḥanīfa, founder of the oldest legal school in Sunni Islam.[2] Hence, Abū Ḥanīfa is seen as the founder of the Māturīdī theological school, whereas Abū Manṣūr al-Māturīdī became known as his brilliant interpreter.[3] It is therefore not surprising that it was the adherents of the Ḥanafī school of law who were the champions of the Māturīdī school of thought. Accordingly, the Muslims of Central Asia, Turkey and the Indian subcontinent,[4] who were already followers of the Ḥanafī school of law, adopted the Māturīdī school of theology.[5]

It is clear from the historical sources that Abū Ḥanīfa had two stances with regards to theology. During his early life he adopted scholastic theology, which his students Bishr b. Ghiyāth al-Marīsī

1 Yusuf, introduction to *Creed of Imam al-Ṭaḥāwī*, p. 22.

2 Oliver Leaman and Sajjad Rizvi, 'The Developed Kalam Tradition', in Winter, ed., *Cambridge Companion to Classical Islamic Theology*, p. 86.

3 Rudolph Ulrich, *Al-Māturīdī and the Development of Sunnī Theology in Samarqand*, Brill: Leiden, 2005, p. 6.

4 Today's modern states of Pakistan, Bangladesh and India.

5 Madelung, *Religious Schools and Sects*, Chapter Two.

(d. 218/833) and Ḥafṣ al-Fard (d. mid-third/mid-ninth century) adopted from him, and at a later stage he opposed it, which his students Abū Yūsuf and Muḥammad followed. Ṭaḥāwī seems to have followed the opinion of the second stage and Māturīdī the first.[1]

In conclusion, it is interesting to note that although the polemics between the early theological schools were frequent, there was only one incident in the history of Sunnism when the ruler backed an inquisition (*miḥna*); this was the Muᶜtazilī inquisition instigated by the Caliph al-Ma'mūn in the third/ninth century. According to Jonathan E. Brockopp, this inquisition was intended to impose a single set of theological doctrines upon the Muslim *Umma* for theological and state centralisation purposes. However, the inquisition failed due to the continuous challenges of theologians like Aḥmad Ibn Ḥanbal, and the result was that no single Islamic school of law or theology has ever dominated Islamic thought. Brockopp emphasises that the significance of the failure of the *miḥna* should not to be underestimated because its success could have led to a rigidly centralised hierarchy in Sunni Islam, similar to that found within other religious traditions.[2] However, Sunni Islam has instead embraced legitimate differences between the legal schools, the theological schools and the various Sufi orders throughout most of its history.[3]

Before turning to the debates that took place amongst early theologians about the articles of faith, a few words must be said about Sufism because its practitioners made important contributions to theological discussions about faith and similar issues.

Sufism and Theology

Many contemporary scholars have regarded Sufism (*taṣawwuf*) to be

1 Māturīdī literature is famously known to have developed as a series of commentaries on Abu Ḥanīfa's theological and jurisprudence work, *al-Fiqh al-akbar.* For further details see Aldosari, 'A Critical edition of Al-Hādī.'

2 Jonathan E. Brockopp, *Islamic Ethics of Life: Abortion, War, and Euthanasia*, Columbia: University of South Carolina Press, 2003, p. 6.

3 Winter, ed., *Cambridge Companion to Classical Islamic Theology*, p. 7.

something alien to the revealed religion of Islam, especially Muslim modernists and the followers of Islam's more puritanical movements, while others have designated it a third denomination of Islam beside Sunnism and Shiᶜism. However, Sufism has long been recognised as an Islamic science, just like theology and jurisprudence, and it was studied and practised by both Sunni and Shiᶜi scholars. According to Majid Fakhry, 'There is little in the early Sufi ideal of life for which a basis cannot be found in the Koran and the traditions [...].'[1] Traditionally, its origins have been said to go back to the Prophet's time, as indicated by the famous *ḥadīth* of Gabriel that was mentioned towards the beginning of this chapter. When the Angel Gabriel asked the Prophet about *islām* and *īmān*, he also asked a third question, what is *iḥsān* (good conduct)? The Prophet replied that *iḥsān* meant 'that you worship God as if you are seeing Him, for though you do not see Him, He, verily, sees you.'[2] Sufis have argued that this part of the *ḥadīth* highlights the immanence of God, Who may be reached through *dhikr* (remembrance of God) and *murāqaba* (meditation).

Thus from the early days of Islam, the practice of *iḥsān* developed into an advanced spiritual science that was referred to as *taṣawwuf*. When this latter term reached the western world, it was anglicised as 'Sufism'. The most famous early Sufis included al-Ḥasan al-Baṣrī (d. 109/728), Rābiᶜa al-ᶜAdawiyya al-Qaysiyya (d. 184/801), Abū ᶜAbd Allāh al-Ḥārith al-Muḥāsibī (d. 242/857), Abū Yazīd al-Biṣṭāmī (d. 261/875), Abū al-Qāsim al-Junayd (d. 297/910), al-Ḥusayn Ibn Manṣūr al-Ḥallāj (d. 309/922), Abū Ḥāmid Ghazālī, Muḥyī al-Dīn Ibn al-ᶜArabī (d. 637/1240), Jalāl al-Dīn Rūmī (d. 671/1273) and Aḥmad Sirhindī (d. 1033/1624). These and other Sufis developed their understanding of spiritual concepts found in the Islamic scriptures, such as divine love, self-examination, mystical union, the divine covenant

1 Fakhry, *History of Islamic Philosophy*, p. 248.
2 Muslim, *Ṣaḥīḥ*, 1.1, http://sunnah.com/muslim/1/1.

and mystical experience.[1] However, it is important to be aware that the Sufis rarely isolated themselves from the wider Muslim society. In fact, many were known to have played an active role within Muslim intellectual discourse and their engagement in it heightened the creative tension between scholars because they brought new perspectives and knowledge.

At times, Sufis were keen to emphasise their 'orthodox' credentials, as in the case of figures like Junayd, Ghazālī and Sirhindī, but others such as Rūmī and Ibn ʿArabī pushed for a more speculative form of Sufism. Yet regardless of this range of expressions of Sufism, they always remained within an Islamic framework.[2] What all of this demonstrates is that it would be a mistake to regard *taṣawwuf* as foreign to Islam, or even as a denomination of it. It is instead an expression of Islam that has always been connected with the ritual, legal and theological dimensions of Islam. Whenever it has been divorced from these dimensions, the majority of Muslim scholars have strongly dismissed it as deviating from Islam.

Early Developments in Islam's Articles of Faith

Following intense theological debates during the first few centuries of Islam over the nature of God and His attributes, a single statement known as the *īmān mujmal* (summary of faith) became the creed accepted by the *Ahl al-Sunna wa'l-Jamāʿa*. It was this: *I believe in God as He is known by His names and His attributes and I accept all of His commands and I assent to it in my heart.*[3] In time, after further reflection and debate, an expanded creedal statement was developed. This was known as the *īmān mufaṣṣal* (detailed expression of faith) and it has been Sunni Islam's basic creed (*ʿaqīda*) since then; it states: *I believe in*

1 Toby Mayer, 'Theology and Sufism', in Winter, ed., *Cambridge Companion to Classical Islamic Theology*, pp. 258–287.

2 Ibid. pp. 270–80.

3 Yasin Ramazan Başaran, 'The Idea of Subjective Faith in al-Maturidi's Theology', *Journal of Islamic Research*, vol. IV, no. 2, December 2011, pp. 167-170. Within the Māturīdiyya theology this text extends to include the words: *and as an expression by the tongue.*

God, in His angels, in His scriptures, in His messengers, in the Last Day (the Day of Judgement), in that good or bad is decided by God the Almighty and I believe in life after death.[1]

Here, it is important to point out that there is a difference between Sunnis and Twelver Shiʿis with regard to the articles of faith. As can be seen in the short treatise on creed called *al-Bāb al-ḥādī ʿashar* (The Eleventh Chapter) by the Twelver Shiʿi theologian Jamāl al-Dīn Ḥasan b. Yūsuf al-Ḥillī (d. 725/1325), Shiʿis have traditionally divided their creed into five articles of faith: *tawḥīd* (divine unity and attributes), *ʿadāla* (divine justice), *nubuwwa* (prophecy), *imāma* (succession) and *qiyāma* (resurrection).[2] Twelver Shiʿis do not place great emphasis on the divine decree as Sunnis do; instead, their focus is on God's infinite justice.[3]

Within Sunnism also there are variations regarding the creed. Although all classical Sunni scholars agreed on the six articles of faith, some added more to the list to elaborate on the first six articles. For example, Ṭaḥāwī lists one hundred and thirty creeds in his book. In so doing, these scholars explained that the original six articles of faith were simply the main foundations of belief in Islam, and that belief actually had many branches. This scheme can be compared to the five pillars of Islam, which are the five core obligatory acts for Muslims that sit alongside a much wider set of prescribed practices that make up the Islamic way of life.

According to Suzanne Haneef, the six articles of faith are not fixed in any sequential order because they are independent and simul-

1 Belief in that good or bad is decided by God and in life after death are always considered together and are not two separate articles of faith. The articles of faith are, therefore, six in number. In a calligraphic tradition dating from the Ottoman period, the text of the *īmān mufaṣṣal* is frequently presented in the shape of a boat, which is popularly known as the *safīnat al-najāt* ('ship of salvation') in Arabic and *amentü gemisi* in Turkish ('ark of belief').

2 Rizvi, 'The Developed Kalām Tradition', in Winter, ed., *Cambridge Companion to Classical Islamic Theology*, pp. 93–94.

3 This will be touched upon in the Chapter Seven.

taneous principles.[1] This is borne out by the fact that all six articles are found scattered across the Qur'ān and *Ḥadīth* literature in varying combinations and ordering. However, it must still be appreciated that the belief in God is considered by Muslims to be absolutely the first article of faith, and that all others derive from it. This is because Islam's main focus has always been on the unity of God, which is expressed through the belief in God as not only the One (*al-Aḥad*) but also the Unique (*al-Waḥid*).[2]

Throughout Muslim history, Muslim scholars have debated over what was required in order to have *īmān* (faith). Is it essentially faith in the heart alone, or is verbal declaration required in addition to that? Alternatively, is the believer obligated to have faith in his heart, declare it verbally and perform good acts? To these questions, each of the main Sunni theological schools answered in a different way. Amongst the Ashᶜarīs, the emphasis was on belief in the heart.[3] For example, the Ashᶜarī scholar Tāj al-Dīn Abū al-Fatḥ Muḥammad b. ᶜAbd al-Karīm al-Shahrastānī (d. 547/1153) wrote that, 'The Ashᶜariyya holds that *īmān* is inner belief; as for its verbal expression and external practice, these are "branches" of belief. Whoever, therefore, believes in his heart, such a one's *īmān* is valid; if immediately afterwards he dies with this *īmān*, he will be regarded as a believer and be saved. Nothing will make him cease to be a believer except the denial of one of these truths. Whoever commits a grave sin, and dies without repentance, his judgement will rest with God.'[4] For the Māturīdīs, however, faith required belief in the heart and its expression by the tongue, as the Māturīdī Najm al-Dīn Abū Ḥafṣ al-Nasafī (d. 536/1142) explained, 'Belief is assent to what he [the Prophet] brought from

1 Suzanne Haneef, *What Everyone Should Know About Islam and Muslims*, Lahore: Kazi Publications, 1979, p. 11.

2 Cafer S. Yaran, *Islamic Thought on the Existence of God*, Washington, DC: Council for Research in Values and Philosophy, 2003, p. 1.

3 See Izutsu, *Concept of Belief*, pp. 182–96.

4 Translation from Halverson, *Theology and Creed*, pp. 21–22.

God and the confession of it.'[1] Lastly, the position of the Atharīs was that faith had to be by heart, word and deed, which the Ashʿarī theologian Juwaynī described as follows, 'The Partisans of Hadith [the Atharīs] hold that faith is cognizance in the heart, confession by the tongue, and acts performed by the limbs and members', but, he continued, 'the doctrines we [the Ashʿariyya] approve is that the real nature of faith is true belief in God, the Exalted.'[2] Thus, although there were slight differences between the theological schools' definitions of faith, no theologian disagreed on the basic definition of *īmān*; namely, that it was the spiritual and intellectual belief in the existence of God.

As a scholarly discipline, the science of theology (*ʿilm al-kalām*) has traditionally been divided into two parts: *jalīl al-kalām*, meaning the 'great' or 'lofty' questions of theology, and *daqīq al-kalām*, the 'minutiae'. The history of Islamic theology began with a focus on *jalīl al-kalām*: these were the metaphysical issues of Islamic faith that involved exploring the meaning of Godhood, celestial beings, the divine decree, the resurrection of the dead and so on. However, later theologians went on to develop what became known as *daqīq al-kalām*. This part of theology dealt with problems of natural philosophy, the most prominent of which was whether the world was eternal or created, and the question of causality. These issues then led theologians to tackle the concepts of space, time, motion and many of other aspects of the physical world.[3]

Part II of this book is specifically concerned with the larger questions of Islamic theology—those of *jalīl al-kalām*. This is because these topics underpin every aspect of Islamic belief and lay the foundation for all other sciences of the *Sharīʿa*. Thus, to understand the Islamic faith well, one needs to begin with *jalīl al-kalām*. However,

1 Ibid., p. 29.

2 Ibid., p. 19.

3 M. B. Altaie, '*Daqīq al-Kalām*: The Islamic Approach to Natural Philosophy', Islamic Philosophy Online, http://www.muslimphilosophy.com/ip/Altaie-Lecture2.pdf, 15 February 2015.

some issues relating to *daqīq al-kalām* (the minutiae of theology) will be touched on in Part II and Part III. This more recent branch of theology is particularly important in modern times because it deals with topics that today fall within the remit of physics and quantum physics. This branch of theology is therefore necessary not only to explain the beliefs of Muslims but also their rational coherence.

To conclude, Part I of this book has introduced the basic tenets of the Muslim creed and has surveyed some of the most important developments related to them in theology in the classical world. Part II—in six chapters—is a detailed account of the six articles of faith in Sunnism and of the classical and contemporary debates that surround them.[1] Even though theology in Islam may appear to be solely about creed and dogma, it will soon become obvious that Muslim theologians engaged not only with discussions of creed but also with the wider social context of issues relating to faith. Part III of this book is a reflection on the state of Islamic theology today and addresses questions about its future. It is hoped that upon finishing this book, readers will feel that they have gained a deeper understanding of the Muslim creed and its significance within Islamic theology.

1 In the Muslim creed, the belief in revealed scriptures is traditionally mentioned before that of belief in prophecy. However, in the chapters of the present book, their order has been reversed. This change has been made because, for the purposes of this study, it is easier for the reader to encounter the subject of prophecy (Chapter Four) before the revealed scriptures (Chapter Five).

PART II
THEOLOGY AND THE ARTICLES OF FAITH

Chapter Two

GOD, MOST HIGH

Islam: an Active Religion of the Twenty-First Century

Although much of the Islamic theological thought presented in this book derives from both classical and modern scholars, it has been written within the context of the western-influenced world in the early twenty-first century. It is therefore important to note the considerable differences between the Muslim world and the West with regards to the impact of religion on modern history. Whereas the western world has experienced major changes brought about by an ever more secular society for more than two centuries, the Muslim world is only recently becoming introduced to this and is reacting in very distinctive ways. Scholars such as J. M. Roberts have noted the colossal changes that the twentieth century witnessed: the demise of empires, the establishment of nation states, the creation of a new global financial system and, especially in Europe, the loss of faith, or the disinterest in the existence of God. Roberts argues that in Europe during the Middle Ages, religious belief was at the root of most people's lives, but now one can find large populations who, for the most part, take no account of God in their daily lives: 'Religion seems to have lost much of the enormous advantage it once possessed as virtually the universal source of consolation, explanation and hope to women and men trapped in an unchanging order.'[1] Even though scholars like Noel Davies and Martin Conway have countered that

1 J. M. Roberts, *The Penguin History of the Twentieth Century: The History of the World, 1901 to the Present*, London: Penguin Books, 1999, p. 845.

such a general viewpoint is questionable, they do recognise that it represents an aspect of change in religious beliefs and practices in at least one section of the global family during the last hundred years.[1]

To understand the perspective of Muslims, it is crucial for the reader to recognise that Roberts's statement is explicitly related to Christianity in Europe (and in some cases to Judaism) but not to Islam, and does not in any way represent a true picture of Muslims in the twentieth century. Nor has such a trend been observed amongst Muslims in the twenty-first century either.[2] From all of the empirical evidence available, it is clear that religious belief is still at the heart of the lives of Muslims, and God is very much a part of everyday life. Muslim faith today is still independent of secular beliefs that are dominated by positivist science and people who believe in their personal autonomy. In fact, such a secular reality is still a rarity amongst Muslims, not a norm.

Allāh Is God

In the world of Islam, God is called *Allāh*, which literally translated means 'the God' in Arabic. Is He the same God as the God of the Judaism, Christianity and other religions? This is a question that I am frequently asked when first talking about God with any non-Muslim audience. One answer to this question is that God for the Muslims is the same God that Jews and Christians worship because the Qur'ān states, 'And dispute ye not with the People of the Book, except with means better (than mere disputation), unless it be with those of them who inflict wrong (and injury): but say, "We believe in the revelation which has come down to us and in that which came down to you; Our God and your God is one; and it is to Him we bow (in Islam)."'[3]

However, the concept of God is not completely identical across the three religions. For Muslims, God is the narrator of the Qur'ān

1 Noel Davies and Martin Conway, *World Christianity in the 20th Century*, London: SCM Press, 2008, p. 282.

2 Pew Research Center report, 'The World's Muslims.'

3 Q.xxix.46.

and in it He repudiates many of the ideas about Him found in other religions. He speaks of Himself as the One, the Unique, the Absolute, the Infinite, the Origin and the End of all things; He is the Creator and the Sustainer; He is the Giver of life and death; thus all things return to Him. Islam categorically declares God to be far beyond possessing any of the attributes of creation that may be ascribed to Him, and does not consider Him to be bound by any of the limitations of human beings or anything else He has created. Thus, God is One, as it says in the Qur'ān, 'Say: He is God, the One and Only; God, the Eternal, Absolute; He begetteth not, nor is He begotten; and there is none like unto Him.'[1]

The core experience of Islam can be described as comprehending the unity of God, where His oneness and His uniqueness are highlighted. In this, the first article of faith and the first pillar of Islam (*shahāda*) coincide; the *shahāda* is to testify that 'There is no god (divinity) but God and Muḥammad is His messenger.' To believe in God as is stated in the first article of faith means to negate any other deity and affirm the belief in the oneness and uniqueness of God. This declaration first removes the notion that anything in creation is worthy of being worshipped and then stresses the existence of God, Who is the only One Who can be worshipped. Some scholars have translated *tawḥīd* as the oneness of God, such as Massimo Campanili's statement that 'Islam is intensely bound up with a burning passion for the oneness of God or *tawḥīd*.'[2] This is correct in as much that Islam stresses *tawḥīd*, but incorrect in the translation of the term as just meaning oneness. This is because the term *tawḥīd* signifies that it is not enough to believe that God is one, since one has also a numerical value, but that He is also unique, since it is that attribute which explains the oneness of God. God is one in the sense that there is no other like Him; thus nothing can be compared to Him. His uniqueness

1 Q.CXII.1–4.

2 Massimo Campanini, *An Introduction to Islamic Philosophy*, Rome: Eulama Literary Agency, 2008, p. 75.

even renders human language inadequate when God is described. One contemporary scholar describes the link between God and His creation as follows: 'There are constant reminders in Qur'ānic verses about God's relation to all existence and how He creates, involves, governs, gives a beginning and end, sufficiently and effectively runs everything with His mercy, power and wisdom. This Qur'ānic perspective of God offers a distinctive perception of reality.'[1]

A Different Concept of God

But how is this different from the perspective of Christianity or Judaism? According to the Qur'ān, the major difference between Christianity and Islam is the Trinitarian notion of God.[2] Numerous verses reject the notion of God incarnated as Jesus, and the Qur'ān instead highlights the uniqueness and oneness of God.[3] Ghazālī explained these verses by stating that Christians had been so dazzled by the divine light reflected in the mirror-like heart of Jesus that they had mistaken the mirror for the light itself and so worshipped it. He argued that the trinity was a Christian error based upon exaggeration:

> When they see that [same perfection] in the essence of the messiah, ʿĪsā [Jesus]—may peace be upon him—and say: he is God; yet they are as mistaken as the one who looks into a mirror and sees in it a coloured image yet thinks that this image is the image of the mirror, and this colour is the colour of the mirror. Far from it! For the mirror has no colour in itself; its nature is rather to receive the image of coloured things in such a way as to display

1 İsmail L. Hacınebioğlu, *Does God Exist? Logical Foundations of the Cosmological Argument*, Istanbul: İnsan Publications, 2008, p. 224.

2 Campanini, *Introduction to Islamic Philosophy*, p. 75.

3 Q.IV.171, V.72–75, XIX.88–93.

> them to those looking at the appearance of things as though they were the images of the mirror—to the point where a child who sees a man in the mirror thinks that the man actually is in the mirror.'[1]

This notion that Jesus is God incarnate is to be found, for example, in the writings of the second-century Christian scholar Clement of Rome, who wrote, 'We must learn to think of Jesus as of God',[2] and also in the writings of the celebrated modern author C. S. Lewis when he wrote of Christ being the Son of God stating, 'Let us not come with any patronizing nonsense about His [Jesus] being a great human teacher. He has not left that open to us. He did not intend to.'[3] Among others, Fakhr al-Dīn al-Rāzī employed a rigorously logical and rational approach to interpretation in his exegesis of the Qur'ān based on the Qur'ānic verses and *Ḥadīth* to refute the possibility that Jesus could partake of the nature of God.[4] In a similar way, but from a perspective different to Rāzī's, Ibn ʿArabī, while highlighting the mystical dimensions of Christ, took care to point out that Jesus

1 Ghazālī, *The Ninety-Nine Beautiful Names of God*, trans. David B. Burrell and Nazih Daher, Cambridge: The Islamic Texts Society, 1992, 153–54.

2 Quoted by McGrath in *Theology: The Basics*, p. 18.

3 Quoted by Armand M. Nicholi in *C. S. Lewis and Sigmund Freud Debate God, Love, Sex, and the Meaning of Life*, New York: Free Press, 2003, p. 88. Unfortunately, we find within Lewis's writings a familiarly hostile Orientalist bias when he compares Muḥammad with other great human teachers to prove that Jesus was not a human teacher of morality but truly the begotten son of God (pp. 87–89): 'If you had gone to Buddha and asked him: "Are you the son of Brahma?" He would have said, "My son, you are still in the vale of illusion." If you had gone to Socrates and asked, "Are you Zeus?" he would have laughed at you. If you had gone to Mohammed and asked, "Are you Allah?" he would have first rent his clothes and then cut your head off. [...] The idea of a great moral teacher saying what Christ said [that Christ is the begotten son of God] is out of the question.' It could be argued that Muslim scholars would strongly insist that in no way does the above description do justice to Muḥammad's character as a great moral and sincere Prophet.

4 Fakhr al-Dīn al-Rāzī, *al-Tafsīr al-kabīr*, [Cairo:] al-Maṭbaʿa al-Bahiyya al-Miṣriyya, [1357/1938], vol. vii, pp. 61–62.

should not be confused with God, but should instead be regarded as the Word of God, the Spirit of God and the slave of God.[1]

Another aspect of Islamic theology that distinguishes it from Jewish and Christian theology concerns the ninety-nine attributes (or names) of God,[2] of which several are not found in the two other Abrahamic faiths. The ninety-nine names of God carry with them both feminine and masculine characteristics as explicitly understood by human cultures, such as mercy and beauty, which are feminine nouns in Arabic, and wrath and power, which are masculine.[3] And yet, the uniqueness and oneness of God, Who is like no other, also refutes the idea of gender. God transcends both the masculine and feminine principle since He is unique and not like His creation. After all, the understanding of male or female is very much a part of the genetic setup of most creatures, and in Islam it is not assumed that God is like the male or female creatures of His dominion.

T. J. Winter states, 'Islamic theology confronts us with the spectacular absence of a gendered Godhead. A theology which reveals the divine through incarnation in a body also locates it in a gender, and inescapably passes judgement on the other sex. A theology which locates it in a book makes no judgement about gender; since books are unsexed. The divine remains divine, that is, genderless, even when expressed in a fully saving way on earth.'[4] Thus, as a name of

1 Muḥyī al-Dīn Ibn al-ʿArabī, *Ibn al-ʿArabi: The Bezels of Wisdom*, trans. R. J. Austin, London: SPCK, 1980, pp. 174–179. For further information on Islam and Jesus see Amjad Hussain, 'Jesus in Islam: The Classic Texts', in Gregory A. Barker and Stephen E. Gregg, eds., *Jesus Beyond Christianity*, Oxford: Oxford University Press, 2010, pp. 115–18.

2 The ninety-nine attributes of God are a list of divine names found in the Qurʾān and often used for devotional purposes. There are a number of these lists of the ninety-nine names with minor variations. Needless to say, the attributes of God are limitless.

3 See Sachiko Murata, *The Tao of Islam*, Albany: State University of New York Press, 1992.

4 T. J. Winter, 'Islam, Irigaray, and the Retrieval of Gender', Masud.co.uk, April 1999, http://www.masud.co.uk/ISLAM/ahm/gender.htm.

God, *Allāh* is understood to be a comprehensive name that does not have a plural or any gendered derived forms. By contrast, the English name *God* has a plural (gods) and a feminine derived form (goddess).

Although God speaks of Himself as 'He' in the Qur'ān, grammarians and exegetes agree that this is in no way 'literal' but is based upon the structure of the Arabic language. Arabic 'has no neuter, and the use of the masculine is normal in Arabic for genderless nouns. No male preponderance is implied, any more than femininity is implied by the grammatically female gender of neuter plurals.'[1] Similarly, Maura O'Neil argues in her book that 'Muslims do not use a masculine God as either a conscious or unconscious tool in the construction of gender roles.'[2] It is clear from Islamic thought that God is not seen as either male or female, since both of these are part of the created order.

As mentioned at the beginning of this chapter, the first part of the *shahāda* specifically deals with the Islamic understanding of God. Gai Eaton argues that the *shahāda* may seem very foreign and perplexing to people who do not know that the whole of the Qur'ān could basically be described as a commentary on these four words (*lā illāha illa Allāh*), or as an amplification of them.[3] To utter these words means to state that there is no other power except Him and that He is like no other. It is to negate the right of any other being to godhead and to affirm that the only one is God. At the same time, it also implies that God is the power behind all things and events that have ever existed or occurred, including time and space, because they exist only because of Him. God is therefore at once transcendent and immanent, infinitely beyond and infinitely close to his creation since He is not only creation's Creator (*al-Khāliq*), Giver of life (*al-Muḥyī*) and Giver of death (*al-Mumīt*), but is also the Sustainer (*al-Rāziq*).[4]

1 Ibid.

2 Maura O'Neill, *Women Speaking, Women Listening: Women in Interreligious Dialogue*, Maryknoll, NY: Orbis Books, 1990, p. 31.

3 Gai Eaton, *Islam and the Destiny of Man*, Cambridge: Islamic Texts Society, 1994, p. 67.

4 Nasr, *Young Muslim's Guide*, p. 23.

According to the late scholar Ismail Raji al-Faruqi, for Muslims, God's ultimacy (besides being metaphysical) cannot be isolated from, or emphasised, at the cost of the axiological. God is the final end in the sense that while everything is sought for another, which in turn is sought for a third and so on, yet God is the ultimate end; in other words, He is the object of all desire. He is therefore unique, because He is the One and no one is like Him, and it is this uniqueness that Muslims bear witness to in their faith.[1] God is self-sufficient in His existence, whereas creation's existence is based totally upon God's. Hence, *tawḥīd* means not merely to accept that God is One, but to affirm the unity of God and actively negate any dualism and idolatry (*shirk*). In Islamic theology, all Sunni scholars have agreed on the unknowable nature of the divine essence, stating that 'God is other than any concept that comes to mind', but also recognising that 'while the essence of God is utterly unlike other essences, it is, nonetheless, not devoid of attributes.'[2]

The Ninety-Nine Beautiful Names of God

Muslim theologians insist that to truly understand the concept of God it is necessary to look at the ninety-nine Qur'ānic attributes simultaneously.[3] In other words, not one single attribute can be understood separately, but all ninety-nine attributes holistically explain the nature of God. God is not just the Most Merciful, the Loving, the Giver of life and the Forgiving, but also the Just, the Distresser, the Giver of death and the Avenger. It is clear that these names could easily belong to two categories: one is gentle and embracing whilst the other instils a sense of awe and fear.[4] From this we may ask how God can have such contradictory qualities. A possible explanation is

1 Ismail Raji al-Faruqi, *Al Tawḥīd: Its Implication for Thought and Life*, Herndon, VA: International Institute of Islamic Thought, 1986, p. 10.

2 Yusuf, preface to *Creed of Imam al-Ṭaḥāwī*, p. 7.

3 Hacınebioğlu, *Does God Exist?*, p. 222.

4 Sachiko Murata and William C. Chittick, *The Vision of Islam*, London: I. B. Tauris, 1996, p. 68.

that the attributes vary due to the complexity of creation and created beings, and their relationship with the divine within space and time. Yusuf Ali (d. 1372/1953), the celebrated exegete and translator of the Qur'ān, argues that these ninety-nine names must be understood in a coherent way. He explains that the ninety-nine names merge into each other just like the night merges into the day:

> To some it may appear strange or even irreconcilable that God should be both Merciful and Just; that He should both protect His devotees and yet ask for their self-sacrifice; that he should command them to return good for evil, and yet permit retaliation under certain restrictions. But such thoughts are short-sighted. Do they not see many inconsistencies in all life, all nature, and all creation? Why, even in such simple phenomena as night and day, the one merges into the other, and no one can tell when precisely the one begins and the other ends. Yet we can see in a rough sort of way that the one gives rest and the other activity, that the one reveals the beauties of the starry heavens and the other the splendour of the sun. In countless ways we can see there the wisdom and the fine artistry of God. And there are subtle nuances and mergings in nature that our intelligence can hardly penetrate.[1]

Ali elucidates that God can therefore be both Just and Merciful since He can understand the subtleties of the immensely complicated human existence, whereas human beings' awareness of all creation is limited. William Chittick uses the examples of God as the Giver of life, the Sustainer and the Giver of death to explain the different facets

1 Q.XXII.180, footnote no. 2841.

of God. He argues that the individual creature come to know God in the guise of specific names at various times. Creatures all around us are given life—from humans and animals to plants, insects and bacteria; they are sustained by an intensely complicated arrangement and then they die. At the same time, all creatures are reborn or recycled into another state: for example, a dead plant may sustain new bacteria and finally give birth to an alternative form of plant life. Muslim theology argues that the subtlety of how creation works does not end here but instead demonstrates that a deeper non-physical reality exists as well. For example, in Islam all new birth is also seen as a death (or, separation) from the previous reality. A creature born into this world, born from the womb of its mother must die (separate) from the life of the womb. In a similar fashion, a person leaving in this world must be born into the next world. Life and death are not seen as contradictory when looked at through such a lens. Consequently, all of the seemingly contradictory attributes of God, such as the Forgiving and the Avenger, must be understood not as contradictory, but as complementary.

Following the same line of reasoning, Sachiko Murata explains the divine name *al-Ḥaqq* (meaning, the Truth or the Real) with regard to what can be regarded as the duality of Creator and creature. She points out that God's reality is seen as absolute whereas creation's reality is relative and intrinsically based upon God's. From this perspective there is no real duality, simply the Real. Everything except God is relative, making God, *al-Ḥaqq*, the only Real.[1] Gai Eaton points out that 'this world is less real than we suppose, but only if we mistake it for the sole reality beyond which there is nothing and again nothing.'[2] All creation at whatever level is therefore in some way 'real', but only in the sense that it represents the Real. Murata puts it this way: 'In respect of God's incomparability everything other than God—the whole cosmos—is false and unreal, but in the respect of

1 Murata and Chittick, *Vision of Islam*, pp. 67–68.

2 Eaton, *Remembering God*, p. 167.

His similarity all things reflect *ḥaqq* to some degree.'[1] In short, everything exists only because of God Who is known as both *al-Ḥaqq* and *al-Ḥayy* (the Living). The Real or the Living is neither a thing nor even a concept, since these are necessarily a part of the materialistic reality; in other words, relative. Thus, when ʿAlī b. Abī Ṭālib, the cousin of the Prophet, was asked, 'Where is God?' he replied, 'He is timeless and spaceless.'[2]

It is argued that *al-Ḥaqq*—and the other ninety-nine names of God—can be known and at the same time remains unknown. Through what is called religious experience and presence, *al-Ḥaqq* is infinitely close and known, and yet at the same time, *al-Ḥaqq* is infinitely beyond human rational comprehension. Material existence is therefore just one of many relative realities, all existing because there is no reality except the Real.

Transcendence and Immanence

Historically, the majority of Muslim theologians were hesitant to use such Christian theological terms as transcendence and immanence since their argument was that God could not be conceptually contained within such limited notions. Their argument followed on to state that God was neither transcendent nor immanent, leading the medieval Egyptian scholar Ibn ʿAtā' Allāh to argue, 'When did He disappear that He needed to be indicated?'[3] In Islam, it would be incorrect to understand the division of Creator and creation as an unqualified separation, since the Qur'ān strongly emphasises God's nearness to His creation. God knows of every creature at every instant, however large or minute the creature or incident might be. This is very strongly felt from verses in the Qur'ān such as, 'Not a leaf doth fall but with His knowledge: there is not a grain in the darkness (or depths) of the earth, nor anything fresh or dry (green or

1 Murata, *Tao of Islam*, p. 121.

2 Habibuddin Ahmed, *The Nature of Time and Consciousness in Islam*, Hyderabad: Islamic Thought and Science Institute, 2000, p. 57.

3 Yusuf, introduction to *Creed of Imam al-Ṭaḥāwī*, p. 15.

withered), but is (inscribed) in a record clear (to those who can read)',[1] and, 'And no female conceives, or lays down (her load), but with His knowledge.'[2] The Qur'ān paints a picture of an immense presence of God with regards to His creation. It is stated in the Qur'ān that God is extremely close to human beings, whom He created: 'It was We Who created man, and We know what dark suggestions his soul makes to him: for We are nearer to him than (his) jugular vein',[3] and that He knows all of creation: 'He is the First and the Last, the Evident and the Immanent: and He has full knowledge of all things.'[4]

As mentioned earlier, in Islam God is described in both the Qur'ān and *Ḥadīth* through the medium of the ninety-nine names, such as the Most Merciful, the Living, the Guide, the Holy, the Self-subsisting, the Wise, the Sovereign King and the Light. In the Qur'ān, Muslims are asked to use these names to call upon Him: 'The most beautiful names belong to Allah: so call on him by them.'[5] These names are also referred to as the attributes of God, and they reflect His immanence and His transcendence.[6] All of the beautiful names are regarded as being connected with each other and with creation in innumerable ways. The theological quest in Islam to understand God and His relationship with creation is pursued through the study of these names and attributes.

It is interesting to note that there are *ḥadīth*s that go beyond this by speaking of God in a more mystical way, for example the Prophet Muḥammad is known to have said, 'Do not abuse time, for God is time.'[7] This *ḥadīth* has been interpreted by the majority of scholars

1 Q.VI.59.
2 Q.XXXV.11.
3 Q.L.16.
4 Q.LVII.3.
5 Q.VII.180.
6 Victor Danner, *The Islamic Tradition: An Introduction*, New York: Amity House, 1988, p. 75.
7 Muslim, *Ṣaḥīḥ*, XL.5, http://sunnah.com/muslim/40 and XL.1, http://sunnah.com/muslim/40, 22 February 2016.

to mean that God is the Creator and Manager of linear time (time related to creation), so anyone who curses time (for example, in its effects on old age) is ipso facto cursing the source of all time, God.[1]

In the Islamic vision of the universe described above, God is always with each individual creature in the capacity of Lord. God is *al-Khabīr* (the All-Aware) in the sense that He is fully aware of all creation, including all human complexities.[2] In this theological world view, the concept of deism has no place in Islam. Deism is a seventeenth-century European philosophical position that argues that the Creator (the Aristotelian prime mover) does not intervene in creation's affairs. Deism is therefore rejected in Islam because of its proponents' contention that God is wholly transcendent and not immanent, meaning that they believe that God exists and is the Creator but that He does not intervene in the world beyond what was necessary to create it. Accordingly, for the deist, God does not literally answer prayers or cause miracles to occur, nor does He have continuous involvement with, or a special presence within, creation.

This idea of God was developed in eighteenth-century Europe through the writings of scholars such as John Locke (d. 1690) and Matthew Tindal (d. 1739) and contributed to the rationalism of the European Enlightenment. Its eventual logical outcome was a position amongst many Enlightenment thinkers that rationalism was superior to revelation, and that in some way revelation had become obsolete.[3] Today, many postmodern thinkers in the West argue that there are 'a variety of "rationalities" which have to be respected in their own right', leading ultimately to the notion that everybody has their own personal truths and that there is no one objective ultimate Truth.[4]

As pointed out in the introduction, this contradicts the Islamic world view. In Islamic theology there is an objective ultimate Truth;

1 Ibid., p. 63.

2 Eaton, *Islam and the Destiny of Man*, p. 62.

3 Alister E. McGrath, *Christian Theology: An Introduction*, 2nd ed., Oxford: Blackwell Publishing, 1997, pp. 214–16.

4 Ibid., pp. 218–19.

what Muslim scholars have had to debate is whether this objective ultimate Truth is only attainable from God's perspective (that is, by humans receiving an external revelation), or it is also possible to understand it from a subjective human perspective. In other words, can human beings come to the conclusion of the existence of the One God by through reason or do they necessarily need revelation from God in order to do so? The scholar Māturīdī accepted that reason alone could lead a person to belief in the One God, even without an external revelation through a prophet reaching one.[1] Thus, he argued that individual human beings could reach the ultimate objective truth through their subjective reasoning. The Muslim scholars defending this idea today would argue that with their innate nature (*fiṭra*), the primordial covenant[2] and reason, all humans can reach this conclusion by themselves if they struggle against selfish desire. Here, we are not talking about the details of rituals and laws that have been revealed, but rather about the knowledge of the existence of *tawḥīd*. Māturīdī did make it clear that even though reason was a source of knowledge, it was subordinate to revelation since revelation was the only source to describe the exact rituals and laws needed for a society. [3] However, the flip side of this belief in the unity of God based upon reason alone is that it becomes incumbent upon all people to reach that conclusion without a prophet in order to attain salvation. On the other hand, the scholar Ashᶜarī held that prophets (and thus, external revelation) were absolutely necessary to reach the objective ultimate Truth and to attain salvation, and therefore belief was not incumbent upon those who were not reached by God's messengers either directly or indirectly.[4]

Hence, this leads the discussion further to the concept of a 'personal God'. What does this word mean in Islamic theology? If God

1 Andrew Rippin, *Muslims: Their Religious Beliefs and Practices*, New York: Routledge, 1990, p. 71.

2 See below for the discussion on the 'primordial covenant'.

3 Ibid.

4 Ibid.

is personal, does that mean He is not transcendent? According to Muhammad Legenhausen, this dichotomy which informs much of Christian theology and western religious studies has no place in Islamic thought.[1] The objective conception of the Real and the subjective experience of an immanent God are but representations of two true realms necessary for the understanding of the divine. The best way to explain this is perhaps through the Qur'ānic verse where the raison d'être for the creation of human beings is stated, 'I have only created Jinns and men, that they may serve Me',[2] and the famous tradition of the Prophet who, speaking on behalf of God said, 'I was a Hidden Treasure and I desired to be known. Therefore I created the creatures so that I might be known'.[3] Islamic tradition is insistent that both ideas lead to the same conclusion: knowing God is to worship Him, and truly worshipping God is to recognise that 'all that is on earth will perish: But will abide (for ever) the Face of thy Lord, full of Majesty, Bounty and Honour.'[4] Consequently, in this world view there is no difference between the immanent and transcendent God.

God in Everyday Life

At this juncture it is important to pause and contemplate the place of God Most High in everyday Muslim life. Eaton says, 'God is sometimes described as *al-Ẓāhir*, translated as the Evident and the Apparent; but such tepid words cannot convey the force of meaning inherent in the word. To a man in the desert the sun is more than simply 'apparent'; it is blazingly and undeniable present and he cannot escape it, such is the actuality of the Divine for the Muslims.'[5] That is why Eaton argues that to bear witness to divine unity (uttering the *shahāda*) is the fountainhead of all Islamic faith and practice.

1 Muhammad Legenhausen, *Contemporary Topics of Islamic Thought*, Tehran: Alhoda Publishers, 2000, pp. 100–01.

2 Q.LI.56.

3 Legenhausen, *Contemporary Topics*, p. 10.

4 Q.XXVII.55–54.

5 Eaton, *Islam and the Destiny of Man*, p. 68.

Ismail Raji al-Faruqi further describes God's place in Muslim life as follows: 'God is centrality in every Muslim thought, Muslim mind and Muslim place. God is not merely an absolute, ultimate first cause or principle but a core of normativeness.'[1] In the Qur'ān it is said, 'Seest thou not that God doth know (all) that is in the heavens and on earth? There is not a secret consultation between three, but He makes the fourth among them,—Nor between five but He makes the sixth,—nor between fewer nor more, but He is in their midst, wheresoever they be: In the end will He tell them the truth of their conduct, on the Day of Judgment. For God has full knowledge of all things.'[2] When speaking to Muslims about God it is therefore crucial to recognise this *immanence* or actuality of the divine presence in everyday life, as well as His transcendence. The Prophet reported that God had said, 'I am as My servant thinks I am. I am with him when he makes mention of Me. If he makes mention of Me to himself, I make mention of him to Myself; and if he makes mention of Me in an assembly, I make mention of him in an assembly better than it. And if he draws near to Me an arm's length, I draw near to him a fathom's length. And if he comes to Me walking, I go to him at speed.'[3]

Thus, to speak to a Muslim of an exclusive transcendent God or an exclusive personal God, and to add in the concepts of scepticism, agnosticism or deism to the debate is to bring in something alien to Muslim thought. For the average Muslim, God simply exists for him or her because they know it to be true; just as the Qur'ān is the word of God and Muḥammad is His Messenger. Historically, Muslim scholars have provided empirical evidence for the integrity and sincerity of Muḥammad from both his followers and his enemies to show why they believed he was the Prophet of God. They have further demonstrated the illiteracy of the Prophet Muḥammad and his limited contact with Jews and Christians and have presented this

1 Al-Faruqi, *Al Tawḥīd*, p. 2.

2 Q.LVIII.7.

3 *40 Hadith Qudsi*, *ḥadīth* 15, http://sunnah.com/qudsi40/15, 22 February 2016.

as the primary reason why it is impossible for him to have borrowed the complex and distinct teachings found in the Qur'ān from the Torah or the New Testament. The beauty, uniqueness and the complex writing style of the Qur'ān have also been used to prove its inimitability.[1]

From this perspective, the above constitutes empirical evidence that the Qur'ān is God's proven word and that Muḥammad is His Messenger, who spoke the whole truth.[2] Anything else is regarded as inconceivable, since it would mean either that Muḥammad did not tell the whole truth or that the Qur'ān is not the 'word of God.' Yet, if the Qur'ān is accepted as the 'word of God' and Muḥammad as His Messenger, why have Muslims felt the need to prove the existence of God? Muslim scholars did debate the proofs for the existence of God, but with the aim to defend the already fully accepted existence of God and never to disprove such a fact. Ibn Khaldūn (d. 808/1406), the Ashʿarī theologian and social historian, wrote on this issue in the eighth/fourteenth century: 'Speculative theologians do not use the (rational) arguments they talk about as do the philosophers, in order to investigate the truth (of the articles of faith), to prove the truth of what had been previously not been known and to make it known. (Their use of rational arguments) merely expresses a desire to have rational arguments with which to bolster the articles of faith and the opinions of the early Muslims concerning them, and to refute the doubts of innovators who believe that their perceptions of (the articles of faith in their interpretation) are rational ones.'[3]

The Theological Positions

However, not all Muslims agreed that rational arguments from outside of revelation were needed to defend the existence of God. For instance, Ibn Rushd (d. 595/1198) divided Muslim scholars into three

1 Abdullah Saeed, *The Qur'ān: An Introduction*, London: Routledge, 2008, p. 52.

2 Ibid., p. 29.

3 Ibn Khaldūn, *The Muqaddimah*, p. 154.

groups according to the position they held on this theological point:
1) The Atharīs (traditionalists) denied that any argument was necessary to prove God's existence. They argued that His existence was basically known through revelation and the Prophet. Thus, they presented empirical evidence based upon scripture and Prophetic tradition to defend the prophethood of Muḥammad and the divinity of the message found within the Qur'ān.
2) The majority of Sufis argued that gaining an understanding of God's existence did not require speculative rationalism, but that those who walked the Sufi path would directly know Him through His presence.
3) Basing their arguments upon the scriptures, the Muʿtazilīs, and their opponents the Ashʿarīs and the Māturīdīs, argued for a rational line of reasoning for the existence of God but each school did so in distinctive ways.

Debates about proving the existence of God in Muslim classical theology have normally utilised two of the three well-known arguments within the philosophical and theological literature; namely, the teleological argument, the cosmological argument and the ontological argument. All of these three arguments for the existence of God are again commonly divided into a posteriori and a priori arguments. An a posteriori argument depends on a rule, principle, assertion or a premise that must be known through human experience within the world, whereas the a priori argument lies or rests on a principle or rule that needs no experience of the world but can be based upon human reflection. It is only the ontological argument out of the three major theistic arguments that is an a priori argument.[1] In classical Muslim theology, the teleological and cosmological arguments were mainly utilised. Yaran states, 'Although there may not be a total consensus, one may say that in Islamic thought, too, there are three traditional or classical arguments. The *kalam* cosmological argument

1 Mustafa Ceric, *Roots of Synthetic Theology in Islam: A Study of the Theology of Abu Mansur Al-Maturidi (d. 333/944)*, Kuala Lumpur: International Institute of Islamic Thought and Civilization, 1995, p. 143.

based on the contingent temporality [*ḥudūth*] of the universe, the *falsafa* cosmological argument based on contingency [*imkān*] of the universe, and the Qur'anic arguments from design [the teleological argument]. The latter was divided into two versions by Ibn Rushd as the argument from providence [*ʿināya*] and the argument from creation [*ikhtirāʿ*].'[1]

Classical Muslim theologians used the teleological (or design) argument to show that through one's sense perception (be it functional or aesthetic) human beings could observe a grand, intricate, complex and harmonious creation of cosmic, spiritual and terrestrial reality that indicated the existence of a Creator. A counter to this kind of design argument was later strongly posited by the Scottish scholar David Hume (d. 1776), who was debating against William Paley's (d. 1805) argument about the 'grand designer.' In his *Natural Theology*, William Paley took the design of a watch as an analogy to explain creation. Hume undermined the use of this kind of analogy by arguing for the dissimilarity between human-made objects and natural objects.[2] Hume may rightly have argued that there are weaknesses in such analogies and that thus the resulting conclusion is suspect, but it is important to note that the Islamic position did not simply rest on this narrow design argument as put forward by Paley. Instead, the Islamic teleological argument also rested on providence, wisdom and interconnection, and speaks of a superb 'fine-tuning' of the universe.[3]

The Muslim teleological argument, which was primarily based upon Qur'ānic verses, was a popular argument found in classical literature, and is even used amongst everyday Muslims today. The argument is that everything was created through design and wisdom; that is, everything is a sign of God's existence. As stated earlier, this argument was not so much to convince Muslims of the existence of

1 Yaran, *Islamic Thought*, p. 195.

2 Victoria S. Harrison, *Religion and Modern Thought*, London: SCM Press, 2012, pp. 176–77.

3 Yaran, *Islamic Thought*, p. 35.

God, but rather to demonstrate the coherence of monotheism. This would then lead believers to contemplate God and glorify Him. The argument within the Qur'ān was that everything was created through design and providence; thus, everything is a sign of His existence.[1] It has been pointed out by Hacınebioğlu that the Qur'ān presents hundreds of verses that speak of evidential signs of the affirmation of the existence of God, and as he says, 'The existence of the universe and the extraordinary beauty, order and wisdom that is manifested in it, is the central evidential sign which the Holy Qur'an constantly draws attention to in its exhortation for mankind to recognise the existence of God.'[2]

This argument is scattered across the text of the Qur'ān in various forms, for example in verses xxv.61, lxxviii.6–16 and lxxx.24–33. Furthermore, the story of the Prophet Abraham's youth in the Qur'ān is used as an example of the human being's rational search for God, first through reason and then divine guidance.[3] 'To reflect' and 'to reason about the signs of the universe' are phrases found scattered across the Qur'ān, where it is considered a spiritual responsibility of human beings to inquire so that they can see the wisdom for the existence of God.[4] In verse ii.164 of the Qur'ān it is stated, 'These are signs for those who use their minds.' For Atharī scholars it was enough that these arguments were in the Qur'ān as proof for anybody who would listen. For the Muᶜtazila and their opponents, the Ashᶜarīs and the Māturīdīs, the words in the Qur'ān, 'who use their minds', were an invitation to use rational arguments to explain the existence of God.

Fakhr al-Dīn al-Rāzī classified four distinct categories of proofs of God's existence:

1) arguments from the creation of the attributes of all created things (teleological argument)

1 Ayman Shihadeh, 'The Existence of God', in Winter, ed., *Cambridge Companion to Classical Islamic Theology*, p. 202.

2 Hacınebioğlu, *Does God Exist?*, p. 36.

3 For instance, see Q.vi.74–82.

4 Yaran, *Islamic Thought*, p. 4.

2) arguments from the creation of things (teleological argument)
3) arguments from the contingency of the attributes of things (cosmological argument)
4) arguments from the contingency of things (Ibn Sīnā's contingency argument).[1]

The teleological argument was therefore the main rational argument developed by the three schools of thought in the eighth century during a period of cultural and political upheaval. It was complemented by the knowledge that Muslim scholars came across when they began translating Greek, Persian and Indian manuscripts, and encountered numerous writings on the teleological argument. For instance, Plato had written about the design argument in his book, *Laws*, as follows: 'To begin with, think of the earth, and sun, and planets and everything',[2] highlighting that the existence of created things must be attributed to a Creator. This would have strongly resonated with Muslim theologians with their knowledge of the Qur'ān and the arguments of God's existence found within it.[3]

Early writers such as the Muʿtazilī theologian and littérateur Jāḥiẓ (d. 258/868) wrote widely about the topic in books such as *The Book of Proofs and Reflection Regarding Creation and Divine Governance*, drawing heavily on Greek sources, whereas Ibādī Imam Qāsim b. Ibrāhīm (d. 245/860) principally used Qur'ānic inspiration to reach the same conclusion in his writings. The Sufi theologian al-Ḥārith al-Muḥāsibī (d. 243/857) used to say that through the universe, inanimate nature, plant life, animal life and human life, from the lowest to the highest, the unity of the universe as creation as well

1 Shihadeh, 'The Existence of God', in Winter, ed., *Cambridge Companion to Classical Islamic Theology*, p. 200–201.

2 Quoted in Yaran, *Islamic Thought*, p. 28.

3 Plato's *Laws* was translated into Arabic and was read and commented on by Muslim theologians. One of the earliest experts on Plato was the philosopher Abū Naṣr Muḥammad al-Fārābī (d. 339/950), whose many works had a profound impact on Islamic scholarship. For Fārābī's compendium of Plato's *Laws*, see Alfarabius, *Compendium Legum Platonis*, ed. F. Gabrieli, London: Warburg Institute, 1952.

as the unity of its Creator may be inferred. Māturīdī also occasionally presented a teleological argument whilst debating the cosmological argument, such as pointing out that 'the components of the world are made in such a way as to serve a certain end of the world as a whole…and that the world as a whole is designed according to the divine wisdom, which is not always obvious to us.'[1] Ibn Ḥazm (d. 456/1064), an Atharī and Ẓāhirī scholar,[2] covered the design argument at two levels: at the cosmic, celestial scale and at the terrestrial, biological scale. He was perhaps one of the first theologians to not only speak of the universe's functionality with regards to the teleological argument, but to also speak passionately about the aesthetic side of the details of the universe. He argued that, when seen from an aesthetic perspective, the universe was unspeakably ingenious in its beauty and variety.[3] Later theologians such as Ghazālī adopted a more holistic approach to the design argument. In his book, *al-Ḥikma fī makhlūqāt Allāh* (The Wisdom in God's Creatures), Ghazālī wrote of the verses in the Qur'ān and the signs in creation: 'It should be apparent to anyone with the minimum of intelligence if he reflects a little upon the implications of these verses, and if he looks at the wonders in God's creation on earth and in the skies and at the wonders in animal and plants, that this marvellous, well-ordered system cannot exist without a Maker who conducts it, and a Creator who plans and perfects it.'[4]

While poets such as the famous Sufi poet Jalāl al-Dīn al-Rūmī (d. 671/1273) wrote impressive poetry to explain the signs of God,[5] other scholars such as Ibn Rushd and Fakhr al-Dīn al-Rāzī set forth arguments from a distinctively different perspective. They

1 Quoted in Ceric, *Roots of Synthetic Theology*, p. 144.

2 An extinct school of jurisprudence, founded by Dāwūd b. ʿAlī b. Khalaf (d. 270/884). The school was known for following the manifest, literal or apparent (*ẓāhir*) meaning of expressions in the Qur'ān and *Ḥadīth*.

3 Cited by Yaran, *Islamic Thought*, p. 34.

4 Ibid.

5 Ibid., p. 90.

advanced the case that the text of the Qur'ān not only supported the argument that creation was a sign of God's existence but also showed that providence could be used to prove His existence. Ibn Rushd highlighted that this kind of design argument originated in the Qur'ān, which is a scripture that requires human beings to reason about creation not only in terms of how it functions but also in terms of providence.[1] Fakhr al-Dīn al-Rāzī argued that with all its inter-connections, the universe is suitable for the existence and needs of all conscious beings. He held that this suitability could not be by mere chance; thus, it necessarily followed that all of this was intended by the One Who is Beneficient.[2] The first argument is that of providence, according to which one may observe that everything in the universe serves a purpose, or is advantageous, for humanity and all other conscious beings. Ibn Rushd speaks of the sun, the moon, the earth and the weather as examples of how the universe is conditioned for human beings. If the universe is so finely tuned, then it speaks of a fine tuner: God. The second argument complements the first and stems from the observation that everything in the world appears to have been made with order and beauty. Plants and animals have a construction that appears to have been designed by someone possessed of wisdom and power. Thus, Ibn Rushd did not only use the design argument but also developed the teleological argument from Qur'ānic verses to include the idea of providence; meaning that God had made the universe in such a way that all of creation could exist and sustain itself.[3] While Fakhr al-Dīn al-Rāzī reasoned that such evidence from the Qur'ān had more than one effect, he stated: '[They] are in one respect evidences, and in other respects, blessings. Such subtle evidences are more efficacious in the heart, and more effective in the soul; for

1 Ibid., p. 31.

2 Cited in Shihadeh, 'The Existence of God', in Winter, ed., *Cambridge Companion to Classical Islamic Theology*, p. 202.

3 Cited in Yaran, *Islamic Thought*, p. 31.

qua evidences they provide knowledge [the mind is assured and enlightened], whereas qua blessings they lead to surrender to the Benefactor, thankfulness to Him and submission to His Majesty's might [the heart and soul find contentment].'[1]

Other Muslim scholars, such as the philosophers Abū Yūsuf al-Kindī (d. 259/873), Abū Naṣr Muḥammad al-Fārābī (d. 339/951) and Ibn Sīnā (d. 980/1037) as well as the theologians Ghazālī and Māturīdī, posited the cosmological argument to demonstrate the existence of God as the First Cause or Necessary Being. However, two distinct cosmological arguments were developed in the Islamic tradition: the first was that of philosophy (*falsafa*) and the second was that of theology (*kalām*). Fārābī and Ibn Sīnā developed the cosmological argument in philosophy to demonstrate the coherence of belief in God. According to this line of reasoning, the universe is considered to be the total of contingent (dependent) beings, and as such is not self-subsistent (it is not able to exist independently of anything external to itself). Due to the universe's contingency, it requires a necessary existent being to sustain it, which is God. Furthermore, Fārabī argued that since it is a matter of fact that the world exists, it then follows that its existence must be due to another being, either contingent or otherwise. However, because a series of contingent beings responsible for a series of creations cannot proceed to infinity, he argued that this series of causes and effects must end in a cause that is self-existent and self-sustaining; in other words, God. Based on this reasoning, Ibn Sīnā continued this argument but placed more emphasis on the concept of contingency. From this reasoning, the philosophers (*falāsifa*) argued for the eternality of the universe. Yaran describes their argument as follows: 'Since the universe is possible of existence, and since what is possible of existence enters into existence only by a cause who makes its existence outweigh its non-existence and continually maintains

1 Quotation from Shihadeh, 'The Existence of God', Winter, ed., *Cambridge Companion to Classical Islamic Theology*, p. 204.

it in existence; then, the universe logically terminates in something necessary of existence, an uncaused first existent, namely, the One God.' Hence, these philosophers adopted the notion of an eternal creation with a first cause and a necessary being.[1]

On the other hand, the proponents of the cosmological argument of theology (*kalām*) accepted a belief in the origination and the temporality of the created universe. It was in fact Kindī, who was known as the father of Muslim philosophy, who was the first to posit the cosmological argument of *kalām* for the existence of God. He argued that the universe had a beginning in time and that the universe could not cause itself to come into existence. Hence, the multiplicity evident in the universe must be caused by something, and the cause of this multiplicity is God. Māturīdī further put forth a seven-point cosmological argument for the existence of the Necessary Being in his book, *Kitāb al-tawḥīd*.[2] Ghazālī further developed this same argument in a number of his books.

This cosmological argument of theology asserts the existence of God based on the contention that everything that comes into existence has a cause and since the universe has come into being and has a series of temporal phenomena in it, these cannot regress infinitely because the acceptance of an infinite series of temporal phenomena leads to meaninglessness. Hence, the series of temporal phenomena must have a beginning, and must have been caused by a being that transcends all creation, space and time. This leads to the conclusion that God is the First Cause or the Creator. Accordingly, the basic structure of the argument is composed of the following four propositions:

1) Everything in the universe that has a beginning must have a cause. Infinite regress is impossible; thus, everything that has a beginning is contingent.

2) The universe has a beginning.

1 Yaran, *Islamic Thought*, p. 200.

2 For more details on his cosmological argument, see Ceric, *Roots of Synthetic Theology*, p. 144.

3) Therefore the beginning of the universe must have been caused by something.
4) The only such cause must be an uncaused cause, the Necessarily Existent One.[1]

The question as to why the first cause must be God was responded to by Ibn Sīnā. He argued that the chain of causes must end with the One who is self-sufficient and not in any need of anything else to give Him existence. He furthered this claim by supporting it with the argument that the concept of 'necessary existence' within the intellect or the mind is the basis for arguing for a Necessary Existent One. Some contemporary scholars have designated this the ontological argument.[2]

It is interesting here to point out that Fakhr al-Dīn al-Rāzī foresaw the criticisms raised by thinkers such as Hume and Immanuel Kant (d. 1804), who disputed that any argument for a cause must be kept within the world of our sense experiences since the argument has an empirical starting point, and consequently to seek to establish an uncaused cause outside the empirical world is wholly unjustified. Fakhr al-Dīn al-Rāzī had in fact already highlighted the same weakness by stating that inevitably all proofs for the existence of God departed from the facts of the world but also have to go beyond them.[3] Thus, he criticised Ibn Sīnā's claim of providing a new proof based on a consideration of existence qua existence exclusively on God; in other words, without the consideration of things other than God. Here Rāzī criticizes Ibn Sīnā for arguing that he had new proof which relied not on any physical evidence (secondery causes), meaning that the existence of God could be proven only through thought without any recourse to the contingent (the created) as evidence. He stated, 'It infers the existence of the necessary existent from the actual existence of the

1 Ibid., p. 166.

2 This idea is further explained below.

3 Anthony Flew, *The Question of God: An Introduction and Sourcebook*, London: Routledge, 2001, p. 71.

contingent', and he argued that one would 'still need to demonstrate that it is other than the physical things perceptible in this world.'[1]

It appears that there is a debate amongst contemporary scholars as to whether Ibn Sīnā advanced the ontological argument or not. It is often claimed that the ontological argument was first posited by the Christian scholar Saint Anselm of Canterbury (d. 1109) during the eleventh century, when he argued that the person who has thought of the concept of God as the Supreme Being cannot then rationally doubt it. This means that this argument is a priori or ontological; that is, it operates in the world of thought without assuming the actual existence of anything. It begins from accepting intellectually the idea that the nature of God is that of which nothing greater can be conceived.[2] The contemporary philosopher Cafer Yaran argues that if the argument posed by Ibn Sīnā was truly along the same lines as the ontological argument of Saint Anselm, then he would not have needed to advance arguments for the existence of God through the principle of causality or the concept of contingent being. Yaran therefore concludes that the best way to look at Ibn Sīnā's argument is to see it as 'a cosmological argument supplemented by conceptual analyses but not by the ontological argument.'[3] Nevertheless, since there is no consensus on whether Ibn Sīnā utilised the ontological argument or not, Toby Mayer argues that it can at least be maintained that Ibn Sīnā could be given credit for being the first person to have advanced an aspect of what we now know as the ontological argument.[4] It is interesting to note that even though Muslims have not formally utilised the ontological argument for the existence of God, the creedal phrase, *Allāh Akbar* (God is Most Great), used by Muslims in their daily prayers is essentially ontological. It implies that God is

1 Quotation from Shihadeh, 'The Existence of God', Winter, ed., *Cambridge Companion to Classical Islamic Theology*, p. 214.

2 Yaran, *Islamic Thought*, p. 189.

3 Ibid., pp. 192–93.

4 Toby Mayer, 'Ibn Sīnā's "Burhān al-Ṣiddīqīn,"' *Journal of Islamic Studies*, vol. XII, no. 1, 2001, pp. 18–39.

greater than anything that can be conceived by human beings; that God is beyond conceptualisation.[1]

Throughout their intellectual history, Muslims have always looked at the universe—be it the whole entity or single individual creation—as something of a revelation or sign of God. Both the teleological and the cosmological argument in Muslim intellectual history have adhered to this perspective. According to the theological view, the whole of the universe exists equally as God's creation because of its common relationship with God. By contrast, to not have a single Creator of cause and effect means either that everything happens by chance, which is illogical in the world view of Islam, or it means that causes themselves are conscious, able and knowledgeable of their effect upon the universe, which is not only meaningless but also makes them godlike. Denying the existence of God means either that other entities make the universe exist or that the universe can exist by itself, making the universe not only a godlike entity but also all of creation as well, down to the tiniest creature, since all entities in the universe co-exist and are interconnected. It has been argued by some that, rationally, it is easier to accept the One God 'instead of accepting the interference of endless godlike things or that we are inhibited by something as impersonal as "chance", which inevitably must lead to "chaos."'[2]

It is important here to highlight again that in Muslim theology these rational arguments were never tools to prove God's existence per se but rather to show a rational coherence in the belief in God. Thus, even if the human argument were perceived to be weak, it in no way means a loss of belief for individual Muslims, since their belief in God does not rely on a profound faith in the 'rightness' of personal human rationalisation, but rather on a profound faith in the Qur'ān as the word of God and Muḥammad as the Messenger of God. It could be argued that if one rational argument put forward is

1 Yusuf, introduction to *Creed of Imam al-Ṭaḥāwī*, p. 15.

2 Hacınebioğlu, *Does God Exist?*, p. 223.

seen to have flaws, then Muslim theologians are simply required to continue to construct and improve their rational arguments to show the coherence of monotheism. This is what a Muslim means when he or she states that the belief in God has never been questioned by Muslims. It must be remembered that even if Muslims strongly value reason and rationality as gifts from God, they do not value it above all other gifts. Reason in Islamic theology is seen as just one tool amongst others, such as revelation, law, theology, philosophy and mysticism, for deepening the human understanding of *al-Ḥaqq*.

The Attributes of God

All of the scholarship produced by the Muslim theological schools during the classical period demonstrates that theologians accepted the oneness and uniqueness of God (*tawḥīd*) and His existence. Any debates that ensued instead were concerned with the Muʿtazilī argument that the attributes of God (such as power, life and knowledge) could not exist on the basis that God was unique and eternally a unity. Ibn Khaldūn described the Muʿtazilīs as a group of people who broadened the interpretation of *tanzīh* (de-anthropomorphism) within theology compared to the work of those Muslims who came before them. The Muʿtazila did this through interpreting such verses as, 'Naught is like Him' (Q.XLII.9) and, 'There is none equal with Him' (Q.CXII.4), which they took to mean the denial of the existence of attributes such as Power, Life and Knowledge.[1] It was argued by Wāṣil b. ʿAṭā', the founder of the Muʿtazila, that if the One God and His attributes were eternal, then this would lead to associations (*shirk*) due to plurality, and thus Wāṣil and all later Muʿtazilī scholars rejected the notion that God has attributes.[2] The Muʿtazilī scholar Abū Hudhayl Muḥammad al-ʿAllāf (d. 235/850) later adopted the view that God could only be described in negatives.[3] This argument of the Muʿtazila

1 See Ibn Khaldūn, *The Muqaddimah*, p. 48.
2 Cited in Danner, *The Islamic Tradition*, p. 144.
3 Rippin, *Muslims*, p. 68.

was clearly intended to defend the oneness of God: therefore, they argued that too much emphasis on the attributes would confer ontological or true existent reality upon them, which in turn would lead to ascribing multiplicity to God. Their argument reiterated that the attributes of God could not be eternal because only God-in-Himself is eternal. Thus, for them, the 'names' of God mentioned in the Qur'ān were not attributes but metaphors, figures of speech or even created modes of divine action.[1]

The Muʿtazila charged those who believed in divine attributes of falling into anthropomorphism (which means believing that God has human attributes) or corporealism (which means believing that God's attributes are corporeal entities that exist within Him).[2] They argued that the verses in the Qur'ān that spoke about God's Hand, Face and God sitting upon the Throne should be interpreted figuratively.[3] They came to argue that when the Qur'ān mentioned God's Hand or Hands, it meant power and grace; His Face meant His existence or essence according to Khayyāṭ (d. 300/913), a later Muʿtazilī scholar. When the Qur'ān mentioned the descent of God, it really meant the descent of certain verses, and sitting on the Throne indicated dominion.[4] Those who countered this argument were the extreme theological groups known as the *Mushabbiha* (Anthropomorphists) and *Mujassima* (Corporealists), who interpreted the aforementioned verses as a corporeal reality. These anthropomorphists argued that the Hand of God was a real appendage and that His Face was a face with human form. The descent of God was also accepted as a corporeal reality, as was God sitting upon the Throne.[5]

The argument which led the Muʿtazilīs to deny that God has

1 Vincent Cornell, 'God in Islam', in Jones, ed., Encyclopedia of Religion, vol. v, pp. 3560–67.

2 Ibid.

3 For instance, see Q.II.255.

4 For instance, see Q.II.272 and Q.VI.52.

5 Georges Anawati, 'Kalām', in Jones, ed., *Encyclopedia of Religion*, vol. VIII, pp. 5059–69.

these attributes caused a confrontation with Aḥmad Ibn Ḥanbal, who argued on the basis of scripture that the attributes of God in no way threatened the unity of God. His was a non-speculative theology based upon the Qur'ān and *Ḥadīth*, which argued for a literal understanding without asking how (*bi-lā kayf*). Thus, Ibn Ḥanbal was defending an unembroidered approach to the text without anthropomorphising God.[1] Ibn Ḥanbal argued that God could only be accepted as He had described Himself in the Qur'ān. In this way, he accepted God's attributes, as well as all such verses that spoke of God's Face, Hand and descent, literally. But at the same time, he strongly argued that the literal text of the Qur'ān emphasised that God was Unique and not comparable to anything in His creation; thus, Ibn Ḥanbal rejected both the figurative interpretations of the Muʿtazilīs and the views of the Anthropomorphists and Corporealists.[2]

It was Ashʿarī in the tenth century who proposed various rationales for supporting the scriptural views of Ḥanbalī theology. However, with regards to God's unity and attributes, he simply said, 'The names of God (exalted is He) are His *ṣifāt*, and it cannot be said of His *ṣifāt* that they are He, nor that they are other than He.'[3] Just like Ibn Ḥanbal, Ashʿarī refused to enter into a rationalistic debate over the issue; he fully accepted the Qur'ān and *Ḥadīth*, which specified that God is One, that God has attributes and that He is eternal without knowing how.[4] Thus, Ashʿarī stated in his creed that 'whoever thinks that God's name is other than He, is in error. That God has Knowledge (*ʿilm*), as He has said, (Qur. 35, 12); ["Not one woman becomes pregnant and brings forth, except by His knowledge."] We maintain that God has Power (*qudra*), as He has said, (Qur. 41, 14); ["and have they not seen that God who created them is stronger than

1 Danner, *The Islamic Tradition*, p. 148.

2 J. Schacht, 'Aḥmad Ibn Ḥanbal', in P. J. Bearman et al., eds., *Encyclopaedia of Islam*, 2nd ed. (*EI²*), 12 vols., Leiden: E. J. Brill, 1960–2005, vol. 1, p. 275.

3 Abū Bakr Muḥammad b. al-Ḥasan Ibn Fūrak, *Mujarrad maqālāt al-Shaykh Abī al-Ḥasan al-Ashʿarī*, ed. Daniel Gimaret, Beirut: Dār al-Mashriq, 1987, p. 10.

4 Fakhry, *History of Islamic Philosophy*, pp. 211–12.

they?"] We maintain that God has Hearing (*samʿ*) and Seeing (*baṣar*) and do not deny it, as do the Muʿtazilites [...].'[1]

Ashʿarī denounced the Muʿtazila for excessive rationalism and for being wilfully ignorant of the Qur'ānic text. He spoke of the verses with regards to God's Hand and Face,[2] and that God sat Himself upon the Throne,[3] as reality but not in the same way that existed in creation. He argued that human beings could not conceive of how God has a hand; thus, the phrase, 'without knowing how and without drawing comparison' (*bi-lā kayf wa-lā tashbīh*) came about. This meant that, according to the Qur'ān, God sits upon His Throne and Muslims should believe in it without needing to know how.[4]

Māturīdī followed in the footsteps of Ashʿarī on the issue of these verses by saying that 'what the text says about God must be believed although human beings cannot know 'how' God is to be conceived as sitting on His Throne.'[5] Later on, one of the leading Māturīdī scholars of the twelfth century, Najm al-Dīn Abū Ḥafṣ al-Nasafī (d. 537/1142), presented a rational defence of the traditionalist view by stating, 'The Originator of the world (*Muhdith*) is God Most High, the One, the Eternal, the Decreeing, the Knowing, the Hearing, the Seeing, the Willing. He is not an attribute, nor a body, nor an essence, nor a thing formed, nor a thing bounded, nor a thing numbered, nor a thing divided, nor a thing compounded, nor a thing limited; and He is not described by quiddity (*mahiya*), nor by modality (*kayfiya*), and He does not exist in place or time, and there is nothing that resembles Him and nothing that is outside His knowledge and power. He has qualities (*ṣifāt*) from all eternity (*azali*) existing in His essence. They are not He nor are they any other than He.'[6]

1 See Duncan B. MacDonald, *Development of Muslim Theology, Jurisprudence, and Constitutional Theory*, New York, Charles Scribner, 1903, p. 294.

2 Q.II.272; VI.52.

3 Q.II.255.

4 Rippin, *Muslims*, p. 70.

5 Quoted in ibid., p. 72.

6 Quoted by MacDonald, *Development of Muslim Theology*, p. 309.

As Nuh Keller explains, there were three categories of God's attributes that were acknowledged within traditional Sunni *kalām* (that is, by the Ashʿarī and Māturīdī schools of theology): firstly, what is necessarily true of God; secondly, what is impossible to attribute to God; and thirdly, what is possible to affirm about God. In addition, each of these categories includes specific tenets of faith, and Keller summarises them as follows:

> The twenty attributes necessarily true of God are His existence; not beginning; not ending; self-subsistence, meaning not needing any place or determinant to exist; dissimilarity to created things; uniqueness, meaning having no partner in His entity, attributes, or actions; omnipotent power; will; knowledge; life; hearing; sight; speech; such that He is almighty; all-willing; all-knowing; living; all-hearing; all-seeing; and speaking—through His attributes of power, will, knowledge, life, hearing, sight, and speech, not merely through His being.
> The twenty attributes necessarily impossible of God are the opposites of the previous twenty, such as non-existence, beginning, ending, and so on.
> The one attribute merely possible of God is that He may create or destroy any possible thing.[1]

As described above, the Sunni schools of theology confronted both the anthropomorphists and those who wanted to understand God figuratively based upon rigid rationalism and analogy, but they did so in different ways. While the Ḥanbalīs confronted them from a purely scriptural position by citing specific verses from the Qur'an and *Ḥadīth*, the Ashʿarīs and the Māturīdīs argued against

1 Adapted from Keller, 'Kalam and Islam.'

these two trends through rational means (although, of course, their arguments were still grounded in the Qur'ān and *Ḥadīth*). Many may argue that the three Sunni schools of thought were being dogmatic and even literalist; however, when looking at it from their perspective, there were only three choices available, and only one that would be mindful of the full meaning found in the scriptures. In other words, accepting God as One, Unique and having attributes. These three choices were as follows:

1) The first choice explained the aforementioned Qur'ānic verses about God within a certain kind of human rationalism. It meant accepting that humankind could fully comprehend the Divine intellectually through human subjective understanding.

2) The second choice accepted these verses anthropomorphically; however, in hindsight, history shows that this led the Anthropomorphists and other similar sects to believe in a corporeal god, which contradicted the primary sources of Islam.

3) The final choice was to refuse anthropomorphism, yet also accept that the Qur'ān was not referring to metaphors or figures of speech but was instead literal; albeit beyond the full comprehension of humankind.

It seems obvious from a Sunni Muslim theological perspective that the first choice would make a human being overconfident and understand God only through rationalism. This would mean that God would be defined by what humans perceive to be possible, which has changed drastically throughout human history. Ultimately, human understanding is confined within time and space, making it subjective, but any transcendent knowledge must be free of such confinement. The second choice would have been a severe departure from the Qur'ānic text that emphasises God's oneness and uniqueness. This choice was in fact adopted by a group which arose in second/eighth century Kufa, and who were referred to by their opponents as the Ghulāt (literally, 'exaggerators'). The group deified ʿAlī b. Abī Ṭālib and his descendants, and because of this they were rejected by both Shiʿis and Sunnis alike.[1] The third and final choice accepts humbly that God can be understood through His attributes, with the understanding that God is infinitely beyond human rational comprehension and yet is also infinitely close.

Ghazālī eloquently explained the Sunni position by stating, 'I hold that the specifying mark of divinity belongs to none but God—the most high and to be held holy—and no one knows it but God, nor is it conceivable that anyone know it except Him or one like Him. And since there is no likeness of Him, He or "His nature" is not known by other than Him.'[2] Ghazālī reasoned that this did not mean that human beings could not know God, but that there were really only two ways of knowing Him: one was to know Him inadequately and the other way of knowing Him was what Ghazali referred to as 'closed', meaning it was inaccessible to humankind.[3] Through the attributes, humans can know God through mentioning His names and attributes, and compare them to what we know ourselves. But this comparison is abruptly cut short when the commandment, '[T]here is nothing whatever like unto Him',[4] is recalled, since it was argued by Ghazālī that God is Living, but not like living things; Powerful, but not like powerful people; and so on with all of God's attributes. Thus, Ghazālī concluded, 'Yet His attributes are too exalted to be likened to ours! So this will be an inadequate knowledge in which imaginings and resemblance are preponderant. So it needs to be complemented by the knowledge which denies any likeness, and which rejects any grounds for commensurability, even though the name be shared.'[5] He argued that the other knowledge was closed because that could

1 History records that many sects arose out of the Ghulāt movement in Kufa. One that survives today is the Nuṣayriyya, who are better known as the ʿAlawīs.

2 Ghazālī, *Ninety-Nine Beautiful Names of God*, p. 35.

3 Ibid., pp. 39–40.

4 Q.XLII.11.

5 Ghazālī, *Ninety-Nine Beautiful Names of God*, p. 40.

only be attained through being 'Lord' and knowing through experience, and so this route was utterly closed for all except God.[1]

The Most Beautiful Names Belong to God

In the Qur'ān it is written, 'The most beautiful names belong to God: so call on him by them';[2] and in a *ḥadīth* the Prophet Muḥammad said, 'God the most high has ninety-nine names—one hundred minus one—and whosoever enumerates them will enter paradise.'[3] The Athariyya, Ashᶜariyya and Māturīdiyya strongly supported the acceptance of the attributes or names of God based upon numerous Qur'ānic verses and *ḥadīth* reports. However, there were differences amongst these scholars as to how to understand the names of God. Bāqillānī (d. 403/1013), the Ashᶜarī scholar, argued that it was possible to come up with alternative names for God through rational consideration—whether revelation affirmed this or not. But the majority of scholars (such as Ghazālī and Fakhr al-Dīn al-Rāzī) argued that God's names could only be derived directly from revelation, although the meaning behind His attributes could be learned by means of reason.

Ghazālī was one scholar who elaborated on the concept of the unity of God and His attributes. He argued that all of the names are interrelated but not synonymous, and that they are intended to be understood in relation to creation. In his book, *al-Maqṣad al-asnā fī sharḥ asmā' Allāh al-ḥusnā* (The Ninety-Nine Beautiful Names of God), Ghazālī discussed each name of God and also explained how each one was related to human beings and to their everyday life. He argued, first of all, that the name *Allāh* was the greatest of all names because it united all attributes of divinity and was not used for anyone other than Him. By contrast, the other ninety-nine names referred only to a single attribute, such as Knowledge or Power, which could be used in creation and could be applied to other than God.

1 Ibid.

2 Q.LXXVI.180.

3 Ghazālī, *Ninety-Nine Beautiful Names of God*, pp. 21–22.

Ghazālī also noted that it was through one's knowledge of, and love for, God's attributes that a person could adopt them. He based this on the following saying of the Prophet: 'You should be characterised by the ninety-nine names of God.'[1] T. J. Winter eloquently explains this statement of Ghazālī as follows: 'When the human being is fully adorned by the names, he or she knows God and becomes a divine agent in the world, as the Qur'an tells the Prophet: "You did not throw when you threw, but God threw [Q.viii.17]."'[2] However, Ghazālī strongly cautioned against interpreting this as a human being attaining the attributes of God, since God's attributes cannot be the attributes of anyone else. It was more correct or accurate, he argued, to state that His servant has attained what is compatible with His attributes. Throughout his book, *The Ninety-Nine Beautiful Names of God*, Ghazālī specifically points out that each attribute is figuratively or generically related to human beings. For example, with regards to the divine name *al-Raḥmān* (the Most Compassionate), humans are asked to show mercy in their dealings with creation so as to embody this attribute of God. Numerous prophetic traditions may be found that highlight an attribute of God amongst creation, such as mercy, forgiveness, guidance, light and justice. Some attributes of God that are His exclusively and more difficult to pursue such as the Resurrector or Raiser of the dead were still dealt with by Ghazālī figuratively to explain their place within creation.[3]

Ibn Taymiyya (d. 726/1326), the celebrated Ḥanbalī scholar, classified belief in God into three theological categories: the unity of lordship (*tawḥīd al-rubūbiyya*), the unity of godship (*tawḥīd al-ulūhiyya*) and the unity of God in His names and attributes (*tawḥīd*

1 Ibid., pp. 49–52.

2 T. J. Winter, 'Jesus and Muḥammad: New Convergences', *Muslim World*, vol. xcix, no. 1, January 2009, pp. 21–39.

3 Ibid.

al-asmā' wa'l-ṣifāt).[1] Unity of lordship refers specifically to all creatures' relationship with God through the term, 'Lord.' This lordship refers to God as the sole Creator, Master, Giver of life and death and the fact that all happenings issue from the Knowledge, Will and Power of God. This lordship highlights creation's response to its Lord through submission, worship, praise and supplication without making anyone or anything associate with God. *Tawḥīd al-rubūbiyya* emphasises that there is only one Creator and Lord. It underlines the uniqueness and exclusiveness of God's work, creation and even the direction of the universe. It is argued that God sustains and maintains creation without any need from it.

Tawḥīd al-ulūhiyya is defined by Ibn Taymiyya as the unified worship of all creation to God and no other. In the Qur'ān it is stated, 'I have only created Jinns and men, that they may serve Me.'[2] Theologians and jurists are unanimous in agreeing that any virtuous action performed sincerely and with a belief in God is an act of worship. This includes any virtuous action such as praying, praising and thanksgiving, as well as mundane actions. This worship is defined as complete love accompanied by complete submission, and is recognised as the inner and outer reality of religion. Performing such worship requires people to direct their worship exclusively to God and it requires that people not take anything or anyone as an object of love of equal or greater importance than God. In the same way, reliance lies ultimately only on God. Even concepts such as harm or good (and which lead to love and fear amongst people) are seen as the domain of God; thus, only God is ultimately to be loved and feared as no other creature can harm you or do you good without His will. Both of the concepts above strongly refute any deistic influence on faith.

The third category, *tawḥīd al-asmā' wa'l-ṣifāt*, means that God

1 See Sophia Vasalou, *Ibn Taymiyya's Theological Ethics*, Oxford: Oxford University Press, 2016, p. 177 and Gerhard Böwering, ed., *The Princeton Encyclopedia of Islamic Political Thought*, Princeton: Princeton University Press, 2013, p. 231.

2 Q.LI.56.

is characterised by all of the attributes in absolute perfection. Even though Ibn Taymiyya expanded on the concept of God's immanence through His attributes, he made it clear that in no way did God's immanence create any possible reduction to divine transcendence. On this topic, Yahya Michot, states that 'no human type can be an image of the divine, but it can be a channel for a theophany in the sense that the divine ethical purposes are fully served and manifested in the one who does heaven's will.'[1]

The vast majority of Muslims agree upon the 'Lordship of God as well as the enumeration of His names, with only slight differences about what can or cannot be considered a name.'[2] As a result of all the debates examined in this chapter and many more that arose across the classical era, the single most popular creedal statement in Islamic theology is what became known as the *īmān mujmal* (summary of faith). It states: *I believe in God as he is known by His names and His attributes and I accept all of His commands and I assent to it in my heart*. It is interesting to note that within the Māturīdī school of theology, this text extends to include the words: *And as an expression by the tongue*.[3] Thus, the affirmation of the existence of God's names and attributes in this creedal statement is a direct consequence of the theological debates that took place in earlier centuries.

In the twenty-first century, when humanity is on the one hand vain about its great progress and on the other laments the destruction and futility that it has brought to the world, it is apt to say that the belief in *tawḥīd* inspires humanity to see itself as it truly is: a servant of God. Islam suggests that humanity's greatest power lies in its selfless service, but to achieve this it needs to know that what

1 Yahya Michot, 'The Image of God in Humanity from a Muslim Perspective', in Richard Harries, Norman Solomon and Timothy Winter, eds., *Abraham's Children: Jews, Christians and Muslims in Conversation*, London: T & T Clark International, 2006, pp. 163–74.

2 Yusuf, preface to *Creed of Imam al-Ṭaḥāwī*, p. 10.

3 Yasin Ramazan Başaran, 'The Idea of Subjective Faith in al-Maturidi's Theology', *Journal of Islamic Research*, vol. IV, no. 2, December 2011, pp. 167–70.

it ultimately serves is neither itself nor anything like itself. The first part of the *shahāda*—'There is no deity'—conveys the meaning that all of the things that one serves, works for and adores (whether it be oneself, ones children, ones spouse, work, aspirations or anything else), only become false when the Truth—the last part of the *shahāda*, 'Except God'—is dismissed for their sake. However, when the Truth is accepted, all of these other aspects of a person's life become a means of worshipping God.

Chapter Three

ANGELS

Do Muslims Believe in Angels?

In the twenty-first century, many people might argue that a belief in angels is an outdated, medieval superstition. Let us first consider the opinions of a Christian theologian, a feminist theorist and a scholar of Reform Judaism because it is useful for the reader to understand how the perception of angels can differ from that of Muslims. Don Cupitt, a contemporary (though controversial) Christian philosopher and theologian, argues that; 'Angels belong to a pre-scientific vision of the world. They are not mentioned in works of science and nobody is likely to discover them. It is usually said that an angel would need a huge breast bone, a keel four-feet deep or more. That's true; but I can't imagine the skeleton of a vertebrate with six limbs.'[1] The French feminist theorist, Luce Irigaray, when asked about the belief in angels, stated, 'Do I believe in angels? No, of course not. Does anyone today?'[2] The scholar Dan Cohn-Sherbok, a rabbi of Reform Judaism, argues that the 'Christian belief in angels was rooted in ancient Judaism. Yet it is a mistake to believe that such beings actually exist. In the past, the faithful conceived of angels as emissaries of the divine but such convictions should now be set aside in favour of a more materialist outlook.'[3]

1 Quoted by Elaine Williams, 'It's the Way He Tells Them', *Times Higher Education*, 19 December 1997, http://www.timeshighereducation.co.uk/story.asp?storyCode=105068andsectioncode=26, accessed 2 December 2008.
2 Ibid.
3 Ibid.

Thus, it is argued that in a modern world whose outlook is rationalistic and materialistic there is no space for angels. This supposition is at odds with popular contemporary culture where angels are artistically represented in books and films as beings of an imagined spiritual world; a portrayal close to that of ancient and medieval times in Europe. Therefore, there is a strange contradiction in western culture between, on the one hand, what individuals enjoy reading about and watching, and on the one hand, what they actually consider to be reality.

Nevertheless, in contemporary western scholarship there are thinkers who argue that there are also ideological reasons for why angels are not believed in anymore, and these reasons move beyond the simplistic notion that this loss of belief was due to the rise of a materialist outlook in the western world. For instance, Richard Bauckham, a professor of New Testament Studies, argues that '[o]ne reason for the decline in belief in angels in the modern period is that they were thought of as a category of beings higher than humans. This was in conflict with modern anthropocentrism, which wanted to see humans as destined to supreme lordship over the whole of creation. It would be a good antidote to human hubris if we could believe in angels again.'[1]

Away with the Stereotype

As stated at the beginning of this book, belief in angels is an article of faith in Islam, and Muslims of the twenty-first century widely accept that angels exist. This is indicated by a recent survey conducted among Muslims by the Pew Research Center in which they specifically asked respondents in all the thirty-nine countries covered by the survey whether they believed in the existence of angels. The survey's conclusion was that a belief in angels is nearly univer-

1 Quoted by Williams, 'It's the Way He Tells Them.'

sal amongst Muslims, even among Muslims in Europe.[1] However, scholars Murata and Chittick explain that when speaking of angels in Islam, 'we need to discard from the outset all those winged little boys shooting arrows or Grecian maidens playing harps that pervade the imagery of modern society.'[2] It is stated in the Qur'ān that angels have varying numbers of wings, and a *ḥadīth* of the Prophet reports that he once saw the Angel Gabriel with six hundred wings.[3] This statement about wings has been understood literally by some Muslims, but as will be discussed later in this chapter, others understand it to represent a metaphysical truth that is not comparable with our mundane experience of what is physically possible.

For Muslims, the belief in angels is based upon the Qur'ānic vision of the universe. It is difficult to explain how 'real' this vision is for most Muslims, but it is possible to do so if one tries to imagine a conception of the world where reality extends beyond the physical world. Beyond the veil that separates the unseen (*al-ghayb*), there are numerous other creations. In this world view, the limitations of empiricism and a materialist outlook are very clear. For example, to demonstrate the holistic Muslim world view, consider how Muslims are obliged to use strict empirical evidence with regards to human interaction: the *Sharīʿa* requires that many human interactions (both legal and illegal) be proven empirically, such as the requirement for witnesses for marriage and divorce, for wills to be documented, for trading to be conducted in accordance with written or oral contracts, and for theft and murder to be empirically proven. However, at the same time, a faith in the unseen—which today is sometimes labelled the 'paranormal'—is a reality for believers based upon their

1 Ibid. The survey asked respondents in all thirty-nine countries whether they believed in the existence of angels. In Southeast Asia, South Asia and the Middle East–North Africa region, the belief in angels is nearly universal. In Central Asia and sub-Saharan Africa, more than seven in ten respondents also say that angels are real. In Southern and Eastern Europe a median of 55% shared this view.

2 Murata and Chittick, *Vision of Islam*, p. 84.

3 Q.xxxv.1; Bukhārī, *Ṣaḥīḥ*, LIX.43, http://sunnah.com/bukhari/59/43.

īmān. This means that rational thinking in Islam is not exclusively based on empiricism. Muslims feel no need to prove the existence of angels as this belief is congruent with the other beliefs in Islam based upon a Qur'ānic world view.

Angels in Islamic Theology

The Arabic word for angel, *malak* (which literally means messenger or envoy), is mentioned ninety times in the Qur'ān.[1] Some of the verses clearly indicate the role of angels as messengers of God. In the Qur'ān it is said, 'God chooses messengers from angels and from men.'[2] One understanding of this verse is that angels are sent as messengers to men such as Moses, John the Baptist and Jesus, who are then entrusted with the responsibility to serve as messengers to their fellow human beings. It could well be asked how is it that these angel-messengers are not easily perceived by people in the same way that God's human messengers are? According to the Qur'ān, the answer is that if angels were clearly seen to walk upon the earth, then all humans would be forced to believe in this phenomenon based upon empirical proof, but a believer must be given free choice to believe in the unseen; that is the true test of belief.[3]

While human messengers like the Prophet Muḥammad delivered the signs of God through revealed scripture (in the Qur'ān, the word for verse is *āya*, 'sign'), the angels may be understood as messengers who deliver the signs of God through creation itself. As illustrated by the teleological argument for the existence of God discussed in Chapter Two, everything created is seen as a sign of His existence. Thus, when angels are reported to descend with every drop of rain, to maintain order, to entrust the soul to an embryo, to serve as the angel of death or as creatures that praise their Lord, they are principally acting as messengers of God as well as literally being signs of God.[4]

1 D. B. MacDonald, *EI²*, vol. VI, p. 216, s.v. '*Malā'ika*.'

2 Q.XXII.75.

3 Q.VI.8–9.

4 Murata and Chittick, *Vision of Islam*, p. 86–87.

In the Qur'ān, angels such as Gabriel, Michael, Hārūt and Mārūt are referred to by their individual names. In the *Ḥadīth* corpus, there are other angels, such as: ʿAzrā'īl, the angel of death; Munkar and Nakīr, who question the dead in their graves; and Isrāfīl, who is responsible for blowing the trumpet on the Day of Judgement.[1] The scholar Jalāl al-Dīn al-Suyūṭī (d. 910/1505) wrote a lengthy description of what could be called the angelology of Islam in his book, *al-Ḥabā'ik fī akhbār al-malā'ik* (The Arrangement of the Traditions about Angels). The book is a compilation of approximately 750 *ḥadīth*s and is followed by a long discourse by Suyūṭī that examines a range of theological issues with regards to angels. Suyūṭī's purpose in this book was to demonstrate, through the corpus of *Ḥadīth*, the existence and function of angels, and their intermediation with God. In the *Ḥabā'ik* we find a lengthy description of the role of angels in people's lives—from birth to death—and of their role in the Afterlife.

Today, for most contemporary Muslims angels are an ever-present meta-reality that is acknowledged within the five daily prayers. All Muslims are required to end their prayers with the greeting, 'Peace be upon you', while turning to the right and then the left, acknowledging the existence of the two angels that are ever present with them. In the Qur'ān and *Ḥadīth* it is stated that each human being is accompanied by two angels who act as record keepers throughout the person's life and who record an individual's sins and good deeds.[2]

According to Islamic theology, the angels were created out of light, but this is understood to be a metaphysical rather than a physical light. It is argued that angels occupy a plane of existence near to God that is beyond human perception. In Islamic theology, the existence of more than one plane of existence in the time/space continuum has always been a reality based on the Qur'ānic vision of

1 Karima Diana Alawi, 'Pillars of Religion and Faith', in Vincent J. Cornell, ed., *Voices of Islam*, London: Praeger Publishers, 2006, p. 34. Please see Chapter Six for more information about Islamic eschatology.

2 Murata and Chittick, *Vision of Islam*, p. 84.

the universe.[1] The angels who exist in such a plane of existence are seen as intermediate agencies between the Will of God and creation. The scholar ʿIzz al-Dīn Kāshānī (d. 735/1335) highlighted the need for Muslims to believe in the existence of angels when he said, 'All believers have faith in the existence of angels, who dwell in the monasteries of holiness and the communities of divine intimacy…'[2]

It has been argued that angels are dissimilar to human beings in the sense that they do not eat, drink, procreate or sleep, and are devoid of sin. Abū Ḥafṣ Nasafī, for example, describes them as servants of God who work only according to His commands and that they are neither masculine nor feminine.[3] According to many statements in the Qur'ān and *Ḥadīth*, angels are capable of metamorphosis; for example, the Angel Gabriel came to Mary in the form of a man to tell her the news of a blessed son. Thus, angels can take the shape of anything that God wills. In the Qur'ān, the absolute obedience of angels to God is strongly stressed, as is their lack of free will. Ghazālī explained the role of angels as follows: 'As for the angels, theirs is the highest level because they are existents whose perception is not affected by proximity or distance. Nor is their perception limited to what is conceivable as close by or far away, since proximity and distance are conceived for bodies, and bodies are the lowest of the categories of existing things. Furthermore, angels are too holy for passion and anger, so their activity is not dictated by passion or anger; rather what moves them to engage in activity is something more exalted than passion and anger, namely, to seek proximity to God the most high.'[4]

1 See Ahmed, *Nature of Time and Consciousness*.

2 Sachiko Murata, 'The Angels', in Seyyed Hossein Nasr, ed., *Islamic Spirituality: Foundations*, London: Routledge and Kegan Paul, 1987, p. 326.

3 Earl E. Elder, ed., *A Commentary on the Creed of Islam: Saʿd al-Dīn al-Taftāzānī on the Creed of Najm al-Dīn al-Nasafī*, New York: Columbia University Press, 1950, p. 127.

4 Ghazālī, *Ninety-Nine Beautiful Names of God*, p. 33.

Angels and Their Origin

Angels play a role in many of the themes of the Qur'ān, especially with regards to creation, revelation and eschatology. 'Muhammad Al-Berkevi [Imam Birgivī] states, "We must confess that God has angels who act according to His order and who do not rebel against Him. They neither eat nor drink, nor is there amongst them any difference of sex. Some are near the throne of God; those are His messengers. Each one has his particular work. Some are on earth, some in heaven, some are always standing, some always prostrate themselves and some laud and praise God. Others have charge of men and record all their actions. Some angels are high in stature and are possessed of great power."'[1] The angels in general are also known (according to the Qur'ān and *Ḥadīth*) to praise and glorify God, to entrust the soul to the embryo and take one's soul at the time of death. They act as intermediaries between the visible universe and God, but it is important to understand that, although they do the bidding of their Lord, they have no individual powers of their own. It is argued that the Islamic concept of cosmos, which encompasses creation, revelation, prophecy, events that occur in the world, worship, spirituality, life and death, cannot be understood without reference to the angels.[2]

Even though angels are created beings, no source speaks of when the angels were created; thus, knowledge about them begins with the account of their witnessing the creation of Adam. As stated in the Qur'ān, they were asked to prostrate in front of the first human being to honour him: 'Behold, thy Lord said to the angels: "I will create a vice-regent on earth." The angels said: "Wilt thou place therein one who will make mischief therein and shed blood? Whilst we celebrate Thy praises and glorify Thy holy name?" He said: "I know what ye know not."'[3] Concerning these verses, the jurist Abū al-Ḥasan

1 Translation from Edward Sell, *The Faith of Islam,* 2nd ed., London: Routledge, 2000, p. 199.

2 Sachiko Murata, 'The Angels', in Nasr, ed., *Islamic Spirituality: Foundations*, p. 324.

3 Q.II.30.

ʿAlī b. Muḥammad al-Māwardī (d. 449/1058) narrated a very interesting tradition from Jaʿfar al-Ṣādiq about the Kaʿba in the holy city of Mecca. In his book, *al-Aḥkām al-sulṭāniyya wa'l-wilāya al-dīniyya* (The Ordinances of Government), he wrote that when God said '"He knew that which they did not know" to the angels, they took refuge in the Throne by circling it seven times and asked for God's forgiveness. He forgave them and instructed them to build a house on earth whereby the children of Adam can take refuge and ask for God's forgiveness as the angels just did around the throne. [...] Thus they [angels] built Him that house, and it became the first house built for humankind. God says "Indeed the first House built for human beings was the one at Beca, a blessed place, and guidance for all beings."'[1]

Various other historical events mentioned in the Qur'ān and *Ḥadīth* involve angels, such as the angels who came to warn Noah about the flood, the angels who visited Abraham in human form to give the good news of the birth of his son, the angels who came in the form of young men to deliver Lot from impending danger, the angels Hārūt and Mārūt who descended upon Babylon, and the Angel Gabriel who came to announce to Mary the birth of Jesus.[2] 'Then We sent to her Our angel, and he appeared before her as a man in all respects.'[3]

Angels and Muḥammad

No account of angels in Islam would be complete without including those who featured in the life of the Prophet Muḥammad. One of Muḥammad's first encounters with an angel took place at the beginning of the revelation of the Qur'ān. For most students of religion, this story should be familiar as it was the meeting between the angelic world and Muḥammad that set the stage for revelation in Islam,

1 Māwardī, *The Ordinances of Government*, trans. Wafaa H. Wahba, London: Garnet Publishing, 2000, p. 174. Beca (or more correctly, Bakka) is a variant of the name 'Mecca' and is mentioned in the Qur'ān (III.96).

2 Abdu'l-Hamid Kishk, *The World of the Angels*, London: Dār al-Taqwa, 1994, pp. 31–41.

3 Q.XIX.17.

the descent of the word of God. At the age of forty, Muḥammad walked up to a cave on Mount Ḥirā' for his habitual spiritual retreat during the month of Ramaḍān. Once inside, he heard a voice saying, 'Recite!' Muḥammad replied that he could not. According to the earliest sources, the voice that Muḥammad heard belonged to an angel who appeared to him in the form of a man; Muḥammad would later come to know this angel by the name of Gabriel. The angel seized Muḥammad and again told him to recite, but once again the Prophet replied that he could not. After a third time, the angel recited, 'Proclaim! (or recite!) in the name of thy Lord and Cherisher, Who created—created man, out of a (mere) clot of congealed blood. Proclaim! And thy Lord is Most Bountiful, He Who taught (the use of) the pen, taught man that which he knew not.'[1] After this encounter, Muḥammad described the revelation of the first verses of the Qur'ān as, 'It was as though the words were written on my heart.'[2] Muḥammad's first reaction to the angel was fear and he fled the cave. But halfway down the mountain, he once again heard something, and this time clearly saw an angel on the horizon who said 'Oh Muḥammad, thou art the Messenger of God, and I am Gabriel.'[3] What did that angel look like? Prophetic tradition describes an immense and powerful creature with wings.

Over the next twenty-three years, Muḥammad continued to see the Angel Gabriel and to be visited by him. At first, this interaction was confined to the revelation of the Qur'ān during Muḥammad's years in Mecca, when he and his community were persecuted by the Meccans. But the Angel Gabriel also taught Muḥammad about many aspects of the religion, including how to perform the ablution and prayers. In 620 CE (three years before the establishment of the *Hijrī* era), and a few years after the first revelation, Muḥammad's Night

1 Q.xcvi.1–5.

2 Quoted by Martin Lings, *Muhammad: His Life Based Upon The Earliest Sources*, Cambridge: Islamic Texts Society, 1991, p. 44.

3 Lings, *Muḥammad*, p. 44.

Journey (*al-Isrāʾ waʾl-Miʿrāj*) took place. On that night, Muḥammad was visited by the Angel Gabriel and taken by him to Jerusalem upon the creature called Burāq, who Muḥammad described as 'a tall white animal somewhat larger than a donkey but smaller than a mule [...] I mounted and rode until I reached Jerusalem.'[1] Muḥammad then prayed in Jerusalem and was taken to various levels of the heavens where he met many messengers who had preceded him, such as Adam, Jesus, John the Baptist, Joseph, Idrīs, Aaron, Moses and Abraham. When Muḥammad reached the highest heaven, even Gabriel had to take leave so that Muḥammad could speak with God alone. This was the moment when he received the five daily prayers from his Lord.[2] The day after this event, Muḥammad told those who followed him about what had happened. When others heard of it, many in Mecca mocked his Night Journey as nonsensical and absurd, and even some of his Companions had reservations about this seemingly fantastical tale. However, Abū Bakr, Muḥammad's closest friend simply said, 'If so he saith then it is true. And where is the wonder of it? He telleth me that tidings come to him from Heaven to earth in one hour of the day or night, and I know him to be speaking the truth. And that is beyond what ye cavil at.'[3] How could such a fantastical tale be a challenge for Abū Bakr's faith when he knew that Muḥammad was receiving divine messages from the Angel Gabriel day and night?

After thirteen years of persecution in Mecca, Muḥammad and his Companions sought refuge in the city of Yathrib, which was later renamed *al-Madīna al-Nabawiyya* (or more commonly in English, Medina), the City of the Prophet. This period of Muḥammad's life featured further encounters with angels, such as additional revelations brought by the Angel Gabriel and angels supporting the believers in various battles. During the first years of Muḥammad's sojourn in Medina, the Muslims did not have permission to fight

1 Kishk, *World of the Angels*, p. 52.
2 Ibid., pp. 52–55.
3 Lings, *Muḥammad*, p. 103.

against the aggressive Meccans, but in the year 2/624 it was revealed to Muḥammad that Muslims could take up arms against their aggressors. The first battle between the Muslims and the Meccans was known as the Battle of Badr. During this battle, God supported the three hundred Muslims with angels led by Angel Gabriel, which ended with a Muslim victory against the one thousand strong force of the Meccan army.[1] 'God had helped you at Badr, when ye were a contemptible little force; then fear God; thus may ye show your gratitude. Remember thou saidst to the faithful: "Is it not enough for you that God should help you with three thousand angels (specially) sent down?" Yea, if ye remain firm, and act aright, even if the enemy should rush here on you in hot haste, your Lord would help you with five thousand angels making a terrific onslaught.'[2]

Many years later in Medina, the Angel Gabriel appeared as a man dressed in clean white clothes who walked straight out of the desert to question Muḥammad about the concepts of *islām* (submission through action), *īmān* (faith) and *iḥsān* (good conduct), as was discussed in the Introduction. This tradition later became one of the most popular *ḥadīth*s in the Muslim world.

The Jinn in Islamic Theology

In the Islamic tradition, another class of intelligent beings who are similar in some ways to the angels are the jinn. But who are they? According to the Qur'ān, God said, 'We created man from sounding clay, from mud moulded into shape; and the Jinn race, We had created before, from the fire of a scorching wind.'[3] From this, Muslim theologians understand that God created the jinn before He created humankind, and that they differ from us humans in that they were created from fire, not clay.

However, it is also evident from the Qur'ān that the jinn are

1 Q.VIII.5–18; III.123.
2 Q.III.123–25.
3 Q.XV.26–27.

similar to humans in some respects; in particular, God states, 'I have only created Jinns and men, that they may serve Me.'[1] Other similarities are suggested by a vivid account of Muḥammad meeting jinn in *Sūrat al-Jinn*:

> Say: It has been revealed to me that a company of Jinns listened (to the Qur'an). They said, 'We have really heard a wonderful recital! It gives guidance to the right, and we have believed therein: we shall not join (in worship) any (gods) with our Lord. There were some foolish ones among us, who used to utter extravagant lies against God; but we do think that no man or spirit should say aught that untrue against God. True, there were persons among mankind who took shelter with persons among the Jinns, but they increased them in folly. And they (came to) think as ye thought, that God would not raise up any one (to Judgment). And we pried into the secrets of heaven; but we found it filled with stern guards and flaming fires. We used, indeed, to sit there in (hidden) stations, to (steal) a hearing; but any who listen now will find a flaming fire watching him in ambush. And we understand not whether ill is intended to those on earth, or whether their Lord (really) intends to guide them to right conduct. There are among us some that are righteous, and some the contrary: we follow divergent paths. But we think that we can by no means frustrate God throughout the earth, nor can we frustrate

1 Q.LI.56.

> Him by flight. And as for us, since we have listened to the Guidance, we have accepted it: and any who believes in his Lord has no fear, either of a short (account) or of any injustice. Amongst us are some that submit their wills (to God), and some that swerve from justice. Now those who submit their wills—they have sought out (the path) of right conduct [...].'[1]

These verses make it clear that, like us humans, the jinn have free will, and that as a result, some of the jinn believe in God while others do not. This account from *Sūrat al-Jinn* also complements verses from *Sūrat al-Aḥqāf*, which describe a group of jinn who were reported to have returned to their people after hearing the recitation of the Qur'ān and to have said, 'O our people! We have heard a Book revealed after Moses, confirming what came before it: it guides (men) to the truth and to a straight path.'[2] This passage has traditionally been understood to refer to a group of jinn who had previously accepted the message of Moses.

During modern times, the identity of the jinn has posed some exegetical problems for Muslim theologians including the twentieth-century Austrian scholar Muhammad Asad (d. 1992), who tried to rationalise any supernatural occurrences in his exegesis of the Qur'ān in a strictly empirical sense. For example, in the verses of *Sūrat al-Jinn* quoted above, Asad interprets Muḥammad's meeting as between him and some human strangers, not jinn. Similarly, on the meaning of the Arabic word *jinn*, which Asad renders as 'unseen beings', he writes:

> [T]he *jinn* are referred to in the Qur'ān in many connotations. In a few cases—e.g., in the present instance and in 46:29–32—this expression may possibly signify '*hitherto* unseen beings',

1 Q.LXXII.1–14.
2 Q.XLVI.30.

> namely, strangers who had never before been seen by the people among and to whom the Qur'ān was then being revealed. From 46:30 (which evidently relates to the same occurrence as the present one) it transpires that the *jinn* in question were followers of the Mosaic faith, inasmuch as they refer to the Qur'ān as 'a revelation bestowed from on high after [that of] Moses', thus pointedly omitting any mention of the intervening prophet, Jesus, and equally pointedly (in verse 3 of the present *sūrah* [Q.LXXII.3]) stressing their rejection of the Christian concept of the Trinity. All this leads one to the assumption that they may have been Jews from distant parts of what is now the Arab world [...] I should, however, like to stress that my explanation of this occurrence is purely tentative.[1]

Thus, rather than interpreting the jinn as a separate class of intelligent beings similar to the angels and humankind, Asad tentatively suggests that they were actually human strangers who were probably followers of the Jewish faith.

Because of the disparity between Asad's writings on the topic and those of classical scholars, it is important to place his thoughts within his twentieth-century context. His positivist and rationalist approach to exegesis seems to reflect that of his contemporary exegetes and theologians in Judaism and Christianity; and as we shall see in the next section, his opinion that the story of Adam and Iblīs was allegorical is similar to the interpretation of his counterparts in Judaism and Christianity.[2]

1 Muḥammad Asad, *The Message of the Qur'an*, Gibraltar: Dar al-Andalus, 1964, p. 506.
2 By way of comparison, see the writings of neo-orthodox theologian Karl Barth (d. 1968).

But Asad was not the only modern Muslim scholar to follow an intensely rationalist approach when it came to the jinn. In early twentieth-century India, Sir Seyyed Aḥmad Khan argued that the *work* of God (by which he meant nature) could not contradict the *word* of God. His interpretation of the Qur'ān went in the direction of doing away with all non-scientific concepts including the jinn—who were reinterpreted as microbes—and the angels—who were described as inner spiritual powers in man, rather than physical beings made of light.[1] As an illustration of the competing interpretations of angels and jinn within the history of Muslim scholarship, the case of Iblīs is instructive, and it is to this that we turn to next.

Iblīs, Angels, Jinn and Infallibility

Based on the discussion about angels at the start of this chapter, it may seem as though angels are understood to be infallible creatures. But how then do Muslims explain the story of Iblīs (who is known as Lucifer in Christianity)?[2] Was he not a fallen angel? Does his story not mean that angels have free will and can indeed make mistakes? Can other angels therefore also be thrown out of the realm of heaven just like he was? What is the opinion of Muslim theologians?

Historically, there have been two interpretations of Iblīs. The first interpretation (which is held by the vast majority of Muslim scholars) is that Iblīs was a jinn. But a small minority have proposed a second interpretation—one that is rooted in the Judeo-Christian tradition; this is the idea that Iblīs was a fallen angel. Only a handful of Muslim scholars have ever agreed with this second interpretation; one such was the exegete ʿAbd Allāh b. ʿUmar al-Bayḍāwī (d. 684/1286).[3] The argument of this minority of scholars who believed Iblīs to be a

1 See Annemarie Schimmel, *Deciphering the Signs of God*, Edinburgh: Edinburgh University Press, 1994, p. 163.

2 In Islam, Iblīs is the personal name of Satan (*Shayṭān*), just as Lucifer is the proper name of Satan before his fall in the Christian tradition.

3 See Sachiko Murata, 'The Angels', in Nasr, ed., *Islamic Spirituality: Foundations*, p. 338.

fallen angel was based upon a literal, linguistic interpretation of the following Qur'ānic verse: 'And behold, We said to the angels, "Bow down to Adam," and they bowed down. Not so Iblis.'[1] These scholars argued that this meant that Iblīs must have been an angel, since it was stated in the Qur'ān that God addressed the angels as a group to prostrate before Adam. However, even Bayḍāwī considered Iblīs to be a specific kind of angel whose story did not compromise the obedience of all angels to God.

Thus, the vast majority of scholars throughout history have considered the idea that Iblīs was a fallen angel to be deeply flawed. They argue instead that by looking at all of the relevant passages on Iblīs in the Qur'ān, it becomes obvious that Iblīs was in fact a jinn. For instance, the prostration of the angels to Adam is found five times in the Qur'ān, but each time it is accompanied by a verse in which the origins of Iblīs are explained in more detail, such as the following: 'Behold! We said to the angels, "Bow down to Adam." They bowed down except Iblis. He was one of the Jinns [...].'[2] Iblīs was also referred to as a jinn in the Qur'ān when he tries to defend his decision not to bow down to Adam. He says, 'I am better than he [meaning, Adam]; You created me of fire and him You created out of clay.'[3]

Scholars have pointed out that there is a discrepancy here between what Iblīs said and what is known about jinn and angels. As mentioned earlier, and as is clearly stated in a *ḥadīth* narrated by ʿĀ'isha, 'The Angels were born out of light and the Jinns were born out of the spark of fire and Adam was born as he has been defined (in the Qur'an) for you [meaning, Adam was fashioned out of clay].'[4] Given the different origins of the angels, jinn and mankind, if Iblīs said in the verse above that God had created him from fire, then that must mean that he could not have been an angel and must have been a jinn.

1 Q.II.34; VII.11; XV.31; XVII.61; XXXVIII.74.

2 Q.XVIII.50.

3 Q.XVIII.50.

4 Muslim, *Ṣaḥīḥ,* LV.78, http://sunnah.com/muslim/55/78.

Likewise, angels are described as not capable of sin or of disobeying God. They are those 'who flinch not (from executing) the commands they receive from God, but do (precisely) what they are commanded.'[1] So how could Iblīs, who refused God's command to bow down to Adam, be an angel? As the Ashʿarī scholar, Saʿd al-Dīn al-Taftāzānī (d. 793/1390), put it, 'If someone objects saying: Did Iblīs not become an unbeliever and he was an angel, the proof of this being that it was valid for him to be made an exception for them? We reply, No he was one of the Jinn and then he strayed from the command of his Lord.'[2]

There have also been grammatical explanations proposed by scholars about Iblīs's origins, such as the grammatical rule of *taghlīb* (meaning for one word to predominate over another) in Arabic. This rule allows the use of the word for the majority grouping in a given context (such as *angels* in the verses above) to include a minority grouping (such as *jinn*), even if that minority were not of the same race, group or gender. In other words, when the Qur'ān refers to the group of angels who bowed down to Adam, the grammarians considered the term 'angels' (*malā'ika*) to indicate both angels and Iblīs, who was the only jinn amongst them. Most Muslim scholars who wrote about this matter (such as Ghazālī and Nasafī) made use of this grammatical argument to prove that Iblīs was a jinn.

Interestingly, the renowned historian and exegete Abū Jaʿfar Muḥammad b. Jarīr al-Ṭabarī (d. 310/923) faithfully reported four different narratives with regards to Iblīs's origin that he had collected from what was loosely referred to as *Isrā'īliyyāt* (Judeo-Christian traditions) and from early Muslim reports.[3] In one tradition, Ṭabarī reported from al-Ḥasan al-Baṣrī that Iblīs was not an angel but a jinn, and that he was the father of all jinn just as Adam was the father of

1 Q.LXVI.6.

2 Quoted by Elder, ed. and tr., *Commentary on the Creed of Islam*, p. 135.

3 See Henry A. Kelly, *Satan: A Biography*, Cambridge: Cambridge University Press, 2006, p. 185. The *Isrā'īliyyāt* will be discussed in more detail in Chapter Five.

humanity. Another of Ṭabarī's traditions of complemented this with a vivid story that is said to have taken place before the creation of Adam in which a host of angels were sent to end a vicious war on earth caused by the jinn. When the war was over, one of the jinn that returned with the angels was Iblīs himself. In heaven he was said to have become a righteous believer and was given a high station never achieved before by an angel or jinn. However, Iblīs's own arrogance later led to his downfall because of his refusal to bow down before Adam. In the third of Ṭabarī's stories, Iblīs was portrayed as an angel by the name of Azazel (*ʿAzāzīl* in Arabic) who belonged to a tribe of angels called jinn. Azazel was said to be in charge of the original inhabitants of the earth (the jinn) and the lower heaven. He was sent out with other angels to overcome the warring parties of jinn, but after his victory he became proud and arrogant, which eventually led to his downfall when he was commanded to bow down before Adam. Here it must be pointed out that those who shared this view, such as Bayḍāwī, argued that this angelic tribe called jinn had free will and were not like the rest of the angels who had no free will. Thus, even this account is not the same as the one represented by the Judeo-Christian account of the fallen angel. Ṭabarī concluded with his own carefully expressed opinion that Iblīs was a jinn and that his disobedience came about only because he was a jinn (due to this form of creation having free will) and not an angel (since angels cannot disobey God).[1] Ṭabarī said:

> In my opinion, the statement most likely to be correct is the one that agrees with God's words: 'We said to the angels: prostrate yourselves before Adam! And they did except Iblīs. He was one of the Jinns. He wickedly disobeyed the command of his Lord.' It is possible that his wickedness in disobeying the command

1 Abū Jaʿfar al-Ṭabarī, *The History of al-Ṭabarī*, trans. Franz Rosenthal, Albany: State University of New York Press, 1989, vol. 1, p. 256.

> of the Lord resulted from his being one of the Jinns. It is further possible that it resulted from his being pleased with himself because he worshipped His Lord so zealously, possessed great knowledge and had been entrusted with the rule of the lower heaven and earth as well as the post of keeper of Paradise. However, it is also possible that there were some other reasons. Knowledge of this subject can be attained only through a report that provides valid proof, but we have no such report, and the difference with respect to the matter is as indicated by the reports transmitted by us.[1]

In the twentieth century, one Muslim scholar who supported the minority opinion that Iblīs was a fallen angel was Muhammad Asad. He agreed with this because he thought that the jinn and angels were created from similar elements—'light and fire being akin' as he put it—and could easily manifest themselves within and through one another.[2] In his exegetical work, *The Message of the Qur'ān*, he interpreted the verse where Iblīs is called a jinn in the following way: '...they all prostrated themselves except Iblīs; he [too] was one of those invisible beings.' Asad argues in the footnotes that, in this case, 'invisible beings' denotes angels.[3]

The case of Iblīs thus demonstrates how, over the centuries and amidst a diversity of opinions, Islamic theology was nonetheless able to reach a consensus based on the careful study of the Qur'ān and *Ḥadīth*, supplemented by additional evidence from wider scholarship, such as other religious sciences and the study of language.

1 Ibid.

2 Muḥammad Asad, *The Message of the Qur'ān*, Gibraltar: Dar al-Andalus, 1964, p. 994 (Appendix III).

3 Ibid., p. 446–47.

Angels and Humankind

So, what does Islam say about angels and their relation to the children of Adam? It is interesting to note that in classical Islamic literature there was an early debate as to whether human beings could potentially reach a higher level of proximity to God than angels. Muʿtazilī scholars argued that angels were superior to human beings—including the prophets. Their proof for this was the consistent references in the Qur'ān to the proximity of angels to God. Furthermore, they contended that the fact that the Angel Gabriel had been the teacher of Muḥammad indicated the superiority of the teacher (namely, Gabriel) to the learner (Muḥammad).[1]

However, the majority of scholars from the Atharī, Ashʿarī and Māturīdī schools of theology all agreed that the Qur'ān's story of the angels bowing down to Adam indicated the possibility that human beings could be superior to angels in terms of their proximity to God. Briefly, the argument of these theologians was that, firstly, the angels were commanded by God to bow down to Adam, which suggested Adam's superiority. Secondly, Adam was more learned than the angels since he knew the names that God is said in the Qur'ān to have taught him, whereas the angels did not. Thirdly, human beings were given the ability to struggle against the like of evil desire, anger and greed; this made obedience more difficult for human beings, whereas angels were obedient in accord with their innate nature. Human beings, therefore, have the potential to be closer to God than angels due to their superior knowledge and their ability to worship God through inner struggle and the application of free will; both of which the angels do not possess. Thus, human beings could potentially be superior to angels and, more specifically, prophets were superior to angels.

By the third/ninth century most Muslims had accepted that prophets were superior to the angels, and believed that ordinary

1 See Edwin E. Calverley and James P. Pollock, eds., *Nature, Man and God in Medieval Islam*, Leiden: E. J. Brill, 2002, pp. 1017–23.

human beings could potentially become superior to angels. Yet scholars such as Ghazālī and Rūmī, echoing a *ḥadīth* of the Prophet, stressed that although humans could become superior to angels, they could also potentially fall far below animals.[1] Gai Eaton, a contemporary Muslim scholar, represents this traditional viewpoint well. He writes, 'For all their splendour, [angels] are "peripheral" beings, in the sense that each represents a particular aspect of the divine Plenitude; no single one amongst them reflects in his nature the totality of God's attributes. The Perfect Man, on the other hand, though far distant from the Light of heaven, stands, as it were, directly beneath the divine axis and mirrors Totality.'[2] It is further argued by Eaton that whereas angels are incapable of sinning and are passive tools of God (as are animals), humans are given the power of choice. Thus, human beings can potentially become like the Perfect Man, or potentially commit monstrous crimes and fall into the deep abyss.[3]

Aside from the question of superiority, the relationship between human beings and angels can be described as one of spiritual fellowship. Indeed several Qur'ānic verses and numerous traditions of the Prophet describe this link between the angels and the believers. In one verse of the Qur'ān it is said, 'The heavens are almost rent asunder from above them (by His glory) and the angels celebrate the praises of their Lord, and pray for forgiveness for (all) beings on earth. Behold! Verily God is He, the Oft-Forgiving, Most Merciful.'[4] And according to one tradition, the angels greet people who are praying the *fajr* prayer[5] with the word 'peace' (*salām*) until the rising of the dawn. Other sources speak of angels granting blessings, praying for mercy and enfolding those performing *dhikr*[6] in their wings and helping people who teach what is good or seek knowledge. In addition,

1 Cited in Murata, *Tao of Islam*, p. 280.

2 Eaton, *Islam and the Destiny of Man*, pp. 184–85.

3 Ibid., p. 172.

4 Q.XLII.5.

5 The dawn ritual prayer (*ṣalāt*).

6 Remembering God.

angels are reported to bless people who bless the prophets and to pray on behalf of people who give charity and who visit the sick.[1]

A vivid picture is drawn of this in the Qur'ān: 'Those who sustain the Throne (of God) and those around it sing glory and praise to their Lord; believe in Him; and implore forgiveness for those who believe: "Our Lord! Thy reach is over all things, in mercy and knowledge. Forgive, then, those who turn in repentance, and follow Thy Path; and preserve them from the penalty of the blazing fire! And grant, our Lord! that they enter the Gardens of Eternity, which Thou hast promised to them, and to the righteous among their fathers, their wives, and their posterity! For Thou art (He), the Exalted in Might, Full of Wisdom. And preserve them from (all) ills; and any whom Thou dost preserve from ills that Day—on them wilt Thou have bestowed mercy indeed: and that will be truly (for them) the highest achievement."'[2]

Spiritual Psychology and the World of Angels, Humans and Animals

The cosmological outlook in Islam has an allotted space for plants, animals, humans and angels in the nature of things. It also specifies that there is a special bond between human beings and the rest of creation, and of course with their Creator. In this sense, the level of angels is something that human beings can attain or even surpass, but at the same time, human beings can fall far from this level, and even fall below the level of animals.

Ghazālī beautifully portrayed the place of humans between the animals and angels as follows:

> Human beings were created at a level between beast and angel, and within them are found a totality of faculties and attributes. In respect of being nourished and growing, they are plants. In respect of sensation and movement,

1 See Kishk, *World of the Angels*, pp. 71–86.
2 Q.XL.7–9.

> they are animals. In respect of their forms and statures, they are like pictures painted on a wall. But the characteristic for which they were created is only the faculty of intellect and the perception of the realities of things.
>
> Those who employ all their faculties in order to reach knowledge and good works through them are similar to the angels and worthy of joining with them and being called lordly angels…
>
> Those who turn their aspiration toward following bodily pleasures and eating as the beasts eat have come down to the horizon of the beasts. Such people become dull like a bull, covetous like a pig, mad like a dog, spiteful like a camel, proud like a leopard, or evasive like a scorpion.[1]

On account of this cosmological world view found in the Qur'ān and *Ḥadīth* and the special position that humans hold within it, a wide range of Islamic literature has sprung up dedicated to the topics of knowledge of the self (*ʿilm al-nafs*) and purification of the heart (*maṭharat al-qalb*). Ghazālī, for example, discussed the concept of the self (*nafs*) in human beings in his book, *The Alchemy of Happiness*. In explaining that true knowledge of God must be based on real self-knowledge, Ghazālī used the famous *ḥadīth* of the Prophet, 'He who knows himself knows God',[2] and the Qur'ānic verse, 'Soon will We show them our signs in the (furthest) regions (of the earth), and in their own souls, until it becomes manifest to them that this is the truth'.[3] He said that this self-knowledge is not the superficial knowl-

1 Quoted in Murata, *Tao of Islam*, p. 280.

2 Ghazālī, *The Alchemy of Happiness*, trans. Claud Field, London: M. E. Sharpe, 1991, p. 5.

3 Q.XLI.53; LI.21.

edge of oneself, meaning 'thy outward shape, body, face, limbs, and so forth', for 'such knowledge can never be a key to the knowledge of God.'[1] Ghazālī described the human as a microcosm and the heart as the sovereign of this world: 'By "heart" I do not mean the piece of flesh situated in the left of our bodies, but that which uses all the other faculties as its instruments and servants. In truth it does not belong to the visible world, but to the invisible, and has come into this world as a traveller visits a foreign country for the sake of merchandise, and will presently return to its native land. It is the knowledge of this entity and its attributes which is the key to the knowledge of God.'[2]

Over the centuries, other Muslim scholars have also spoken clearly about the need for human beings to reach a state of peace and contentment based on purification of the heart. This may be achieved by combatting the two types of diseases of the heart. The first disease, referred to as *shubuhāt* (obfuscations), is related to impaired understanding; for example, if someone is fearful that God will not provide for them. This is seen as a disease since a sound heart should have knowledge and trust in God, and not doubt or anxiety. This disease is connected to the soul or the self and its ardent attachment to what is ephemeral, instead of to the unseen world. The second category of disease, *shahawāt* (appetites), is related to the basic desires of the self and to when these desires exceed the natural state, such as when people live only to satisfy their basic urges.[3] Now, since angels are recognised as being close to God, and since the soul or heart belongs to the world of the unseen (*ghayb*), the highest level and most lasting human experience is that of the soul; whereas the other faculties are necessary in this life but are ultimately transitory.

1 Ghazālī, *Alchemy of Happiness*, p. 5.

2 Ibid.

3 Hamza Yusuf, *Purification of the Heart: Translation and Commentary of Imam al-Mawlud's* Matharat al-Qulub, [no place]: Starlatch Books, 2004, p. 5–7.

To conclude, it is clear that to envision Islam's creation story, Islamic theology, spirituality, worship or concepts of the Afterlife without referring to those beings known as angels would be impossible.

Chapter 4

PROPHETS AND MESSENGERS OF GOD

Islam, the Primordial Religion

As stated in the Introduction, Muslims do not view Islam as a fifteen-hundred-year-old religion, but rather as a far more ancient faith that has been revealed in various forms throughout human history. The word *Islam* in this sense denotes not only the final form of the religion revealed to Muḥammad, but also any faith revealed before him that subscribed to monotheism. *Islam* in this context means 'submission to God'; the messengers who were sent by God before Muḥammad (and their followers) are therefore described in the Qur'ān as *muslimūn* (the ones who submit to the One God).[1] The Islamic tradition describes all of these faiths as individually tailored by God for their time and society but reiterating the same message that there is only the One God. In other words, the prophets and messengers of God were not each given a new message; instead, they were given one that has always been a reiteration of the first message so that human beings may be reminded and encouraged to reflect about the proper understanding of God.

The classical exegetical scholar Ṭabarī explained this perspective of Islamic history by affirming that the *dīn* (or 'religion') of all the messengers was the same in terms of declaring the oneness and uniqueness (*tawḥīd*) of God and confirming what previous messengers had proclaimed. However, despite this continuity, the situations of each messenger—and consequently the content of their transmitted commands and prohibitions—have differed. Fakhr al-Dīn al-Rāzī

1 Lumbard, 'Prophets and Messengers of God', in Cornell, ed., *Voices of Islam*, p. 103.

further explained this statement of Ṭabarī's by arguing that it was the creed (*ʿaqīda*) that stayed the same while the applied laws were what changed.[1] Thus, in Islamic theology, the Prophet Muḥammad is never seen as the founder of Islam but as the last in a long line of messengers beginning with the primordial prophet, Adam (in Arabic, Ādam).[2] Therefore, each revelation to every prophet and messenger of God throughout the history of monotheism is recognised as a form of Islam (submission to God). As the Qur'ān says, 'And We sent no messenger before you but We inspired him [saying]: There is no God save Me, so worship Me.[3]

What Is a Prophet or a Messenger?

The cosmology of the Qur'ān and *Ḥadīth* ultimately describes the relationship between contingent human beings and God, the Real (*al-Ḥaqq*). God intervenes in the universe in all spheres of existence, including a series of revelations to humanity through His chosen prophets. According to the famous Ashʿarī scholar Imām al-Ḥaramayn al-Juwaynī, prophecy only begins upon God's declaration to the one He selects: 'You are my apostle',[4] and, as Joseph Lumbard has stated, 'The means by which the prophets and messengers bring this message is revelation (*waḥy*).'[5]

So what is a prophet (*nabī*)? It is common to misunderstand the word *prophet* in our contemporary times for someone who prophesises the future. However, in Islam, the Arabic term *nabī* has no such connotations, even though some prophetic messages have been connected to future events. The root of the word *nabī* in Arabic derives from two meanings: to give news and to be exalted by God. Thus, a prophet in Islam is not in any way divine but is considered to be an

1 Ṭabarī, *History of al-Ṭabarī*, vol. VIII, p. 495 and Rāzī, *al-Tafsīr al-kabīr*, vol. XII, p. 48.

2 Arshad Khan, *Islam, Muslims and America*, New York: Algora Publishing, 2003, p. 136.

3 Q.XXI.25.

4 Imām al-Ḥaramayn al-Juwaynī, *A Guide to Conclusive Proofs for the Principles of Belief*, trans. Paul E. Walker, Qatar: Garnet Publishing, 2000, p. 193.

5 Lumbard, 'Prophets and Messengers of God', in Cornell, ed., *Voices of Islam*, p. 102.

exceptional (and mortal) human being favoured by God to convey His instructions to people. In addition to the term prophet (*nabī*), Islamic primary sources also frequently use the term messenger (*rasūl*); this term means a person who conveys a specific message.

Most scholars in Islam have argued, on the basis of the overall usage in the Qur'ān, that the term *nabī* is wider in its scope than *rasūl*. Whereas *nabī* (prophet) denotes every person chosen by God to receive a message, *rasūl* (messenger) refers to the relatively small number of prophets who were chosen to receive an oral and/or a written scripture that is the foundation of a revealed religion and a sacred law. Thus, a messenger is always also a prophet but not vice versa. For example, the most well known of the prophets who were also messengers in Islamic theology were Adam, who was the first prophet and messenger, Noah (Nūḥ), Abraham (Ibrāhīm), Moses (Mūsā), Jesus (ᶜĪsā) and Muḥammad, who is accepted as the last prophet and messenger of God. Others who were prophets but not messengers included Ishmael (Ismāᶜīl), Isaac (Isḥāq), Jacob (Yaᶜqūb) and Joseph (Yūsuf), all of whom followed the scriptures and laws given to the Prophet Abraham. Prophets such as Aaron (Hārūn), Samuel (Shamwīl) and John the Baptist (Yaḥyā) all followed the main scripture and laws given to the messenger Moses. In all, the *Ḥadīth* literature records that Muḥammad spoke of there being 124,000 prophets chosen by God from all nations from the time of Adam to himself, whereas he only said that 313 or 315 of these were messengers.[1]

It is believed that all prophets were given the same first part of the *shahāda*, 'There is no deity but the One God', but the second part of it—'Muḥammad is the Messenger of God'—was different in each epoch and in each nation. In other words, each people was sent its own individual messenger and they followed rites and laws revealed for their specific time.

It may be asked if there were ever any female prophets. Islamic theology appears to have two possible answers to that question. On

1 See Murata and Chittick, *Vision of Islam*, p. 133–34.

one side, Māturīdī argued that being male is a condition for prophethood, and consequently, maintained that it was not possible for a woman to be a prophetess. However, Ashʿarī contended that being male was not a condition for the role and so being a female did not prevent someone being a prophet(ess).[1]

One topic that follows from the definition of a messenger or prophet in traditional theology is the question of the necessity of revelation.

Why Did God Reveal Himself to Humankind?

Although, as the Qur'ān and *Ḥadīth* indicate, God is immanent as well as transcendent, this does not mean that He manifests Himself in any way, or that He incarnates Himself as a human being. For various classical Muslim theologians, this is the raison d'être of prophetology or prophecy.[2] For example, the early Muʿtazilī theologian Jāḥiẓ, who stressed the importance of studying prophecy (and who pioneered the genre known as 'proofs of prophecy'), thought that prophecy was needed because humankind was filled with such diversity—ranging from varied geographical settlements to intellectual abilities. He argued that this diversity would always create tension and aggression amongst humankind. Thus, he considered prophecy to be the answer to the ever-present social evils as prophets instituted laws that brought order to human relations. Jāḥiẓ saw the succession of prophets sent by God to be a continuous repetition of sacred history, or of the narrative that began with the first prophet, Adam.[3]

The philosopher Kindī furthered this argument by contending

1 Shams al-Dīn Aḥmad b. Sulaymān ibn Kamāl Pāshā, 'The Disagreements between the Ashʿarīs and Māturīdīs', Marifah.net, http://marifah.net/articles/disagreementsbetweenasharisandmaturidis-ibnkamalbasha.pdf, accessed 15 August 2014.

2 In Islamic theology, the definition of the role of a prophet, the prophetic institution, the possibility or the necessity of its existence, the demonstrations of its existence, the manner in which it operates and so on is called *nubuwwa*, which in English is rendered as 'prophetology' or 'prophecy'.

3 Tarif Khalidi, *Images of Muhammad*, New York: Doubleday, 2009, pp. 175–207.

that the truth of Muḥammad's prophethood could be syllogistically demonstrated and that the 'superiority of the revealed truth over human wisdom is an instance of the privileged status of the prophets, who are God's spokesmen and the bearers of a "divine science" transcending human capability.'[1] Hence, the need of human beings for revelation is ultimately based on the fact that they are imperfect, and therefore neglectful and forgetful by nature. Thus, revelation and the need for prophecy is, in the end, simply a reminder of the message originally brought by Adam, the first of the messengers.[2]

On the other hand, theologians such as the Atharī scholar Ibn Ḥazm defined prophetology as God's sending a select group of people—His prophets—to humanity; He bestowed upon them excellence for no other reason than that it was His will, and He directly communicated knowledge to them without their having to learn or seek it.[3] The Māturīdī scholar Nasafī called the sending of messengers an act of wisdom by God, and the Ashʿarī scholar Taftāzānī agreed with this in his commentary on Nasafī's creed, calling it a consequence arising from God's wisdom.[4] By contrast, Ibn Sīnā gave this topic a social twist by arguing philosophically that prophecy was a requisite for the spiritual guidance of the general populace (who he referred to as 'the common people') and that it was a socio-political necessity. Furthermore, he stated that only prophets were capable of introducing laws necessary for human well-being through divine guidance.[5]

However, Ibn Sīnā's reasoning was rejected by the Ashʿarī scholar Fakhr al-Dīn al-Rāzī, who argued:

1 Fakhry, *History of Islamic Philosophy*, p. 70.

2 Seyyed Hossein Nasr, *Ideals and Realities of Islam*, Cambridge: Islamic Texts Society, 2001, pp. 22–23.

3 F. Rahman, *Prophecy in Islam*, London: George Allen and Unwin, 1958, p. 93.

4 Earl E. Elder, ed., *A Commentary on the Creed of Islam: Saʿd al-Dīn al-Taftāzānī on the Creed of Najm al-Dīn al-Nasafī*, New York: Columbia University Press, 1950, p. 128.

5 See Ayman Shihadeh, *The Teleological Ethics of Fakhr Al-Dīn al-Rāzī*, Leiden: Brill, 2006, pp. 130–31.

> What is the meaning of your saying, 'Since people in this world need a lawgiver, his existence will be necessary (*wājib*)'? … If you mean that it is obligatory on God to create and existentiate him (as the Muʿtazila say, 'Compensation is "obligatory" upon God,' i.e. that if He does not deliver it, He will deserve blame), then that will go against what the *falāsifa* claim in the first place.
>
> However, if you mean that since the existence of the prophet brings about the order of this world, and since it has been proved that God is the source of every perfection and good, it will be necessary that God causes that person to come into being, then this too is false. For we say: Not all that is most advantageous (*aṣlaḥ*) to this world will happen necessarily in this world. For had the people of this world been naturally disposed to goodness and virtues, that would have been more advantageous than their present condition; yet that is not the case. Therefore, it is conceivable for the existence of the prophet to be more advantageous than his non-existence, yet for [no prophet] to ever exist!
>
> If he [Ibn Sīnā] meant something else, then that ought to be explained, so that we may investigate its plausibility or falsehood.[1]

It is not that Fakhr al-Dīn al-Rāzī thought it was inconceivable that some divine acts were performed for the advantage of humankind, but rather that he argued that unaided reason alone had no means

1 Shihadeh, *Teleological Ethics*, pp. 131–32, citing Fakhr al-Dīn al-Rāzī, *Sharḥ al-ishārāt wa'l-tanbīhāt*, Cairo: [no place], 1325 AH, vol. II, p. 106.

of arriving at a more detailed knowledge of this beyond affirming it as a possibility. This was because all of the classical Ashʿarī scholars maintained that not all of God's commands and acts that affected humans were necessarily aimed at human advantage.[1]

Consequently, Fakhr al-Dīn al-Rāzī turned his attention away from the topic of the purpose of prophecy to the matter of how to prove prophecy itself. He postulated that the only way to prove that a person was a prophet and carried the station of prophecy was by affirming God's unconstrained will and His absolute omnipotence, and by documenting the prophet's miracles. He argued that alongside the proof from miracles, there was the prophet's character: 'The second way to proving the prophecy of [Muḥammad], peace be upon him, is the inference (*istidlāl*) from his character traits, acts, judgements and conduct. Although each of these alone does not indicate prophecy, their combination is known, with certainty, to be found only in prophets. This was the preferred way of Jāḥiẓ and was adopted by Ghazālī in his book, the *Munqidh*.'[2]

All Muslim theologians and philosophers seem to agree that human beings are in need of divine guidance, and that prophecy is there to guide them. Tarif Khalidi, a contemporary academic, appears to encounter the same theological issue when writing about the *Sīra* (the life of the Prophet). He argues that the human being is described in the Qur'ān as a soul that is forgetful, inconsistent, impatient, fickle and frivolous. On the other hand, a believer is a soul that is steadfast, patient and remembering. In consequence, he argues that the portrait of the human being in the Qur'ān ends up being a fluctuation between these two states, where human beings are not necessarily sinners but instead frivolous. Human beings are represented as individuals who cannot be judged with blanket statements but are instead portrayed

1 Ibid.

2 Shihadeh, *Teleological Ethics*, p. 134, citing Fakhr al-Dīn al-Rāzī, *Muḥaṣṣal afkār al-mutaqaddimīn wa'l-muta'akhkhirīn* ...., ed. H. Atay, Cairo: [no place], 1991, p. 491. The full title of the work by Ghazālī mentioned here is *al-Munqidh min al-ḍalāl*.

as fragmented persons who have deeply divided personalities in need of discipline. Hence, only guidance, patience, and steadfastness can lead one from the darkness to the light.[1] It may be argued that it is these same human qualities that lead to the need for a messenger from the Divine. Thus, proper guidance through the prophets has existed from the beginning of humankind's journey, and classical and modern scholars agree that the purpose of the messengers and prophets is to guide and help their fellow human beings to come to know themselves, and by doing so, to come to know God.

The Turkish theologian and the final Shaykh al-Islām of the Ottoman Caliphate, Muṣṭafā Ṣabrī Efendī (d. 1373/1954), argued in a similar fashion to Fakhr al-Dīn al-Rāzī when faced with questions about prophecy in modern times. In fact, he argued against his Muslim contemporaries who were trying to justify prophecy through rational proof. He contended that although one could make a case for the existence of God through rational means, one could only do the same for prophecy on the basis of the existence of God. He wrote: 'Firstly, the existence of God is established by a necessary rational proof, then the rational contingency of *al-samʿiyāt* (knowledge received from the Divine Source) such as Prophethood, miracles and the Hereafter are established on the basis of God's existence. Finally, their actual occurrence is established through reports of prophets supported by miracles from God and from these with regard to whom falsity is not conceivable.'[2]

Not surprisingly, there were very few scholars in Islamic history like the philosopher Abū Bakr Muḥammad b. Zakariyyā al-Rāzī (d. 312/925) who argued that human reason was enough to know God's will, and that, consequently, there was no need for prophets.[3] The vast majority of Muslim scholars of his period rejected this view

1 Khalidi, *Images of Muhammad*, pp. 21–22.

2 Faruk Terzić, 'The Problematic of Prophethood and Miracles: Mustafa Sabri's Response', *Islamic Studies,* vol. XLVIII, no. 1, Spring 2009, pp. 5–35.

3 Yahya Michot, 'Revelation', in Winter, ed., *Cambridge Companion to Classical Islamic Theology*, p. 182.

and considered it to be an extreme form of rationalism. Instead, they remained resolute in their belief that prophets and messengers were elected by God to receive revelation.[1] For instance, Juwaynī specifically argued against such excessive rationalism in his book, *Kitāb al-irshād* (A Guide to Conclusive Proofs), that even if it were conceded that rationality alone can lead to knowing good and evil, still none of the proofs attested by reason about good and evil can exclude what the Prophet proclaimed. He argued that this was analogous to using several rational proofs to support a single objective.[2] Juwaynī continued the debate by arguing that the prophets had also been sent to specify what believers needed to do in order to conduct their lives righteously. He compared a prophet to a physician who was able to identify the precise cure for an ailment. He made use of this same analogy to explain that a prophet—just like a physician—is needed to identify foods and medicines for people so as to distinguish them from deadly poisons. Even though experience gained through trial and error could lead to the same information, the long period of time it would take could cause irrevocable injuries and losses.[3]

The debate over prophecy and reason focused on whether reason alone was enough to believe in God, or if a prophet was necessary to believe in God and to understand what God required from the believer. At the time, this debate over prophecy and reason must have been significant because it prompted the scholar Ibn Ṭufayl (d. 580/1185) to compose the first philosophical novel as a way of addressing the subject. Entitled *Ḥayy Ibn Yaqẓān* (which in its later Latin translation was known as *Philosophus Autodidactus*, 'The Self-Taught Philosopher'), the book immortalised the eponymous protagonist throughout Islamic civilisation.[4] *Ḥayy Ibn Yaqẓān* is an allegorical novel in which the protagonist grows up alone, secluded on an island and raised by his fellow

1 Ibid., pp. 182–83.

2 Juwaynī, *Guide to Conclusive Proofs*, pp. 165–66.

3 Ibid., p. 166.

4 See Ibn Ṭufayl, *Ibn Tufayl's Hayy Ibn Yaqzan: A Philosophical Tale*, trans. Lenn Evan Goodman, Chicago: University of Chicago Press, 2009.

creatures (animals). By the time he becomes a grown man, he has used his senses and reason (that is, empirical proof) to discover the world around him, and by means of his senses and reason, Ḥayy discovers science, morality and the One God. Through this fictional story, Ibn Ṭufayl argued that it was possible for a human being to discover God only by using his intelligence, and by means of rationality and natural mysticism to reach the truth about the 'One True Being'. In the narrative, Ḥayy is led to the highest spiritual station through reason alone. The story then proceeds to tell us about Ḥayy's meeting with the character Absāl, a new arrival at the secluded island. For Ḥayy, their meeting leads to a curious clash of mysticism, philosophy, theology and law.

Ibn Ṭufayl demonstrated thorough the eyes of his protagonist that it was possible for philosophy and dogma to co-exist in harmony. However, he concluded his narrative by also demonstrating that prophecy and religious tradition were a necessity for the majority of human beings because they could only comprehend guidance in the form of a rites and religious traditions. But the elect few (such as philosophers) were able to seek the hidden meaning of scripture through 'illuminative wisdom' rather than by means of religious tradition.[1] Because he concluded that philosophical mysticism had pre-eminence over religious tradition, Ibn Ṭufayl's philosophical novel was strongly denounced by theologians.

It was the Ashʿarī scholar Ibn Nafīs (d. 686/1288) who wrote a rebuttal of Ibn Ṭufayl's arguments in the form of another philosophical novel called *Risālat Fāḍil bin Nāṭiq* (The Treatise of Fāḍil bin Nāṭiq) or *al-Risāla al-Kāmiliyya fī al-sīra al-nabawiyya* (The Treatise of Kāmil on the Prophet's Biography) and in Latin, *Theologus Autodidactus* (The

1 Ibid. Ibn Ṭufayl was a neo-Platonic scholar following in the footsteps of Ibn Sīnā, and the neo-platonic concept of rationalism and its relation to revelation was rejected by most of the Muslim theologians but was later on a key concept of the renaissance in the West.

Self-Taught Theologian).[1] Interestingly, even though the author was an Ashʿarite, many of the views in this book appear to share a Māturīdī perspective.[2] The novel is an account of the protagonist's demonstration of the reasonableness of Islamic beliefs through the events of his life. Ibn Nafīs's protagonist, Kāmil, is very similar to Ibn Ṭufayl's Ḥayy since both begin their stories in seclusion on a desert island. However, it seems that since Ibn Nafīs was also a physician, he began the work by describing how Kāmil was spontaneously generated in a cave as a fully mature youth on a remote desert island through a natural phenomenon.[3] Ibn Nafīs's description of this spontaneous generation would today be called 'science fiction' without a doubt; however, it has been argued by Nahyan A. G. Fancy that this was mainly the author's subtle way of signalling the theological concept of bodily resurrection.[4] The story then goes on to describe how Kāmil—now a youth—discovers the world around him through his senses and faculty of reason (in other words, by empirical proof).[5] After a few years, this knowledge leads him to utilise the teleological and cosmological arguments to convince him of the existence of God; however, when he begins to reflect on what claim God has on him as a creature (in other words, in terms of worship and obedience),

1 See Ibn al-Nafīs, *Theologus Autodidactus,* ed. M. Meyerhof and Joseph Schacht, Oxford: Oxford University Press, 1968.

2 According to Māturīdī thought, belief in the One God was obligatory for human beings and it came before revelation by the mere fact of their having reason. By contrast, the Ashʿariyya thought that human beings should believe in God due to revelation, not simply because they are endowed with reason.

3 Ibid., pp. 39–40.

4 Cited in 'Arabic Literature', *New World Encyclopedia*, http://www.newworldencyclopedia.org/entry/Arabic_literature, accessed 8 March 2016. The notion of physical bodily resurrection was one of the main major disagreements between theologians and philosophers.

5 He is self-taught (*autodidactus*) in all of the sciences. Once again, this informs us about the preoccupations of the author Ibn al-Nafīs as a man of science. See Ibn al-Nafīs, *Theologus Autodidactus*, pp. 40–44.

he is at a complete loss.[1] It is at this time that he comes across other people (all of them believers) who have been stranded on the island; by communicating with them, he learns about religion, society and culture. From these interactions, Kāmil deduces the need for a society to have a God-given law, 'a law by which all disputes are settled',[2] and this in turn rationally leads to the need for a prophet.[3]

The vast majority of Muslim theologians, however, agreed that God would not communicate His message directly to every human being through their faculty of reason. It was argued instead that the prophets were chosen by God as a special favour: 'The Prophet is a human being who enjoys special connection with God which is above the connection that occurs to every rational being while inferring about his Lord through the proofs of the cosmos. He receives revelation from Him, and this revelation is greater than the inspiration of the world's sciences to scientists and of grand projects to great people. This level of humanity is not achievable, but is characterized by being a special favour from God for those whom He chooses from among His servants.'[4]

Thus, according to Islamic theology, the position of messenger and prophet cannot be acquired; it is only bestowed by God. It is also acknowledged that the prophets and messengers were chosen by God before the creation of the world of forms.[5] They were then born into different communities throughout human history in order to re-establish the relationship between creation and the Divine. This is the context in which the famous *ḥadīth* of the Prophet narrated by Abū Hurayra should be understood: 'They said: "O Messenger of God (peace and blessings be upon him)! When was the Prophethood

1 Ibid., p. 44. The Ashʿarī and Māturīdī schools of theology both agree that the religious sciences (rituals, laws, and so on) can only be truly confirmed through revelation, not reason.

2 Ibid., p. 45.

3 Ibid., p. 31.

4 Terzić, 'The Problematic of Prophethood', p. 12.

5 On this, please see Chapter Six.

established for you?" He said: "While Adam was between soul and body."'[1] In the Qur'ān, it is stated that messengers were sent by God to all human communities: 'For We assuredly sent amongst every people a messenger, (with the command), "Serve God, and eschew evil."'[2]

The issue of the 'humanity' of the prophets and messengers—as opposed to an angelic nature—is something that the Qur'ān addresses in a number of verses as it was one of the reasons the pagan Arabs rejected the message of Muḥammad. In his commentary on the Qur'ān, the exegete Ismāʿīl Ibn Kathīr (d. 774/1373) narrated reports from Ibn ʿAbbās that when God sent Muḥammad as a messenger, some of the pagan Arabs denied him and said that God was too great to send a human being as a messenger. The Qur'ānic verses below convey God's answer:

> What kept men back from belief when guidance came to them, was nothing but this: they said, 'Has God sent a man (like us) to be (His) messenger?' Say, 'If there were settled, on earth, angels walking about in peace and quiet, We should certainly have sent them down from the heavens an angel for a messenger.'[3]
> And the messengers whom We sent before thee were all (men) who ate food and walked through the streets: We have made some of you as a trial for others: will ye have patience? For God is One Who sees (all things).[4]
> Nor did We give them bodies that ate no food, nor were they exempt from death.[5]

1 Abū ʿĪsā Muḥammad al-Tirmidhī, *Jāmiʿ al-Tirmidhī*, XLVI.3609, http://sunnah.com/urn/634700, accessed 19 February 2016.

2 Q.XVI.36.

3 Q.XVII.94–95.

4 Q.XXV.20.

5 Q.XXI.8.

> Say: 'I am no bringer of new-fangled doctrine among the messengers, nor do I know what will be done with me or with you. I follow but that which is revealed to me by inspiration; I am but a warner open and clear.'[1]

It is important to highlight that, in addition to prophets, Muslims believe that God can directly address anything in the universe—such as the earth, animals, insects and even humans who are not prophets. Numerous Qur'ānic verses and *ḥadīth*s speak of this kind of communication.[2] The theologian Ibn Taymiyya called this an 'equivocal' form of revelation, a lesser form of revelation where the announcement is confined strictly to the addressee. In a similar way, the Islamic tradition recognises that some dreams can offer divine guidance. The Prophet Muḥammad is reported to have said, 'A good dream (that comes true) of a righteous man is one of the forty-six parts of prophetism.'[3] Thus, dreams are accepted not only as having psychological importance, but also as possessing a spiritual reality that may offer a valuable source of wisdom, understanding and inspiration. Throughout Islamic history, Muslim scholars such as Ibn Khaldūn, Ibn ʿArabī and Rūmī have shown great interest in dreams, and have accepted dreams as a part of the wider reality which is weaved into the daily life of human beings.[4]

The Inerrancy of the Prophets

This brings us to the notion of knowledge in Islamic theology. In Islamic thought, knowledge is separated into two categories: acquired knowledge and revealed knowledge. Acquired knowledge is the product of sense perception, which leads to reasoning and reflec-

1 Q.XLVI.9.

2 For example, see Q.XCIX.5 (revelation to the earth), Q.LXII.12 (revelation to the sky), Q.XVI.69 (revelation to bees).

3 Bukhārī, *Ṣaḥīḥ*, XCI.2, http://sunnah.com/bukhari/91, accessed 22 February 2016.

4 Ibn Khaldūn, *The Muqaddimah*, pp. 80–83.

tion and the time-honoured experimentation of a given theory until it is recognised as fact and categorised.[1] On the other hand, revealed knowledge is based upon revelation (*waḥy*) from God and is not seen as a product of reason, reflection or even inspiration. It is believed that revelation is poured directly into a prophet's heart and that this message is unerring. In the Qur'ān, revealed knowledge is portrayed as a guidance that has been accessed by humanity through a prophet: 'It is not fitting for a man that God should speak to him except by inspiration, or from behind a veil, or by the sending of a messenger to reveal, with God's permission, what God wills: for He is Most High, Most Wise.'[2] According to the scholar Ibn Taymiyya, the first part of this Qur'ānic verse refers to when God speaks to a prophet through inspiration or a vision. The second part refers to a prophet being addressed by God behind a veil, which is what happened to Moses at Sinai, where God spoke to Moses but he could not see Him. The last part of this verse refers to when God sends His angels as messengers to reveal the message to a prophet or messenger. All of this indicates that prophets are divinely elected and that they have a quintessential duty to implement this message.[3]

This leads us to the concept of the inerrancy (*ʿiṣma*) of the prophets. For the last fourteen hundred years, Islamic theologians have been discussing the idea of the purity of revelation that is free from human contamination and subjective motivation. As Joseph Lumbard has observed, 'The reception of an unerring message is not particular to the Prophet Muḥammad. All Prophets are preserved from erring in the reception and deliverance of the messages revealed to them by God.'[4] It does not mean that they are not human, or infallible or free from human weakness; it means that they are protected (*maʿṣūm*) from

1 Ibid., p. 381.

2 Q.XLII.51.

3 Michot, 'Revelation', in Winter, ed., *Cambridge Companion to Classical Islamic Theology*, pp. 182–83.

4 Lumbard, 'Prophets and Messengers of God', in Cornell, ed., *Voices of Islam*, p. 102. For Qur'ānic reference, see Q.LXII.26–28.

moral decadence and sin, and from error when conveying the divine message with which they have been entrusted.

Inerrancy was acknowledged as a very important criterion for the station of prophets and messengers. The followers of a prophet had to trust them fully so as to adopt the divine guidance that they transmitted, which meant that in theological writings, prophets were recognised as being protected from sin throughout their entire life, not only during their prophetic mission. This was argued on the basis that it would be easy for people to mistrust a person who claimed prophethood but who had led a life without probity.[1]

In dogmatic handbooks from the classical era, theologians from the Ashᶜariyya and Māturīdiyya schools argued that prophets had four necessary attributes: they had to be truthful, trustworthy, intelligent and engage in preaching the divine word.[2] The two schools also agreed that there were four more attributes that a prophet could never possess because they were the opposite of the four listed above; they were: lying, treachery, feeblemindedness and concealing what they had been ordered to reveal. It is, however, possible for a prophet to experience any human state that does not detract from their rank, such as eating, sleeping, marrying or having an illness that is not repellent to others.[3]

By contrast, in early Muᶜtazilī writings it was argued that prophets could commit sins out of negligence, but later on in Muᶜtazilī thought scholars seemed to argue that prophets could not sin at all because of God's absolute justice. At the time when the Ashᶜariyya school was led by the theologian Bāqillānī, it was argued that the inerrancy of the prophets meant that they were protected from intentionally lying with respect to their message, and that they were protected from major transgressions and grave sins. The Ashᶜarīs seem to have

1 Lumbard, 'Prophets and Messengers of God', in Cornell, *Voices of Islam*, p. 106.

2 Annemarie Schimmel, *And Muhammad is His Messenger*, Chapel Hill: University of North Carolina Press, 1985, p. 57.

3 As summarized by Keller, 'Kalam and Islam.'

had two differing views about the possibility of prophets committing lesser sins. Their first opinion was that they could do so absent-mindedly, and their second opinion was that prophets were protected from such lapses, in addition to protection from major sins.[1] However, the Māturīdīs disagreed with the Ashᶜarīs on this issue and argued that prophets were preserved from all sin. For instance, Abū Ḥanīfa, who was the forerunner of the Māturīdīs, wrote in his *al-Fiqh al-akbar*, 'The Prophets, peace and blessings be upon them, are infallible of all sins, whether major, minor, or disbelief, and of all that is detestable/distasteful. It may be, however, that they commit insignificant lapses and inaccuracies... And Muḥammad, peace and blessings be upon him, is His beloved, His worshipper, His Messenger, His Prophet, His pious one, and His Chosen One. He never worshipped idols, he never associated anything with Allah, not even for a blink of an eye, and he never committed a sin, major or minor, ever.'[2]

The prophets and messengers were also acknowledged by the vast majority of Muslim theologians to possess qualities that cannot be imitated. The most well known of these are miracles (*muᶜjizāt*), which only the prophets of God can perform, and then only by leave of God. Such well-known miracles include the raising of the dead by Jesus, the parting of the Red Sea by Moses and many others attested to in the Qur'ān. An example is to be found in the following verses:

> Behold! the angels said: 'O Mary! God giveth thee glad tidings of a word from Him: his name will be Christ Jesus, the son of Mary, held in honour in this world and the Hereafter and of (the company of) those nearest to God;

1 Nuh Keller, 'Ashari and Maturidi School of Islamic Belief', Reflections of a Traveler [blog], February 3, 2007, https://baraka.wordpress.com/2007/02/03/ashari-and-maturidi-school-of-islamic-belief/, accessed 15 August 2014.

2 Creed 47 and 48 in Abū Ḥanīfa, *al-Fiqh al-akbar*, comments and trans. by Muhammad bin Yahya Ninowy, http://www.central-mosque.com/aqeedah/fiqakbar.pdf, accessed 1 April 2014.

> He shall speak to the people in childhood and in maturity. And he shall be (of the company) of the righteous.' She said: 'O my Lord! How shall I have a son when no man hath touched me?' He said: 'Even so: God createth what He willeth: When He hath decreed a plan, He but saith to it, "Be," and it is! And God will teach him the Book and Wisdom, the Law and the Gospel, And (appoint him) a messenger to the Children of Israel, (with this message): "I have come to you, with a sign from your Lord, in that I make for you out of clay, as it were, the figure of a bird, and breathe into it, and it becomes a bird by God's leave: And I heal those born blind, and the lepers, and I quicken the dead, by God's leave; and I declare to you what ye eat, and what ye store in your houses. Surely therein is a sign for you if ye did believe."'[1]

The Historical Cycle of Revelation

Islamic theology lays great stress on the idea that all revealed religions belong to the same historical cycle. All messengers are seen by Muslims as brothers in faith. In the Qur'ān, it is maintained that *Islām* (in the sense of the submission of one's mind, body and soul to the One God) is the only religion that God has revealed through time.[2] All of the messengers of God are therefore called *Muslims* (meaning that they literally submitted to God) and all revealed religions that came before Muḥammad were revealed to messengers who relayed the teachings they had received from God. Hence, in the Qur'ān, Noah is recognised as a Muslim,[3] Abraham and Ishmael pray to God

1 Q.III.45–49.

2 Q.III.85.

3 Q.X.72.

in the hope that their descendants would be Muslims,[1] the children of Jacob (Israel)[2] testify to being Muslims like their ancestors Abraham, Ishmael and Isaac,[3] Joseph is indicated as being a Muslim,[4] Moses commands his people to be Muslims,[5] Solomon is recognised as a Muslim[6] and Jesus's apostles testify that they are Muslims.[7] Though the prophets and others are described as Muslims in the Qur'ān, there is a difference when it comes to the actual name of a particular revelation. It is believed by Muslim scholars that the name of Islam designating the final faith revealed to Muḥammad—and Muslims as the followers of this faith—was given by God himself in the Qur'ān.[8] While Jews, Zoroastrians and Christians are referred to in the Qur'ān as the People of the Book (*Ahl al-Kitāb*). The name of each of the religions is understood to be of human invention—either highlighting a founding prophet's name or, in the case of Judaism, adopting the name of the nation of Judea.[9]

Thus, God revealed only one religion (namely, the way of submitting to the One God) and, periodically, He sent messengers with different laws and interpretations of that one religion. Prophets continued to be chosen by God to lead people back to the original teachings up until the last prophet, Muḥammad, who brought the final law and interpretation which superseded all previous ones. In the Qur'ān, Muḥammad is given the title the Seal of the Prophets

1 Q.II.128.

2 According to the Hebrew Bible, God gave Jacob the name Israel. See Genesis 32:28–29 and 35:10. This name has been accepted in Islamic tradition.

3 Q.II.133.

4 Q.XII.101.

5 Q.X.84.

6 Q.XXVII.44.

7 Q.III.52.

8 Q.XXII.78.

9 Under the Babylonians, and later the Persian, Hellenistic and Roman empires, the nation previously known as the Kingdom of Israel became known as 'Judea' and its people 'Judean' (*Yehudim*). For more information on this subject see Eliezer Segal, *Introducing Judaism*, London: Routledge, 2009, pp. 4–5.

(*Khātam al-Nabiyyīn*), meaning that he was the last human being to receive such guidance and revelation.[1] Muḥammad elaborated on this title in his farewell sermon, saying, 'O people, no prophet or messenger will come after me and no faith will be born after me.'[2] It is a major part of Islamic theology to accept Muḥammad as the Seal of the Prophets, meaning that there will be no new *Sharīʿa* after Muḥammad, nor any new religion or prophet. This is the reason why movements such as the Bahá'í faith in nineteenth-century Iran, the Aḥmadiyya in late nineteenth-century India and the Nation of Islam in the twentieth-century United States—all of whom claimed new prophets and continuing revelation from God—have been considered heresies by both Sunni and Shiʿi theologians.[3]

As discussed above, Islamic theology does not present any obstacles to accepting the messengers and prophets from the other Abrahamic religions that predated Muḥammad. For instance, in the Qur'ān, a number of prophets and scriptures are identified as being related to the line of revelation finally given to Prophet Muḥammad. 'We have sent thee inspiration, as We sent it to Noah and the messengers after him: we sent inspiration to Abraham, Ishmael, Isaac, Jacob and the Tribes, to Jesus, Job, Jonah, Aaron, and Solomon, and to David We gave the Psalms. Of some messengers We have already told thee the story; of others We have not; and to Moses God spoke direct.'[4]

It has even been postulated by many Muslim scholars throughout the centuries that, based upon the general message of the Qur'ān and *Sunna*, it is possible that most—if not all—of the world's religions that were established before the lifetime of the Prophet Muḥammad are remnants of the teachings of previous revelations.[5] According to

1 Q.xxxiii.40.

2 Translation from Lumbard, 'Prophets and Messengers of God', in Cornell, ed., *Voices of Islam*, p. 102, citing Muḥammad Ibn Hishām, *al-Sīra al-Nabawiyya*.

3 Schimmel, *And Muhammad is His Messenger*, p. 189.

4 Q.iv.163–64.

5 Wan Adli Wan Ramli, 'A Critical Study of Liberal Interpretations of the Qur'an on the Concept of "Religious Pluralism,"' Ph.D. thesis, University of Wales, Lampeter, 2011, p. 174.

Yahiya Emerick, there are a number of criteria that a religion must meet in order to be considered as having been revealed by God.[1] Primarily, a religion would have to have been revealed before the time of Muḥammad because, as mentioned above, Muḥammad is recognised as the last prophet, and so any religion that began after his lifetime is viewed as a human construct. Many theologians have therefore argued that all religions taught before Jesus's message qualify as religions revealed by God, but not any that were founded between the time of Jesus and Muḥammad. The Prophet Muḥammad is reported in a tradition to have said, 'I am most akin to Jesus Christ amongst the whole of humankind, and all the prophets are of different mothers but belong to one religion and no prophet was raised between me and Jesus.'[2]

However, there are other criteria as well. Muslim theologians insist that an in-depth investigation of religion's rituals, doctrine and history is necessary with contextual study to scrutinise any accumulation of human, rather than divine, elements that a religion may have acquired over the centuries. Numerous Muslim theologians who have studied other religions have argued that such figures as Buddha, Zoroaster, Lao-Tzu, Confucius and Hammurabi may have been prophets of God,[3] although these theologians have stressed that these are just theories and cannot be fully proven with the data available.[4]

This attempt to integrate the founders of other faiths into the Islamic world view demonstrates Islamic theology's inclusivity with respect to earlier religions. It also highlights the embedded historical attitude of respect, tolerance and inquiry within Islam into these faiths whilst upholding the teachings of the Qur'ān and *Ḥadīth* as the

1 Yahiya Emerick, *The Complete Idiot's Guide to Understanding Islam*, ALPHA: A Pearson Education Company, 2002, p.182.

2 *Bukhārī, Ṣaḥīḥ,* XLIII.189, http://sunnah.com/muslim/43/189.

3 On this, see Annemarie Schimmel, *Islam: An Introduction*, Albany: State University of New York Press, 1992, p. 82.

4 Ibid.

culmination of revealed religion. Nevertheless, Islamic theology also stresses exclusivity in the case of religions established after the lifetimes of Jesus and Muḥammad. Those movements are largely seen as human constructs that may have been based upon earlier revealed religions.

Prophets in the Sources

Twenty-five prophets are mentioned by name in the Qur'ān, including the Prophet Muḥammad. With the exception of the Prophet Muḥammad and a few ancient Arabian prophets, most of twenty-five prophets also feature in the Hebrew Bible and in the New Testament. However, when comparing the stories about them in the different scriptures, it becomes obvious that there are significant divergences when it comes to particular events. Moreover, some of the individuals referred to as prophets in the Qur'ān are not given the same title in the Hebrew Bible or New Testament. For example, David is portrayed as a king in the Hebrew Bible: 'David sent messengers to the men of Jabesh-gilead and said to them [...] "For Saul your lord is dead, and the house of Judah has anointed me king over them."'[1] But according to the Qur'ān, he was a prophet: 'We gave him Isaac and Jacob: all (three) guided: and before him, We guided Noah, and among his progeny, David [...] These were the men to whom We gave the Book, and authority, and prophethood.'[2] It is also important to appreciate the philological problem here with regards to the terms prophet and messenger, given that these concepts are understood differently in Islamic tradition compared to the Judeo-Christian one.

In Islamic theology, which uses the Qur'ān and *Ḥadīth* as primary sources, the Hebrew prophets are not presented as they are in the Hebrew Bible—where they are portrayed as men who were, at times, ecstatic, in a trance and even involved in immoral situations (at least, as defined by Islam). Rather, Islamic theology views the Hebrew prophets as human beings who were highly moral indi-

1 2 Samuel 5–7.
2 Q.VI.84–89.

viduals and who were granted freedom from grave sins and immoral acts by God. In Muslim eyes, although these prophets may at times have been vulnerable and persecuted by their own people, they were always supported by God.

Since it is not possible to discuss all twenty-five of the Islamic prophets in the present work, this section will only discuss a few of these prophets beginning with the first, who, according to Islamic theology, was Adam.

ADAM. Whereas the Judaic-Christian traditions portray Adam as a fallen man, and Eve as the reason for his fall (and in Christianity Jesus was heralded as the saviour for that very fall), Islamic tradition presents Adam as the first of all the prophets. In the Qur'ān, the event that led to Adam and Eve being expelled from the Garden of Eden, and their progeny being banished to the world, is clearly described as the shared fault of both of them when they succumbed to the temptation of Satan. In the Qur'ān it is stated, 'Then did Satan make them slip from the (garden), and get them out of the state (of felicity) in which they had been. We said: "Get ye down, all (ye people), with enmity between yourselves. On earth will be your dwelling-place and your means of livelihood—for a time."'[1]

In the Islamic tradition, Adam's banishment from the Garden is interpreted as representing the consequences of forgetting and breaking the covenant between him and God. However, the story in the Qur'ān goes on to recount how both Adam and Eve begged for God's forgiveness and mercy, and once their pleas were accepted, God promised guidance for all of their progeny: 'Then learnt Adam from his Lord words of inspiration, and his Lord turned towards him; for He is Oft-Returning, Most Merciful. We said: "Get ye down all from here; and if, as is sure, there comes to you guidance from me, whosoever follows My guidance, on them shall be no fear, nor shall they grieve."'[2]

1 Q.II.36.
2 Q.II.37–38.

ABRAHAM, ISHMAEL AND ISAAC. This revelation from God to Adam set into motion the cycle of God's revelations to His prophets. Between the time of Adam and Abraham, numerous prophets and messengers were sent by God. However, the figure of Abraham stands out clearly within the Muslim tradition. He is portrayed by the sacred scriptures in Islam as a pure monotheist, a prophet whose many traditions were renewed by the Prophet Muḥammad. Abraham is described in the Qur'ān as a prophet to whom it was promised that his offspring would maintain the line of prophecy: 'When he [Abraham] had turned away from them and from those whom they worshipped besides God, We bestowed on him Isaac and Jacob, and each one of them We made a prophet.'[1] The main difference between the Judaic-Christian tradition and Islamic theology in their portrayal of Abraham lies in their respective claims about the legacy of prophecy between Abraham's two sons, Ishmael and Isaac.

In the Hebrew Bible, Isaac is presented as the son who is granted the legacy of Abraham, whose line continues with the Prophet Jacob and the twelve tribes of Israel. Indeed, the Jewish historian Titus Flavius Josephus (d. c. 100 CE) went as far as to describe Isaac as Abraham's only begotten and legitimate son, even though Abraham is described in the Book of Genesis as having married Hagar and as having a son named Ishmael.[2] Although the Qur'ān also contains an extensive account of the descendants of Isaac (all the way down to Jesus), it is made clear in it that God's covenant with Abraham not only continued through the Prophet Isaac and his progeny but also through the Prophet Ishmael and his progeny. It was from the line of the Prophet Ishmael that the Prophet Muḥammad was descended, and this specific link between the Prophets Abraham, Ishmael and Muḥammad is highly visible in the Qur'ān and in the *Ḥadīth* literature, whereas the portrayal of Ishmael in the Hebrew Bible is scant and inconsequential.

1 Q.XIX.49.

2 Genesis 3 and 16, as cited by M. M. al-Azami, *The History of the Qur'anic Text from Revelation to Compilation*, Leicester: UK Islamic Academy, 2003, pp. 211–12.

The second point of difference between the Hebrew Bible and the Qur'ān with regards to the two sons of Abraham is the famous sacrificial event. The Hebrew Bible describes this event in detail, and names Isaac as the son who Abraham was willing to sacrifice upon the command of God. However, the descriptions of this same event in the Qur'ān and the *Ḥadīth* name Ishmael as the sacrificial son:

> He [Abraham] said: 'I will go to my Lord! He will surely guide me! O my Lord! Grant me a righteous (son)!' So We gave him the good news of a boy ready to suffer and forbear. Then, when (the son) reached (the age of) (serious) work with him, he said: 'O my son! I see in vision that I offer thee in sacrifice: Now see what is thy view!' (The son) said: 'O my father! Do as thou art commanded: thou will find me, if God so wills one practising patience and constancy!' So when they had both submitted their wills (to God), and he had laid him prostrate on his forehead (for sacrifice), We called out to him 'O Abraham! Thou hast already fulfilled the vision!' Thus indeed do We reward those who do right. For this was obviously a trial. And We ransomed him with a momentous sacrifice. And We left (this blessing) for him among generations (to come) in later times: 'Peace and salutation to Abraham!' Thus indeed do We reward those who do right. For he was one of our believing servants. And We gave him the good news of Isaac—a prophet, one of the Righteous. We blessed him and Isaac [...].[1]

1 Q.xxxviii.99–109.

This event is celebrated by Muslims every year during the Feast of Sacrifice (*ʿĪd al-ʿAḍḥā*), which comes at the end of the Ḥajj (pilgrimage) season. On the day, every Muslim is advised by the Islamic scriptures to sacrifice an animal, such as a ram, to commemorate the willingness of Abraham to sacrifice Ishmael and God's mercy when He accepted a ram in exchange for Ishmael. It is also important to note that most of the rites involved in the Ḥajj are linked to events from the lives of Abraham, Hagar and Ishmael. According to the sources, the Ḥajj and its rites were performed by Abraham and his family and the practice continued up to Muḥammad's time, by which point it had become bound up with paganism. The story of the establishment of the Ḥajj is that during one of Abraham's visits to Mecca, where Hagar and Ishmael had settled earlier, he was commanded by God to build the sanctuary of the Kaʿba at Mecca, and he established the annual Ḥajj there.[1] Muslims continue to remember and practise these rites revived by the Prophet Muḥammad as the 'legacy of Abraham'. In the Qur'ān it is stated:

> Behold! We gave the site, to Abraham, of the (Sacred) House, (saying): 'Associate not anything (in worship) with Me; and sanctify My House for those who compass it round, or stand up, or bow, or prostrate themselves (therein in prayer). And proclaim the pilgrimage among men: they will come to thee on foot and (mounted) on every kind of camel, lean on account of journeys through deep and distant mountain highways; That they may witness the benefits (provided) for them, and celebrate the name of God, through the days appointed, over the cattle which He has provided for them (for sacrifice): then eat ye

1 In another verse, Q.II.125, it is specified that the command to 'purify My house' was addressed to both Ishmael and Abraham.

> thereof and feed the distressed ones in want.'[1] [Abraham said:] 'O our Lord! I have made some of my offspring to dwell in a valley without cultivation, by Thy Sacred House; in order, O our Lord, that they may establish regular prayer: so fill the hearts of some among men with love towards them, and feed them with fruits: so that they may give thanks. O our Lord! truly Thou dost know what we conceal and what we reveal: for nothing whatever is hidden from God, whether on earth or in heaven. Praise be to God, Who hath granted unto me in old age Ishmael and Isaac: for truly my Lord is He, the Hearer of Prayer!'[2]

MOSES AND AARON. Another very prominent figure in the Qur'ān besides Abraham is the Prophet Moses; he is mentioned by name more times than any other prophet. For the most part, the depiction of Moses[3] in the Hebrew Bible and the rabbinical tradition known as the Oral Torah is similar to that in the Qur'ān and *Ḥadīth*. However, this is not the case with regards to Moses's brother, Aaron.[4] Aaron was the elder brother of Moses, and in both the Qur'ān and the Torah he is either portrayed as the helper[5] or the mouthpiece[6] of Moses. Yet in the Qur'ān, Aaron is also recognised as a prophet,[7] whereas in the Hebrew Bible, Aaron is described as a consecrated priest of the Temple in Jerusalem, making him the founder of the hereditary

1 Q.XXII.26–28.

2 Q.XIV.37–39.

3 Please see Chapter Five on the sacred scriptures for more details.

4 See S. B. Noegel and B. M. Wheeler, *The A to Z of Prophets in Islam and Judaism*, Lanham: Scarecrow Press, 2010, pp. 1–3.

5 Q.XX.29–30.

6 Hebrew Bible, Exodus 4:16.

7 Q.IV.164; XIX.53.

priesthood. A further difference between the Judeo-Christian and Islamic traditions concerns the story of Aaron and the golden calf. In the Hebrew Bible, Aaron is described as the person responsible for constructing a golden calf for the Hebrews in order to console them during Moses's journey to Mount Sinai.[1] By contrast, several verses in the Qur'ān indicate that a person known as Sāmirī was the culprit who made the golden calf.[2] Furthermore, although Moses is said to have rebuked Aaron for not preventing the people from worshipping the golden calf (since he had left Aaron in charge during his absence), the Qur'ānic text states that Aaron did admonish those worshippers, but they refused to listen. It also states that Aaron defended himself against Moses's anger and rebuke, saying that the only reason he had not gone further in reprimanding the people was because he did not want to create divisions amongst the Children of Israel in the absence of Moses.[3]

LOT. There are similarities between the Hebrew Bible and the Qur'ān with respect to the story of Lot (*Lūṭ*). In both scriptures, Lot is recognised as the nephew of Abraham who migrated with him to Canaan. However, in the Qur'ān, Lot is portrayed as a prophet of God, whereas in the Hebrew Bible, he is not ascribed a prophetic role.[4] The Hebrew Bible narrates how Lot was tricked (due to alcohol) into having incestuous relations with his two daughters, who argued that there were no men available for them.[5] This event, which—according to the Hebrew Bible—occurred after the destruction of Sodom and Gomorrah, is not mentioned at all in the Qur'ān. Accordingly, that story is seen as false in Islamic theology because it is clear from the Islamic scriptures that Lot was a prophet, and prophets are examples of righteousness. For instance, Ibn Ḥazm, who is recognised

1 Hebrew Bible, Exodus, 32:1-6.

2 Q.xx.85–87.

3 This story may be found in various parts of the Qur'ān, especially Q.xx.83–99 and vii.148–55.

4 See Noegel and Wheeler, *The A to Z of Prophets*, pp. 194–96.

5 Hebrew Bible, Genesis 19:30–36.

as having been one of the first Muslim scholars to engage in what became known in modern Europe as biblical criticism, argued that besides the moral and ethical issues of this story, there were also internal contradictions in the text. He inquired, for example, as to how it could be considered credible that the daughters of Lot could say, '[O] ur father is old, and there is not a man in the earth to come in unto us after the manner of all the earth', when their own uncle, Abraham, and his people lived only three miles away.[1]

DAVID. King David is prominent in both the Hebrew Bible and in the Qur'an, and his defeat of Goliath is mentioned in both. However, there are major differences between the two religious traditions regarding David. For example, in the Qur'ān and *Ḥadīth*, David is known as a prophet, a messenger and a king, who was the recipient of the revealed book known as the Psalms (*Zabūr*). While in the Judeo-Christian tradition, he is anointed as a king by the Prophet Samuel,[2] but there is no mention of him being a prophet like Samuel himself. In addition, the passages of Psalms are attributed to him and are not considered a revelation from God.[3]

The major difference between the two traditions is linked to the story in the Hebrew Bible of David taking for himself a married woman named Bathsheba.[4] Bathsheba becomes pregnant, and in order to hide her pregnancy from her husband, Uriah, David sends

1 Genesis 19:31 cited in Ghulam Haider Aasi, *Muslim Understanding of other Religions: A Study of Ibn Hazm's* Kitāb al-Faṣl fi al-Milal wa al-Ahwā' wa al-Niḥal, New Delhi: Adam Publishers, 2007, p. 113.

2 See Hebrew Bible, 1 Samuel 16:1–13. The Prophet Samuel is also mentioned in the Qur'ān II.246–47 but not by name, only as 'their prophet': 'Hast thou not Turned thy vision to the Chiefs of the Children of Israel after (the time of) Moses? They said to a prophet (That was) among them: "Appoint for us a king, that we May fight in the cause of God..." and their Prophet said to them: "God hath appointed Talut as king over you." They said: "How can he exercise authority over us when we are better fitted than he to exercise authority, and he is not even gifted, with wealth in abundance?"'

3 See Noegel and Wheeler, *The A to Z of Prophets*, pp. 76–78.

4 According to the Hebrew Bible, Bathsheba was the mother of Solomon.

Uriah back to the battlefront so that he may be killed on the battlefield. The son that is born to David and Bathsheba dies in childbirth, and this event is presented in the Hebrew Bible as a punishment from God.[1] Also, a prophet named Nathan reprimands David for the alleged adultery with Bathsheba. This whole biblical tale is rejected by Islamic tradition and is not found in the Qurān,[2] although it should be noted that some rabbinical traditions based upon the Oral Torah have argued that David never committed adultery because Uriah and Bathsheba were considered divorced from the moment that Uriah first set off for war.[3]

SOLOMON. After David, the Hebrew Bible continues chronologically with the story of his son, Solomon, who became king of Israel after David and built the First Temple in Jerusalem. Both the Hebrew Bible and the Qur'ān allude to the special gifts given to Solomon by God, and both the Talmud and the Islamic scriptures describe Solomon's control over supernatural forces. The Hebrew Bible portrays him as a wise king with wealth and power, which is very similar to his characterisation in the Qur'ān.[4] However, the Qur'ān describes Solomon as a prophet whereas the Hebrew Bible does not attribute that title to him. Nevertheless, in the Hebrew Bible, Solomon is shown as having a theophoric dream where God grants him what he needs to reign.[5]

The main difference between Solomon's portrayal in the two traditions lies in what the Hebrew Bible describes as Solomon's falling into sin in older age, including idolatry and turning away from Yahweh. Ultimately, this leads to his kingdom being torn apart by civil war during the reign of his son Rehoboam, and ending with the creation of two separate nations: Israel to the south and Judah to

1 Hebrew Bible, 2 Samuel 12:14.
2 Azami, *History of the Qur'anic Text*, p. 218.
3 Hebrew Bible, 2 Samuel 11:1–26.
4 See Noegel and Wheeler, *The A to Z of Prophets*, pp. 308–09.
5 Hebrew Bible, 1 Kings 3:4–15.

the north.[1] The various allegations made in the Hebrew Bible against King Solomon, such as offering sacrifices to idols and killing Joab, his cousin, are not found in the Qur'ān and are strongly rejected by Muslim theologians.[2]

JESUS. As quoted above, a tradition of the Prophet Muḥammad reports that he said, 'I am most akin to Jesus Christ amongst the whole of humankind, and all the prophets are of different mothers but belong to one religion and no prophet was raised between me and Jesus.'[3] For Muslims, this means that Jesus was the last prophet before Muḥammad and that he is recognised as the last of the prophets from the line of Isaac and Jacob; in other words, the children of Israel. The story of Jesus is to be found in the New Testament, which is a compilation of the four Gospels and Paul's writings about Jesus's life, statements and the early church. It is beyond the scope of this chapter to compare the portrayal of Jesus in the New Testament and Church tradition with that in the Islamic tradition. Instead, the present discussion will focus on how Jesus is understood in Islamic theology.

In the Qur'ān, Jesus is described as a servant and messenger of God: 'Christ disdaineth not to serve and worship God.'[4] It also records that he said, 'I am indeed a servant of God: He hath given me revelation and made me a prophet; and He hath made me blessed wheresoever I be, and hath enjoined on me prayer and charity as long as I live; (He) hath made me kind to my mother, and not overbearing or miserable; So peace is on me the day I was born, the day that I die, and the day that I shall be raised up to life (again)!'[5] In addition, Jesus is referred to in the Qur'ān as the 'Word of God' (*Kalimat Allāh*).[6] He is recognised as having been aided by the Holy Spirit (which is another name for the Angel Gabriel) and is given the title

1 Hebrew Bible, 1 Kings 11:4–13.
2 Aasi, *Muslim Understanding*, p. 113.
3 Bukhārī, *Ṣaḥīḥ*, XLIII.189, http://sunnah.com/muslim/43/189.
4 Q.IV.172.
5 Q.XIX.30–33.
6 Q.III.45; IV.171.

of Messiah (*Masīḥ*). However, verses from the Qur'ān and reports from the *Ḥadīth* literature explicitly reject the idea of Jesus being the Son of God, or God incarnate. For instance, the Qur'ān includes the following verses on this topic:

> In blasphemy indeed are those that say that God is Christ the son of Mary.[1]
> And the Christians call Christ the son of God. That is a saying from their mouth; (in this) they but imitate what the unbelievers of old used to say.[2]
> It is not befitting to (the majesty of) God that He should beget a son. Glory be to Him! when He determines a matter, He only says to it, 'Be,' and it is.[3]

In the Qur'ān and *Ḥadīth*, the divinity of Jesus is denied, as are his crucifixion and resurrection. Instead, the Qur'ān states that Jesus was raised up into the Divine Presence without being crucified. 'That they said (in boast), "We killed Christ Jesus the son of Mary, the Messenger of God"; but they killed him not, nor crucified him, but so it was made to appear to them, and those who differ therein are full of doubts, with no (certain) knowledge, but only conjecture to follow, for of a surety they killed him not. Nay, God raised him up unto Himself; and God is Exalted in Power, Wise.'[4]

Over the past fourteen centuries, Muslim scholars have debated the differences between Islam and Christianity regarding the divinity and crucifixion of Jesus. For instance, Ghazālī employed a spiritual metaphor to point out that, while Jesus was extremely important as a chosen messenger, his shining divine light should not to be con-

1 Q.v.17; v.72.
2 Q.ix.30.
3 Q.xix.35.
4 Q.iv.157–58.

fused with the source of that light (God Himself). He argued that any claim of union between man and God was inherently false since it was not possible that one being could at the same time be another. The only exception was if the meaning of the words used was given a metaphorical value, as poets may do. Hence, the claim of union by a poet should never be taken literally; rather, such a union means that one is so close to another that one begins to lose oneself entirely in the other. This is loosely called a 'union'.[1]

Ghazālī further argued that this kind of poetic licence could be observed in the case of the Sufi Abū Yazīd,[2] who used poetry to speak of how all of his desires and concerns were sloughed off just like a snake sloughs off its skin, whereby he realised that he was He (by which he meant God). By this Abū Yazīd meant that once all that could signify 'I' was erased, nothing remained other than God. In which case, nothing existed in his heart but the majesty and beauty of God and His beauty. Hence, any expression such as 'I am He' or 'he is He' is the poet's way of saying 'as though he were He'. However, Ghazālī argued that there was a danger here for anyone who was unable to understand the subtle difference between them, because when such a person looked at the perfection that shone through his essence, he might begin to think that he was He, and so begin publicly to proclaim, 'I am the Truth'.[3] Ghazālī continued:

> Such a one commits the same error as the Christians, when they see that [same perfection] in the essence of the messiah, ʿĪsā [Jesus]—may peace be upon him—and say: he is God; yet they are as mistaken as the one who looks into

1 See Ghazālī, *Ninety-Nine Beautiful Names of God*, pp. 151–53.

2 Abū Yazīd Ṭayfūr al-Bisṭāmī (d. 261/874–5), who was also known by the name Basṭāmī, was a Persian Sufi known as one of the most important early teachers of Sufism. He was one of the first to speak of annihilation of the self in God (*fanā' fī Allāh*).

3 See Ghazālī, *Ninety-Nine Beautiful Names of God*, p. 153.

> a mirror and sees in it a coloured image yet thinks that this image is the image of the mirror, and this colour is the colour of the mirror. Far from it! For the mirror has no colour in itself; its nature is rather to receive the image of coloured things in such a way as to display them to those looking at the appearance of things as though they were the images of the mirror—to the point where a child who sees a man in the mirror thinks that the man actually is in the mirror. In a similar way, the heart is devoid of images and shapes in itself, yet its state is to receive the meaning of shapes and images and realities. So whatever inheres in it is as though it were identical with it, but it is not actually identical with it [...] Now the claim of the one who said 'I am the Truth' either means what the poet means when he said: 'I am whom I desire, and the one I desire is I', or he says it in error, as Christians err in thinking that divinity is united with humanity in Jesus.[1]

Other Muslim scholars who rejected that Jesus could partake of God's nature were Fakhr al-Dīn al-Rāzī, who employed a rational approach based upon the Qur'ān and *Ḥadīth*; Ibn ʿArabī who, although highlighting the mystical dimension, took care to point out that Jesus should not be confused with God;[2] and Ibn Kathīr (d. 737/1373), the famous Shāfiʿī scholar, traditionist and exegete, who refuted the crucifixion and resurrection in his *Tafsīr al-Qur'ān al-ʿaẓīm* (Commentary on the Great Qur'an).[3]

1 Ibid., pp. 153–54.
2 Cited in Gregory A. Barker and Stephen E. Gregg, eds., *Jesus beyond Christianity*, Oxford: Oxford University Press, 2010, pp. 107–110 and 115–19.
3 Ibid., pp. 119–23.

However, there is far more than refutation involved in Muslim accounts of Jesus. Throughout their history, Muslims have shared with Christians a love for Jesus; they believe in his virgin birth, in his miracles and they expect his return at the end of time. Many theologians have collected traditions about Jesus in order to enrich their understanding of this spiritual messenger. The traditionist and exegete Ṭabarī illustrates the closeness felt by Muslims with Jesus, whom they affectionately call the Spirit of God (*Rūḥ Allāh*). Ṭabarī dealt in detail with Jesus's life in his exegesis, not only collecting information about Mary's childhood and the early life of Jesus from the Qur'ān and *Ḥadīth*, but also from the Hebrew and Aramaic traditions, such as the Talmud and the non-canonical Christian Gospels. Narratives such as these were termed *Isrā'īliyyāt* because they concerned the ancient Israelites. Muslim scholars accept them only when they do not contradict the Qur'ān or the *Ḥadīth*. From as early as the eighth century CE, the image of Jesus as an ascetic who rejected both material things and rigid legalism for a life of silence, poverty and fasting started to emerge within Muslim literature. Later, many Sufi scholars explored the deep spiritual lessons in traditions associated with Jesus. For example, Rūmī and others viewed Jesus as both a healer of the heart and a beacon of truth in a world that was ever more closely oriented towards the material and the mundane.[1]

According to the Qur'ān, Jesus's miracles, wisdom and his knowledge of the Torah were demonstrated as early as the time of his birth, and continued throughout his life: 'Then will God say: "O Jesus the son of Mary! Recount My favour to thee and to thy mother. Behold! I strengthened thee with the Holy Spirit, so that thou didst speak to the people in childhood and in maturity. Behold! I taught thee the Book and Wisdom, the Law and the Gospel and behold! thou makest out of clay, as it were, the figure of a bird, by My leave, and thou breathest into it and it becometh a bird

1 Cited in Barker and Gregg, eds., *Jesus beyond Christianity*, pp. 112–14.

by My leave, and thou healest those born blind, and the lepers, by My leave. And behold! thou bringest forth the dead by My leave."'[1]

Finally, it is important to recognise that, in Islam, the image of Jesus as a historical figure of the first century CE has always been accompanied by that of him as the eschatological Messiah who will return at the end of time. The Prophet Muḥammad is reported to have said, 'By Him in Whose Hands my soul is, surely (Jesus,) the son of Mary will soon descend amongst you and will judge mankind justly (as a Just Ruler) [...].'[2] In the vast majority of Muslim exegetical and *Ḥadīth* literature, the dominant interpretation of the sources has been that Jesus will return to earth, fight the Antichrist, marry and have children. Then he will live an everyday life as a prophet of God and will even die a natural death.[3]

Thus, all of the prophets named in the Qur'ān are very significant figures within Islam; they are understood by Muslims to have been sent by God to manifest God's complete message and each fully represented the path of God for their era. Similarly, Muḥammad represented the complete message for his time (which includes the present era). Since Muslims recognise themselves as the *Umma* of the Prophet Muḥammad (the Community of Believers who follow Muḥammad), the focus of their loyalty and emulation is Muḥammad's *Sunna* (way, deeds and manner). This is so not because he was more 'complete' than other prophets, but because he is recognised by Muslims as the prophet for this age and because he is regarded as the 'Seal' of the all the prophets. Indeed, Muḥammad himself emphasised, 'Do not prefer some prophets to others.'[4]

To conclude this section on the prophets mentioned in the Qur'ān, it is worth noting that the gender of prophets was an issue that was

1 Q.v.110.

2 Bukhārī, *Ṣaḥīḥ*, LX.118, http://sunnah.com/bukhari/60/118, accessed 22 February 2016.

3 See Hussain, 'Jesus in Islam: Closing Reflection', in Barker and Gregg, eds., *Jesus beyond Christianity*, p. 140.

4 Bukhārī, *Ṣaḥīḥ*, LXXXVII.54, http://sunnah.com/bukhari/87/54, accessed 22 February 2016.

discussed by Muslim scholars. In particular, Ibn Ḥazm argued that women had also been prophets; however, he restricted messengership (*risāla*) to men only. He argued that since Mary,[1] Sarah,[2] Asiya[3] and the mother of Moses[4] had all received communication from God (either through word or inspiration), they should be included amongst God's prophets. Yet despite his careful reasoning, Ibn Ḥazm was in a minority; the majority of Sunni theologians have disagreed with his arguments.[5]

There are a number of other figures from non-Abrahamic religions who—despite not being named in the Qur'ān—were accepted as prophets within Islamic tradition and it is to them that we turn next.

God's Prophets beyond the Abrahamic Tradition

As mentioned above, in the Qur'ān there are twenty-five prophets referred to by name; there are also other prophets mentioned but not named. Aside from this, both the Qur'ān and *Ḥadīth* literature contain many general references to the fact that prophets have been sent to all nations throughout time. For instance, in the Qur'ān it is stated:

> We have sent thee inspiration, as We sent it to Noah and the Messengers after him: we sent inspiration to Abraham, Ishmael, Isaac, Jacob and the Tribes, to Jesus, Job, Jonah, Aaron, and Solomon, and to David We gave the Psalms. Of some messengers We have already told thee the story; of others We have not; and to Moses God spoke direct.
>
> Not a messenger did We send before thee

1 Mother of Jesus.

2 Mother of the Prophet Isaac.

3 The adoptive mother of the Prophet Moses and wife of Pharaoh.

4 She was known as Jochebed.

5 See Barbara Freyer Stowasser, *Women in the Qur'an, Traditions, and Interpretation*, Oxford: Oxford University Press, 1996, p. 77.

> without this inspiration sent by Us to him:
> that there is no god but I; therefore worship
> and serve Me.
> Nothing is said to thee that was not said to the
> messengers before thee.
> We sent not a messenger except (to teach) in
> the language of his (own) people, in order to
> make (things) clear to them.[1]

The acknowledgement in Islamic theology that all revealed religions belong to the same historical cycle and that God has only ever revealed one faith with many different laws and paths has meant that the adherents of other religions—such as Christianity, Judaism, Zoroastrianism, Hinduism, Buddhism and other religious groups—have generally been regarded by Muslims as followers of earlier authentic expression of the one religion that was later altered by people who introduced varied beliefs and practices into the original revelation. As Jacques Waardenburg has put it, 'The prophetical religions were seen to be, to the extent that they rejected idolatry, not wholly false. The revelations on which they were based were thought to be inherently true but to have been tainted by people in the course of history, resulting in a betrayal of the divine, revelatory, primordial religion (Urreligion) common to all. In order to restore this primordial, monotheistic religion, Muḥammad was sent to bring a conclusive revelation. Once memorised and written down, the Qur'ānic revelation channelled by Muḥammad, was held to have remained authentic and pure.'[2]

At this juncture it is important to introduce the topic of Muslim categorisations of religions and their adherents. In the Qur'ān, Christians and Jews were referred to as the People of the Book (*Ahl al-Kitāb*). It is from this basic recognition of other religions that many

1 Q.IV.163–64; XXI.25; XLI.43; XIV.4.

2 Jacques Waardenburg, *Muslim Perceptions of Other Religions,* New York: Oxford University Press, 1999, p. 22.

Muslim scholars were inspired to study and write about the other faiths they came across. Ibn Ḥazm, for example, wrote an extensive book entitled, *Kitāb al-faṣl fī al-milal wa'l-ahwā' wa'l-niḥal* (A Critical History of Religions, Sects and Philosophical Schools), in which he tried to categorise and analyse the religions and ideological philosophies of his period. His description of the five different denominations of Judaism that existed during his time is very interesting. He described them as:

1) The Sāmiriyya (Samaritans), a minority who differed from the majority of Jews in not accepting Jerusalem as the Holy City. They had their own version of the Torah and they did not accept any prophets after Moses and his successor, Joshua.

2) The Ṣadūqiyya (Zadokites), a minority who lived in Yemen and differed from the majority of Jews in calling Uzayr (the biblical Ezra) the son of God.

3) The ʿAnāniyya (Karaites), who were the followers of the second-/eighth-century Iraqi Jew ʿAnan ben David. The members of this anti-rabbinical movement only believed in the legitimacy of the written Hebrew Bible and not the rabbinical tradition. At the time of Ibn Ḥazm, they were mostly found in Syria, Iraq, Egypt and the Iberian Peninsula.

4) The Rabbāniyya (Rabbanites), who were the followers of rabbinical Judaism and represented the majority of Jews during Ibn Ḥazm's time.

5) The ʿĪsāwiyya, who were the followers of the Persian Jew, Muḥammad b. ʿĪsā al-Iṣfahānī. They believed that the message of Jesus was intended only for the Children of Israel and that the revelation of Muḥammad was intended only for the Children of the Prophet Ishmael. The adherents of this group, that Ibn Ḥazm personally encountered, were mostly from the elites of the Persian Jewish society.[1]

Many scholars also wrote extensively about religions besides Judaism and Christianity. For example, the influential jurist Shāfiʿī

1 Aasi, *Muslim Understanding*, pp. 81–82.

considered Zoroastrians to be People of the Book and not just among the 'protected people' (*Ahl al-dhimma*), which was a different theological category.[1] As Hamza Yusuf has observed, 'Many modern Muslims may regard Buddhists to be amongst the polytheists, believing them to be idolatrous due to the profusion of images and statues of the Buddha; early Muslim scholars of comparative religion had a very different view.'[2] In fact, due to the early Islamic conquest of areas such as Afghanistan, India and Turkic Central Asia, Muslims came into contact from very early on with Jains, Hindus and Buddhists; theologically and legally, Muslims had to engage with the status of other religions and of their adherents.

Legally, other religions and their adherents were generally granted official status as protected persons, or *dhimmī*s; that is, they were granted official protection by Muslim rulers.[3] An important case that illustrates this is the famous 'Brāhmanābād Settlement' reached in 92/711 between Hindus, Jains and Buddhists in Sind (now modern-day Pakistan) and the Umayyad general Muḥammad b. al-Qāsim al-Thaqafī (d. 106/725). It is recorded that after consulting with his scholars, Muḥammad b. al-Qāsim replied to their request for freedom of religious practice as follows:

> The request of the chiefs of Brahmanabad about the building of Budh and other temples, and toleration in religious matters, is just and reasonable. I do not see what further rights we can have over them beyond the usual tax. They have paid homage to us and have undertaken to pay the fixed tribute [*jizya*] to the Caliph. Because they have become *dhimmī*s we have no right whatsoever to interfere in their lives and

1 Reza Shah Kazemi, *Common Ground between Islam and Buddhism*, Louisville, KY: Fons Vitae, 2010, p. 11.

2 Hamza Yusuf, 'Buddha in the Qur'ān', in Kazemi, *Common Ground*, p. 114.

3 Kazemi, *Common Ground*, pp. 7–8.

> property. Do permit them to follow their own religion. No one should prevent them.[1]

He is also reported to have said, 'The temples [lit. *al-Budd*, but referring to the temples of the Buddhists and the Hindus, as well as the Jains] shall be treated by us as if they were the churches of the Christians, the synagogues of the Jews, and the fire temples of the Magians.'[2]

Although this single case did not mean that all Muslim rulers followed the same practice—in fact, at times atrocities were committed by some Muslim rulers—it nonetheless set a theological and legal precedent that was generally followed in Central Asia, India and the Far East. In these regions, Buddhists and Hindus were seen to be akin to the People of the Book and were given legal recognition accordingly.[3] One consequence of this was that early Muslim scholars studied other faiths in order to contextualise them, primarily for legal reasons but also for the purposes of theological inquiry, such as whether any of the figures venerated in these faiths could possibly have been a prophet of God. As Franz Rosenthal has justly observed, 'The comparative study of world religions has been rightly acclaimed as one of the great contributions of Muslim civilization to mankind's intellectual progress.'[4]

By the second/eighth century, Muslim historians, geographers and travellers focused on seven great ancient civilisations in their works: the Persians, Chaldeans, Greeks, Egyptians, Turks, Indians

1 Ibid., p. 8, citing Gobind Khushalani, *Chachnamah Retold: An Account of the Arab Conquest of Sindh*, New Delhi: Promilla, 2006, p. 156.

2 Quotation from Kazemi, *Common Ground*, p. 8, who cites Abū al-Ḥasan al-Balādhurī, *Futūḥ al-buldān*, Beirut: Maktabat al-Hilāl, 1988, pp. 422–23.

3 However, due to the variation within all of these faiths, some of their denominations constituted clear idolatry in Muslim eyes and were therefore not granted this status.

4 Franz Rosenthal, 'Preface', in Bruce B. Lawrence, *Shahrastānī on the Indian Religions*, The Hague: Mouton, 1976, p. 5.

and Chinese.[1] Just two decades after the Prophet's death, areas of the Sasanid empire in Persia had been conquered, which included eastern regions where Buddhism had a wide following. As early as the year 42/663, the Umayyads had captured the area around Balkh in northern Afghanistan and they went on to conquer the rest of Afghanistan and West Turkistan, where Buddhism had spread. The conquest of Sasanid Persia then led the Arabs to Central Asia where Turkic peoples resided, and they were mostly followers of either Buddhism or Shamanism.

The Umayyad conquest of Balkh provides an insightful illustration of early Muslim interactions with Buddhism as the city housed the famous Buddhist monastery and stupa Nava Vihara.[2] As Alexander Berzin explains, 'The Arabs allowed followers of non-Muslim religions in the lands they conquered to keep their faiths if they submitted peacefully and paid a poll tax (*jizya*). Although some Buddhists in Bactria and even an abbot of Nava Vihara converted to Islam, most Buddhists in the region accepted this *dhimmī* status as loyal non-Muslim protected subjects within an Islamic state. Nava Vihara remained open and functioning. The Han Chinese pilgrim Yijing (I-ching) visited Nava Vihara in the years around 60/680 and reported it flourishing as a Sarvastivada center of study.'[3] It seems that for at least one or two centuries, Buddhism and faiths other than Islam remained the main religion of the populace in the eastern lands the Umayyads had conquered and which the Abbasid dynasty later ruled.

1 Hilman Latief, 'Comparative Religion in Medieval Literature', *American Journal of Islamic Social Sciences*, vol. XXIII, no. 4, Fall 2006, pp. 28–62.

2 A stupa is a place of worship for Buddhists and is normally a mound-like structure, many of which are said to contain Buddhist relics. The word derives from Sanskrit and literally means 'heap'.

3 Alexander Berzin, 'Historical Sketch of Buddhism and Islam in Afghanistan', Berzin Archives, November 2001 (revised December 2006), http://www.berzinarchives.com/web/en/archives/study/history_buddhism/buddhism_central_asia/history_afghanistan_buddhism.html, accessed 15 August 2014.

The first detailed Muslim account of the Nava Vihara monastery was written by the second-/eighth-century Umayyad author ʿUmar b. al-Azraq al-Kirmānī a few decades after that of Yijing's in 60/680. Kirmānī's comprehensive account of the monastery of Nava Vihara was preserved in an abridgement of the fourth-/tenth-century work, *Kitāb al-buldān* (Book of Lands), by the Persian historian and geographer Ibn al-Faqīh al-Hamadhānī (d. 289/902). As Berzin explains in the following quotation, Kirmānī's account of Nava Vihara indicates that the Umayyads were respectful in their dealings with non-Muslim religions:

> [Al-Kirmani] described it [Nava Vihara] in terms readily understandable to Muslims by drawing the analogy with the Kaaba in Mecca, the holiest site of Islam. He explained that the main temple had a stone cube in the center, draped with cloth, and that devotees circumambulated it and made prostration, as is the case with the Kaaba. The stone cube referred to the platform on which a stupa stood, as was the custom in Bactrian temples. The cloth that draped it was in accordance with the Iranian custom for showing veneration, applied equally to Buddha statues as well as to stupas. Al-Kermani's description indicates an open and respectful attitude by the Umayyad Arabs in trying to understand the non-Muslim religions, such as Buddhism, that they encountered in their newly conquered territories.[1]

Under the Abbasids and their administrators, the Barmakids, who were originally a family of Buddhist administrators at Nava Vihara—many Buddhist and Hindu scholars were invited to Baghdad

1 Berzin, 'Historical Sketch of Buddhism'.

from India and Afghanistan. As an indication of the interest in these non-Muslim religions, Ibn al-Nadīm's (d. 387/998) famous *Fihrist* (literally, an index or list of books)[1] included a list of Buddhist works, many of them medical books, but amongst them was an Arabic account of Buddha's previous lives known as the *Kitāb al-Budd* (Book of Buddha).[2] In the *Fihrist*, Ibn al-Nadīm mentioned the Buddha as a possible prophet of God who was sent to the people of *al-Hind*.[3] In addition, an anonymous treatise on the religious beliefs of the Indians was in circulation by the end of the second/eighth century and Ibn Nadīm is said to have reported that he saw one copy of it in the handwriting of the philosopher Kindī, and another written in 248/863 by an Indian scholar for Yaḥyā b. Barmak.[4]

In the following centuries, many Muslim travellers and geographers wrote about India and composed brief accounts of the various religious denominations found there.[5] *Al-Hind* or *al-Sind* was the Arabic term for India from as early as the Prophet's lifetime. In his first historical compendium, *Murūj al-dhahab* (The Meadows of Gold), the historian Masᶜūdī (d. 283/956) described the nation of Hind as extending from the mountains of Khurāsān and Sind to Tibet (*Tubbet*).[6] The Persian geographer Ibn al-Khurradādhbih (d. 299/912) gave a report about the various types of Indian castes and their forty-two religious denominations in his book *Kitāb al-masālik wa'l mamālik* (The Book of Roads and Kingdoms).[7] Another account was written by the Persian geographer Abū Saᶜīd

1 His index, composed in 377/938, was intended to include all books ever written in the Arabic language on every branch of knowledge up until his time.

2 Berzin, 'Historical Sketch of Buddhism.'

3 Kieko Obuse, 'The Muslim Doctrine of Prophethood in the Context of Buddhist-Muslim Relations in Japan: Is the Buddha a Prophet?', *Muslim World*, vol. C, no. 2–3, April/July 2010, pp. 215–32.

4 Fakhry, *History of Islamic Philosophy*, p. 33.

5 For instance, see M. S. Khan, 'A Twelfth Century Arab Account of Indian Religions and Sects', *Arabica*, vol. XXX, no. 2, June 1983, pp. 199–208.

6 Cited in Latief, 'Comparative Religion', p. 31.

7 Ibid.

Gardīzī (d. 452/1061) in his book *Zayn al-akhbār* (The Ornament of Histories). He praised the inhabitants of India for their sciences, saying, 'Among [their] wonders [are their] mathematics, geodesy, geometry and astronomy, in which their science and authority have reached a degree impossible to explain.'[1] Gardīzī then proceeded to classify their beliefs and philosophies into ninety-nine divisions which he simplified into forty-two denominations. He described these groups in detail and mentioned some of their names as Shamanī or Būdī (Buddhist), Bāsdīv or Vāsudeva (Brahman Vaishnavites), Kālī or Kāpālikas (Shaivites) and Rāmāni (Followers of Rama).[2]

Another early account of India by Sulaymān al-Tājir dating from the third/ninth century, entitled *Akhbār al-Ṣīn wa'l-Hind* (An Account of China and India) was compiled in approximately 236/851 but became more widely known after being incorporated into Abū Zayd al- Sīrāfī's (d. 338/950) collection of Arab travel accounts known as the *Silsilat al-tawārīkh* (The Chain of Histories). In it, Tājir briefly informed the reader of the cultural connections between the two lands, specifically highlighting how Buddhism in China and other Chinese religious traditions had originated in India. He compared the belief systems in India and China and stated that both affirmed their belief in communication with their idols, he saw similarities in the mystical aspects of their respective faiths and noted that people in both lands believed in metempsychosis (the transmigration of the soul).[3]

During this period, there was also a concerted response from Muslim theologians against the Hellenistic and Indian proponents of the idea that revelation was not required, and hence that prophecy was neither necessary nor needed. It was in this context that the philosopher Kindī wrote a treatise justifying the prophets' legitimacy

1 Translation from V. Minorsky, 'Gardīzī on India', *Bulletin of the School of Oriental and African Studies,* vol. XII, no. 3–4, 1948, pp. 625–40.

2 Ibid.

3 Latief, 'Comparative Religion', p. 33.

entitled 'Refutations of the Arguments of the Atheists', which was directed against those who denied prophecy.[1] All of the works mentioned here demonstrate that Muslim society under the Umayyads and Abbasids was one which was intellectually cross-cultural and in which there was constant engagement with other civilisations through politics, trade, culture and religion.

Following these early descriptions of engagements with faiths other than Judaism, Christianity and Zoroastrianism made by geographers, travellers and traders, the first Muslim scholar to study the subject in detail was the polymath Abū al-Rayḥān Muḥammad al-Bīrūnī (d. 439/1048). He spent a total of thirteen years in India and in recent times has been acclaimed as the founder of the comparative study of religion. He travelled to India from Central Asia during the fifth/eleventh century as part of the invading army of Sultan Maḥmūd of Ghazna (r. 388–421/998–1030). As Bīrūnī was a versatile scientist and writer, who was well-versed in several languages including Sanskrit, and an enthusiastic traveller, his duties for Sultan Maḥmūd included exploring the sciences, geography, customs, literature, philosophical thought and religious traditions of India.

Bīrūnī wrote numerous books on natural science, one of which was his famous work *Kitāb fī taḥqīq mā li'l-Hind min maqūla maqbūlah fī al-ʿaql aw mardhūla* ('The Book Confirming What Pertains to India, Whether Rational or Despicable', more commonly known simply as 'India'), which was completed in approximately 420/1030.[2] This book detailed his travels in India and his research not only on the religion and the traditions of India, but also on the nation's scientific contributions. Arthur Jeffery described Bīrūnī's contribution to the study of religion as scrupulous and focused on the scientific principles of completeness, accuracy and unbiased treatment.[3] Bīrūnī praised

1 Fakhry, *History of Islamic Philosophy*, p. 70.

2 See Muḥammad b. Aḥmad al-Bīrūnī, *Tārīkh al-Hind*, trans. Edward C. Sachau as *Alberuni's India*, 2 vols., repr., Delhi: Low Price Publications, 2003.

3 A. Jeffery, 'Al-Biruni's Contribution to Comparative Religion', in *Al-Biruni: Commemorative Volume*, Calcutta: Iran Society, 1951, p. 126.

the Hindus as being 'excellent philosophers, good mathematicians and astronomers.'[1] He analysed India's religious traditions in detail, especially Hinduism. He wrote less on Buddhism, perhaps because it had largely disappeared from Northern India (where Bīrūnī conducted most of his research) by that time. In Bīrūnī's *India*, he wrote, 'This book is not a polemical one [...] My book is nothing but a simple historic record of facts.'[2] He continued: 'I have [...] written this book on the doctrines of the Hindus, never making any unfounded imputations against those, our religious antagonists, and at the same time not considering it inconsistent with my duties as a Muslim to quote their own words at full length when I thought they would contribute to elucidate a subject. If the contents of these quotations happen to be utterly heathenish, and the followers of the truth, i.e. the Muslims, find them objectionable, we can only say that such is the belief of the Hindus, and that they themselves are best qualified to defend it.'[3]

Interestingly, Bīrūnī saw Hinduism as being monotheistic in nature and he pointed to references to the One Unique God within Hindu texts. He therefore saw the polytheism of Hinduism as an example of the deviation from strict monotheism common to pre-Islamic faiths. He argued that whereas the general populace (the *ʿāmma*) perceived their religion through the lens of polytheism, the elites (the *khāṣṣa*)—by which he meant the theologians and philosophers—apprehended it in more profound manner which, at times, led to a more monotheistic outlook. Bīrūnī demonstrated great sophistication when he argued that idolatry did not only come in one form, explaining that 'the pagan Arab, Greeks, Romans and Indians have a tradition of idols but some think the idol is an actual deity, others see it as a mediator to God, other think of it as interces-

1 Quotation from Latief, 'Comparative Religion', p. 35.

2 Ibid., p. 39.

3 Hilman Latief, 'Comparative Religion in Medieval Muslim Literature', *American Journal of Islamic Social Sciences*, vol. XXIII, no. 4, Fall 2006, pp. 39–40, citing Edward Sachau, tr., *Alberuni's India*.

sor with God, or His manifestation or His representation whereas others see it only as a memorial'.[1] Once Hinduism and Buddhism were understood in this more nuanced way, it became possible for Muslim theologians to consider whether any of the major figures in these religions, such as the Buddha, could qualify as prophets.

The second major Muslim scholar to look at eastern religions in details was the Ashᶜarī theologian Tāj al-Dīn Abū al-Fatḥ Muḥammad al-Shahrastānī (d. 547/1153). Eric J. Sharpe, a contemporary scholar of religious studies writes of Shahrastānī, 'The honour of writing the first history of religion in world literature seems in fact to belong to the Muslim Shahrastānī, whose *Religious Parties and Schools of Philosophy* describes and systematizes all religions of the then known world, as far as the boundaries of China.'[2] Shahrastānī's major contribution to comparative religion was his book *Kitāb al-milal wa'al-niḥal* (Religious Parties and Schools of Philosophy). Although he never travelled to India himself, Shahrastānī obtained information on Indian religions and traditions through now lost intermediates, with additions from classical Muslim sources. The book first of all sets forth a detailed discussion of the sectarian divisions within Islam and then deals with the various Greek philosophical schools. The text then continues with a description of the beliefs and ritual observances of several non-Muslim religious groups, including Jews, Christians, Magians, Buddhists and Hindus.

Shahrastānī also suggested that Buddha may possibly have been the Prophet Khiḍr (Khaḍir). He wrote, '[The Buddhists believe that] Buddha is a person from this world who is born and does not marry, eat, drink, age, or die. The first Buddha to manifest in the world is known as Shakyamuni, which means "honourable and noble". [...] They [the Buddhists] emerged in India due to the special qualities of that land and its topography as well as the fact that among its peoples are those who excel in spiritual exercises and self-mastery. Based

1 Latief, 'Comparative Religion', pp. 46–48.

2 Quoted by Latief, 'Comparative Religion', p. 29.

upon their description of the Buddha, if they are accurate, it would seem that he is none other than Khadir, whom Muslims acknowledge, upon him be peace.'[1] In the recent book *Common Ground between Islam and Buddhism*, Hamza Yusuf proposes several reasons why Shahrastānī may have identified Khiḍr, a sage mentioned in the Qur'ān, with the figure of Buddha. Yusuf argues that there are numerous examples drawn from Qur'ānic exegesis, *Ḥadīth* and classical theology that can be used to show the parallel teachings of Buddha and Khiḍr. In addition, Yusuf points out that it is important to highlight that with Shahrastānī's 'status as an authoritative imam and his knowledge of Buddhism and Islamic theology, it is even singularly noteworthy that he should suggest the possibility of the Buddha being the Qur'ānic sage, al-Khadir'.[2]

Shahrastānī is known to have approached his study of the Hindu faith sensitively and to have employed an analytical approach to Hinduism which was unique. He was the first scholar to describe both Hinduism and Buddhism as Sabians.[3] The Sabians, who are mentioned in the Qur'ān, are seen in Islamic tradition as a historic religious community that had monotheist inclinations. Shahrastānī also devoted a great deal of attention to prophecy with regards to Hinduism. He wrote a refutation of the beliefs of the Brahmans who believed in God but not in prophecy, and he went as far as identifying Shiva and Vishnu as possible messenger angels.[4]

During the following centuries, many scholars continued to study Buddhism and Hinduism. One was Rashīd al-Dīn Faḍl Allāh (d. c. 718/1318), who was known as the Physician (*Ṭabīb*). He served as grand vizier to the Īlkhānid court in Persia and wrote the famous *Jāmiᶜ al-tawārīkh* (Compendium of Chronicles), in which he discussed

1 Quotation from Shahrastānī's *Kitāb al-milal wa'l-niḥal*, cited by Yusuf, 'Buddha in the Qur'ān', in Kazemi, ed., *Common Ground*, p. 119.

2 Ibid., pp. 118–22.

3 Bruce B. Lawrence, 'Shahrastānī on Idol Worship', *Studia Islamica*, vol. XXXVIII, 1973, p. 66. Also see Yusuf, 'Buddha in the Qur'ān', in Kazemi, ed., *Common Ground*, p. 115.

4 Bruce B. Lawrence, 'Shahrastānī on Idol Worship', p. 69.

Buddhism and its features.[1] In reading this and other medieval Arabic works, it becomes clear that Muslim scholars did entertain the possibility that the founders and key figures of other faiths had in fact been messengers of God. Pre-Islamic figures who were recognised as possible prophets of God by Muslims over the centuries included the Babylonian King Hammurabi (r. 1792–1750 BCE), Lao Tzu (sixth century BCE) and even Confucius (d. 478 BCE). The Indian Muslim scholar Aḥmad al-Sirhindī (d. 1033/1624), also known as Imam Rabbānī, argued that there were figures in Indian history who may have been prophets of God, but he was hesitant to name any of them. K. H. Qadiri argues that many Muslim Indian theologians of this era showed a similar reluctance to name Hindu demi-gods as prophets.[2] However, Mīrzā Maẓhar Jān-i-Janān (d. 1195/1781), a distinguished Sufi scholar of Delhi, clearly asserted that the Vedas (Hindu scriptures) were divinely inspired and that Hinduism had begun as a monotheist faith. He then proceeded to argue that Krishna and Rama, called 'avatars' in the Hindu faith, could be regarded within the Islamic tradition as messengers, prophets or saints. However, he also highlighted that this faith—like all others—had been abrogated by the coming of the Prophet Muḥammad. Furthermore, he did not consider it appropriate to pass any judgement on the pre-Islamic Indians, nor did he consider it incumbent upon his fellow Muslims to decide whether those people had attained salvation or not. He argued that this was also the case for all of the pre-Islamic peoples of Persia and other nations.[3]

As this discussion has clearly shown, Muslim scholars were some of the first to lead the way in the comparative study of religion and were more successful in their research than any of their contempo-

1 Imtiyaz Yusuf, 'Islam and Buddhism Relations from Balkh to Bangkok and Tokyo', *Muslim World*, vol. C, no. 2–3, April/July 2010, pp. 177–86.

2 K. H. Qadiri, *The Prophets of India*, Patna: Khuda Baksh Oriental Public Library, 1992, pp. 4–5.

3 Yohanan Friedmann, 'Medieval Muslim Views of Indian Religions', *Journal of the American Oriental Society*, pp. 219–20.

raries from other religions. However, it must be acknowledged that there were practical inaccuracies in some works from the past, such as Rashīd al-Dīn Faḍl Allāh's writings on Buddhism.[1] However, this does not detract from the achievement of Muslim scholars, throughout history, who have tried to establish a theology of world religions in which the scriptures and figures of other faiths were studied in a more sympathetic way than any other religious tradition had previously done.

In contemporary times, a number of scholars have discussed the unnamed prophets of the past. The well-known scholar Syed Sulaiman Nadvi (d. 1372/1953) wrote in his biography of the Prophet Muḥammad, quoting various scholars, that, 'According to the teachings of the Prophet, it is necessary to believe that in countries such as China, Iran or India, there appeared prophets before the advent of Prophet Muḥammad. No Muslim can really deny to the people in these lands, the truth of faiths ascribed to the figures venerated by them. It is not only possible but probable that Vedic Rishis of old, and Rama, Krishna, Buddha and Mahavira of India, Zoroaster of Persia and Confucius of China may have been the messengers the Qur'ān is referring to.'[2]

The late Muhammad Hamidullah (d. 1422/2002) observed that the Buddha could possibly be regarded as one of the earlier prophets. It is interesting to note that according to Buddhism, the term 'Buddha' is a title rather than a given name, as with the Arabic terms *rasūl* and *nabī*. Accordingly, Buddhist tradition mentions twenty-seven Buddhas who may have appeared over a period of five thousand years. However, the

1 On this, see Yusuf, 'Islam and Buddhism Relations', p. 179 and Alexander Berzin, 'Historical Survey of the Buddhist and Muslim Worlds' Knowledge of Each Other's Customs and Teachings', Berzin Archives, August 2009, http://www.berzinarchives.com/web/en/archives/study/islam/general/historical_survey_knowledge.html, accessed 22 February 2016.

2 Shiblī Nuʿmānī and Sulaymān Nadvī, *Sīrat al-Nabī* [in Urdu], Lahore: Maktaba Tamir-i-Insaniat, 1975, cited in Abdul Basit, *The Global Muslim Community at a Crossroads*, Santa Barbara, CA: Praeger, 2012, p. 57.

Buddha that is normally recognised as a possible unnamed prophet in Islam is Siddhārtha Guatama Buddha (d. 483 BCE); this is an especially prevalent opinion amongst Muslims in South and Southeast Asia.[1] Similarly, Prince Ghāzī b. Muḥammad of Jordan recently wrote in the foreword to the book, *Common Ground between Islam and Buddhism*, that 'the Buddha, whose basic guidance one in ten people on earth have been in principle following for the last 2500 years, was, in all likelihood—and God knows best—one of God's great Messengers, even if many Muslims will not accept everything in the Pali Canon as being authentically attributable to the Buddha. [...] It seems to us then that the Umayyads and the Abbasids were entirely correct in regarding Buddhists as if they were '*ahl al-kitāb*' (people of a revealed scripture). This is in fact how millions of ordinary Muslim believers have regarded their pious Buddhists neighbours for hundreds of years, despite what their scholars will tell them about doctrinal difference between the two faiths.'[2]

Muḥammad and the Importance of the Sunna

As has been made clear in this chapter, all of the prophets recognised by Muslims were people who submitted to God and who were chosen for the purpose of helping other human beings learn how to fully submit to God. Although these prophets lived in different times and places throughout history, and were chosen to convey God's message to diverse peoples in various languages, Islam considers their mission to have been one and the same. Expounding upon this universality of the prophets and his role within it, the Prophet Muḥammad said, 'The similitude of mine and that of the Apostles before me is that of a person who built a house quite imposing and beautiful and he made it complete but for one brick in one of its corners. People began to walk round it, and the building pleased them and they would say: "But for this brick your building would have

1 Obuse, 'Muslim Doctrine of Prophethood', p. 215.
2 Kazemi, *Common Ground*, pp. xv–xvi.

been perfect." Muḥammad (may God bless him and grant him peace) said: "And I am that final brick.""[1] As noted previously, Muslims recognise Muḥammad as the Seal of the Prophets, and because Islam and Muḥammad's message from God are considered not to have deviated from the original message like earlier religions, the Prophet's life and practice have a special status for Muslims.

Thus, for the *Umma* of Muḥammad the imitation of his 'Beautiful Model'[2] by each Muslim is a means of taking on the attributes of the Prophet.[3] The famous jurist Imam Shāfiʿī described the importance of the *Sunna* of the Prophet as follows, 'God said: "The believers are only those who have faith in God and His Messenger without wavering, and strive for the sake of God by means of their property and their persons. They are the ones who are sincere [Q.XLIX.15]." 'Thus, 'God prescribed that the perfect beginning of the faith, to which all other things are subordinate, is the belief in Him and then in His Messenger. For if a person believes only in [God] and not in His Messenger, he cannot be described as one who has "perfect faith"; he must have faith in His Messenger together with Him. [...] God has imposed the duty upon men to obey His divine communications as well as the *Sunna* of His Messenger.'[4]

The term *sunna* is an Arabic word meaning 'path' or 'custom relating to norms and practices' of a people or a person. During Muḥammad's own lifetime, the *Sunna* began to be understood exclusively as the way of the Prophet, embodied in what he said, what he did and in what he approved of through explicit or tacit confirmation. The Prophet's way informs every aspect of the *Sharīʿa*, from sources dealing with what is obligatory (*wājib*) to the forbidden

1 Muslim, *Ṣaḥīḥ*, book 43, *ḥadīth* 23, http://sunnah.com/muslim/43/23, accessed 22 February 2016.

2 The Qur'ān refers to the Prophet as the 'Beautiful Model' (*uswa ḥasana*); see Q.XXXIII.21.

3 See Schimmel, *And Muhammad Is His Messenger*, p. 55.

4 Cornell, *Voices of Islam*, p. 128.

(*ḥarām*). Over time, the term *Sunna* came to be employed for two auxiliary purposes. Firstly, the term *Sunna* is utilised by legal theorists to denote acts of worship that are not obligatory, but which are recommended (*mandūb*).[1] Secondly, in jurisprudence, *Sunna* was the name associated with the body of information preserved in the *Ḥadīth* and it was used to distinguish this evidence from that found in the Qur'ān. Hence, the *Sunna* is the way of the Prophet and it has been generally understood by Muslims to be the precedents set by Muḥammad that are worthy of imitation by all Muslims. The link between the *Sunna*—or the *Ḥadīth*—and the Qur'ān in the person of the Prophet was emphasised by his wife ᶜĀ'isha in her description of him as the living Qur'ān. This was reported by Yazīd b. Yabnus who said, 'We went to ᶜĀ'isha and said, "*Umm al-Mu'minīn* [Mother of the Believers], what was the character of the Messenger of God, may God bless him and grant him peace, like?" She replied, "His character was the Qur'ān."'[2]

1 In other words, such an act is rewarded in the Afterlife, but its omission is not punished. In the context of Islamic law, recommended acts are contrasted with obligatory acts, which are rewarded in the next life and their omission leads to punishment in the next life.

2 Bukhārī, *Ṣaḥīḥ*, xiv.308, http://sunnah.com/urn/2203080.

Chapter Five

THE SCRIPTURES

Meaning of the Term Scripture

As Ghulam Haider Aasi succinctly observes, 'The distinguishing characteristic of a Muslim is his firm belief that the Qur'ān is the word of God; the Speech of God (*Kalām Allāh*) *verbatim*. The Qur'ān, as revelation from God, embodies His will and His Guidance *par excellence*. It provides man [with] norms and basic principles relating to all aspects of life. Therefore, the Qur'ānic teachings also play a very prominent role in shaping a Muslim's approach to the understanding of other religious traditions.'[1]

In the Qur'ān, *kitāb* is the term used for 'book' or 'scripture' and this term has a general as well as a particular meaning. The general meaning refers to all of God's revelations to humankind. The Qur'ān and the *Ḥadīth* refer to a Preserved Tablet (*Lawḥ Maḥfūẓ*)[2] and, theologically, the term denotes the celestial sphere wherein the Qur'ān is preserved. Elsewhere, it is referred to as the Mother of the Book (*Umm al-Kitāb*): 'We have made it an Arabic Qur'ān that you may understand. Truly, it is the Mother of the Book, in Our Presence, lofty and full of wisdom.'[3] There are also allusions to the Preserved Tablet in the *Ḥadīth* literature, such as: 'God created the preserved tablet from a white pearl with a ruby surface; its pen and its writing being of light—upon which all worldly affairs are laid

1 Aasi, *Muslim Understanding*, p. 1.

2 Q.LXXXV.21–22, 'But this is an honoured Qur'ān, [inscribed] in a Preserved Tablet'.

3 Q.XLIII.3–4.

out'; and, 'God sent down the Qur'ān all at once from the Preserved Tablet to the place of glory in the lowest heaven. Then He sent it down according to the various occasions, over thirteen years, to the Prophet.'[1] The particular meaning of 'book' (*kitāb*) applies to all the individual revelations revealed to God's messengers throughout human history: 'This Qur'ān is not such as can be produced by other than God; on the contrary it is a confirmation of (revelations) that went before it, and a fuller explanation of the Book—wherein there is no doubt—from the Lord of the worlds.'[2]

In this context, book or scripture does not necessarily mean a physical book that has been revealed. In fact, the meaning of the term also includes revelation in the form of a structured message that has been sent by God and is clearly distinct from human speech, and is yet transmitted through the language of a messenger. This is precisely the case with the Qur'ān: 'Qur'ānic rhythm and assonance alone confirm that it is meant to be heard. But the oral nature of the Qur'ān goes beyond euphony: the significance of the revelation is carried as much by the sound as by its semantic information.'[3] In fact, since its revelation, the importance of the oral nature of the Qur'ān—and its recitation—has always been emphasised. Consequently, it would be a mistake to treat it exclusively as a written text. 'When reading the Qur'ān it is crucial to remember that the text was originally intended to be read [recited] aloud and that is still its most effective form. Recitation to an audience gives the text a dimension that does not come across in silent reading.'[4]

Aside from the Qur'ān, what are the scriptures that Muslims are asked to believe in? According to the Qur'ān and the *Sunna*, Muslims are asked to believe in all of the scriptures revealed to God's mes-

1 Translations from Oliver Leaman, ed., *The Qur'an: An Encyclopedia*, London: Routledge, 2006, p. 506.

2 Q.x.37.

3 K. Nelson, *The Art of Reciting the Qur'an*, Cairo: American University in Cairo Press, 2001, p. xiv.

4 J. Rodwell, *The Koran*, [no place]: Everyman Library, 1994, p. xix.

sengers throughout human history (whether named or unnamed). For instance, in the Qur'ān it is said, 'We have sent thee inspiration, as We sent it to Noah and the messengers after him. We sent inspiration to Abraham, Ishmael, Isaac, Jacob and the Tribes, to Jesus, Job, Jonah, Aaron, and Solomon, and to David We gave the Psalms.'[1] Twice, the Qur'ān refers to an unidentified scripture revealed to the Prophet Abraham—the *Ṣuḥuf Ibrāhīm*, which is sometimes translated as the Scrolls of Abraham.[2] However, the four scriptures explicitly named in the Qur'ān are the Torah (*Tawrāt*), which was revealed to Moses; the Psalms (*Zabūr*), which were revealed to David; the Gospel (*Injīl*), which was revealed to Jesus; and the Qur'ān itself, which was revealed to Muḥammad.[3] Muslims therefore understand the Qur'ān to be God's final revelation in a similar way to how they accept the Prophet Muḥammad as the Seal of the Prophets. This understanding is based on the words of the Qur'ān itself: 'Step by step, He has sent the scripture down to you [Muḥammad] with the truth, confirming what went before; He sent down the Torah and the Gospel as a guide for people. He has sent down the distinction [between right and wrong].'[4]

For Muslims, revealed scripture has traditionally been understood as being the literal word of God. For example, Ibn Taymiyya stated that the Word of God (*Kalām Allāh*) was what the messengers had received and transmitted from God.[5] What humans say about God or what they attribute to Him and what they attribute to a messenger after his death would therefore not qualify as scripture on account of it being of human origin. Thus the traditional Muslim definition of scripture requires that anything considered revelation must strictly come from God Himself. As a consequence, what in Judaism and Christianity is indirectly attributed to God, or said to be inspired

1 Q.IV.163.

2 Q.LXXXVII.9–19; Q.LIII.36–62.

3 Cornell, ed., *Voices of Islam*, p. 36.

4 Q. III.3–4.

5 Saeed, *The Qur'an*, p. 153.

reports about various figures in the Bible, is not considered revelation by the majority of Muslims. However, if material is directly attributed to God (such as when God spoke to Moses), then such a communication may be regarded as revealed scripture. Furthermore, for Muslims, the language a scripture is revealed in must remain unchanged. This means that any translation—being a product of human endeavour—is not considered the *very* Word of God.

In the Qur'ān, three words are used to signify the idea of religion: these are *dīn*, *milla* and *umma*. According to Aasi, the three terms have distinct but related meanings within the Qur'ānic world view. *Dīn* has a generic meaning of primordial religion or faith, *milla* is what can be termed a religious tradition or community and *umma* denotes a community that is based upon a revealed religious and moral norms, but at the same time constitutes a socio-political entity.[1] In the Qur'ān, all of the communities that were sent messengers and revelation prior to the *Umma* of Muḥammad are described as *Ahl al-Kitāb* (literally, People of the Book), meaning a people who have been given a divine writ or revelation.

These scriptures that were revealed prior to the Qur'ān are believed to have been sent to particular groups of people and nations. By comparison, Islamic theologians consider the Qur'ān to be the only scripture intended for all of humanity. The three other scriptures named in the Qur'ān, the Torah (*Tawrāt*), the Psalms (*Zabūr*), and the Gospel (*Injīl*), are therefore understood as having been primarily addressed to the tribes of Israel. 'It was We who revealed the law (to Moses): therein was guidance and light. By its standard have been judged the Jews, by the prophets who bowed (as in Islam) to God's will, by the rabbis and the doctors of law: for to them was entrusted the protection of God's book, and they were witnesses thereto [...]'; 'And in their footsteps We sent Jesus the son of Mary, confirming the Law that had come before him. We sent him the Gospel: therein was guidance and light, and confirmation of the Law that had come

1 Aasi, *Muslim Understanding*, p. 38.

before him: a guidance and an admonition to those who fear God.'[1] It is generally considered by Muslims that none of the earlier revelations have been preserved in their original form, and so they are not obliged to believe in those books as they are found today.

However, there have been differences amongst Muslim theologians (including within the same theological school) on this issue of the distortion (*taḥrīf*) of scriptures by previous religious communities. One opinion is that the extant versions of the Hebrew Bible and the New Testament that have survived till today cannot be at all identified as the revealed scriptures of *Tawrāt*, *Zabūr* and *Injīl*. This is because these sacred scriptures have been altered so much that all that is left is the human version of them. A second theological opinion claims that distortion did not occur within the text of the scriptures, but in the interpretations given to them by religious communities. Finally, a third opinion is that although *taḥrīf* may be generally confined to the interpretation of the scriptures, direct distortion of the text may also have occurred through changes, additions and omissions.[2] This third opinion is the one that is followed by the majority of Muslims today. Thus, Muslims have normally regarded the scriptures of other faiths to be divine revelation that has been distorted over time.[3]

The Tawrāt, Zabūr, Injīl and Qur'ān

THE TAWRĀT. The sacred book of the Jews today, the Hebrew Bible (which is known by Christians as the Old Testament[4]), consists of twenty-four books according to the rabbinical tradition. The Hebrew Bible is divided into three sections: the Torah (the Pentateuch, consist-

1 Q.v.44, 46.

2 Aasi, *Muslim Understanding*, p. 38.

3 Abdullah Saeed, 'The Charge of Distortion of Jews and Christian Scriptures', *Muslim World*, vol. XCII, Fall 2002, pp. 419–36.

4 The Old Testament is edited from the same textual source (it is primarily based on the Hebrew Bible) but it varies in the number of books it contains, its numbering, the addition of passages and so on, according to the various Church traditions. It should also be noted that there are multiple versions of the Old Testament.

ing of five books), the Nevi'im (Prophets) and the Ketuvim (Writings). These three sections are collectively known by the acronym *Tanakh*. Orthodox Jews[1] make a distinction between the revelation of the Torah and the rest of the Hebrew Bible. They claim that the first five books were directly spoken to Moses from God, while the other two sections were less directly inspired. It is believed that the books of the Nevi'im were inspired through the gift of prophecy and that those of the Ketuvim were written under the influence of the Holy Spirit (which is considered a lesser degree of inspiration than prophecy[2]).

The first five books of the Hebrew Bible are collectively known as the Torah; they are: Genesis, Exodus, Leviticus, Numbers and Deuteronomy. The dominant figure in the Torah is Moses, who is referred to in the third person. The chronological narrative traces the genesis of the world and humanity then focuses on Abraham and his descendants through Isaac, all the way to the exodus of the Children of Israel from Egypt under Moses. All of the primary Jewish laws are found in the Torah in the form of divine commandments. The second part of the Hebrew Bible, Nevi'im, is commonly translated as 'prophets' or 'divinely revealed works'. It includes the books of Joshua, Judges, Samuel, Kings, Isaiah, Jeremiah, Ezekiel, Hosea, Joel, Amos, Obadiah, Jonah, Micah, Nahum, Habakkuk, Zephaniah, Haggai, Zechariah and Malachi. The third part is the Ketuvim, meaning 'writings', which includes books such as the Psalms, Proverbs, Job, Song of Songs, Ruth, Lamentations, Ecclesiastes, Esther, Daniel, Ezra, Nehemiah and Chronicles.

1 The main division within Judaism today is between the Orthodox and non-Orthodox denominations. The Orthodox consider themselves to be those who follow Jewish law to the letter, whereas non-Orthodox Jews mostly belong to the Reform and Conservative movements. These two more recent movements within Judaism were deeply influenced by the European Enlightenment and have challenged many of the core values of traditional Judaism, including the idea of direct revelation from God.

2 The Karaites, the anti-rabbinical Jewish tradition disagrees with the divisions of this of hierarchy of revelation; instead, they insist that all forms of revelation in the Hebrew Bible are equal.

It seems, however, that there are differences of opinion between Orthodox and non-Orthodox Jews in their understanding of the authorship of the Torah. As already mentioned, according to the Orthodox position, the five books of the Torah were dictated to Moses by God. On the other hand, non-Orthodox Jews and modern biblical scholars[1] strongly argue that there are a number of different sources in the Pentateuch, some of which even post-date Moses. They argue that the five books have been collected and assembled from separate documents that were composed and modified by different circles representing diverse religious ideologies.

Most Muslim scholars who have studied the Hebrew Bible recognise the distinction made by Jews between the Torah (which was given to Moses) and the rest of the books of the Hebrew Bible; however, this does not mean that the other parts of the Hebrew Bible are not accepted by Muslims. Indeed, in the Qur'ān it is clearly stated, 'We have sent thee inspiration, as We sent it to Noah and the Messengers after him: we sent inspiration to Abraham, Ishmael, Isaac, Jacob and the Tribes, to Jesus, Job, Jonah, Aaron, and Solomon; and to David We gave the Psalms. Of some messengers, We have already told thee the story; of others We have not; and to Moses God spoke direct.'[2] Hence, because these other books of the Hebrew Bible may have originally been revealed to Israelite prophets, the books have never been totally disregarded by Muslim scholars. In fact, as early as the fifth/eleventh century, Ibn Ḥazm's studied the Torah and the rest of the Hebrew Bible.[3] In his book *Kitāb al-faṣl fī al-milal wa'l-ahwā' wa'l-niḥal*, which was a very detailed historical criticism of the Pentateuch, he reached very similar conclusions to those of non-Orthodox Jews and modern biblical scholars about the authorship of the Hebrew Bible. He

1 Secular modern biblical criticism is a field of study that arose during the seventeenth century and was pursued by Christian and Jewish scholars influenced by the European Enlightenment.

2 Q.IV.163–64.

3 Aasi, *Muslim Understanding*, p. 106.

ended his remarks on the topic by stating that although he believed the original Torah to have been given to Moses by God, that version of the scripture had not survived amongst the Jews of his day due to the major alterations and additions that had accumulated in the text over the centuries.[1]

THE ZABŪR. The *Zabūr*, which according to Islamic sources was given to the Prophet David, is traditionally accepted by Muslims to be the book of Psalms, which is part of the Ketuvim in the Hebrew Bible. The Arabic term *Zabūr* is mentioned nine times in the Qur'ān in reference to the scripture revealed to David.[2] However, there seems to be a lack of written research on whether the Psalms and the *Zabūr* are in fact identical. There are a number of correspondences between the two that indicate a possible common origin. The Book of Psalms consists of one hundred and fifty psalms divided into five parts or books. The psalms address praise, pleading and thanks to God, as well as articulate passionate trepidation and adoration of Him. There are also prayers attributed to King David for his son Solomon and a prayer attributed to Moses.[3] One verse of the Qur'ān reminds the reader, 'Before this We wrote in the Psalms, after the Message (given to Moses): My servants the righteous, shall inherit the earth';[4] and two verses in the Psalms state, 'But the meek will inherit the land and enjoy peace and prosperity';[5] and, 'The righteous will inherit the land and dwell in it forever.'[6] When compared side by side, it is apparent that these verses both state that the righteous will inherit the earth (in Islam righteousness is synonymous with humbleness, or being meek), and they indicate that the Psalms may be identifiable as the *Zabūr*.

Furthermore, according to Jewish rabbinical writings and

1 Ibid., pp. 86–114.

2 Noegel and Wheeler, *The A to Z of Prophets*, p. 350.

3 See the Hebrew Bible, Psalms 72 and 90 respectively.

4 Q.XXI.105.

5 Hebrew Bible, Psalms 37:11.

6 Hebrew Bible, Psalms 37:29.

the Midrash,[1] the Psalms were written by King David under the influence of the Holy Spirit.[2] The Talmud[3] accepts that David included psalms that were recited by other people, such as the Prophet Moses and Asaph,[4] without questioning the final authorship of King David.[5] The Hebrew Bible states, 'The Holy Spirit sometimes rested on King David before he commenced singing and playing hymns, and he was in fact prompted to the hymns by the Holy Spirit that rested upon him. At other times, the Holy Spirit kept away from him, but came upon him as soon as he gave himself up to hymns and praises.'[6] However non-Orthodox Jews and Biblical scholars argue that the Psalms were actually created by a number of authors from various historical periods in addition to King David. The merit of this argument is particularly apparent in relation to Psalm 137, which refers to the Babylonian exile of the Jews from the kingdom of Judea. This event took place

1 The Midrash contains a series of discourses on a vast range of subject matter compiled by Jewish rabbis since 200 CE. The corpus is mostly focused on the elucidation of the content of the scriptures by looking into the recurrence or comparison of words and situations. For more information see William G. Braude, *The Midrash on Psalms*, New Haven, CT: Yale University Press, 1959.

2 In the Hebrew Bible, this is called the 'Spirit of Yhwh' and the 'Spirit of Elohim', and it is not to be confused with the idea of the Holy Spirit as part of the Trinity in Christianity. In the Talmud and Midrash, the expression 'Holy Spirit', or 'Spirit of the Lord' (*Ruaha-Kodesh*), is used. It is sometimes employed instead of *Shekinah*, which indicates God's Majestic Presence. See Joseph Jacobs and Ludwig Blau, 'Holy Spirit', in Isidore Singer, ed., *The Jewish Encyclopedia*, New York: Funk and Wagnalls, 1901–1906, available online, http://www.jewishencyclopedia.com/articles/7833-holy-spirit, accessed 20 February 2016.

3 The Talmud is the primary source of Jewish religious law alongside the Hebrew Bible in Orthodox Judaism. It is also known as the Oral Torah.

4 Asaph is identified as a scribe and musician who was commanded by King David to worship God through song in 1 Chronicles 15:16–17.

5 See Talmudic passage (Bava Batra 14b).

6 Midrash Psalms 24; see Samuel Rapaport, ed., *Tales and Maxims from the Midrash*, London: Routledge, 1907, p. 204, available online, http://www.sacred-texts.com/jud/tmm/tmm17.htm, accessed 20 February 2016. The Midrash on Psalms is a commentary on the Book of Psalms.

in 586 BCE, which was some 384 years after King David's death.[1]

THE INJĪL. Whereas the *Tawrāt* and *Zabūr* can in places be identified with parts of the Hebrew Scriptures, the *Injīl* presents a much more complex situation. The discussions and polemics between Muslims and Christians on the topics of Jesus, the Trinity, crucifixion and resurrection are extensive; however, very little has been said about the *Injīl*. The Arabic word *Injīl* is believed by scholars to be a transliteration of the Greek or Ethiopic words for gospel, which literally mean 'good news'.[2] *Injīl* is mentioned twelve times in the Qur'ān to denote the Holy Writ or book that was revealed to the Prophet Jesus. These verses make it very clear that the *Injīl* was a revelation (a scripture) given to him: 'And in their footsteps We sent Jesus the son of Mary, confirming the Law (*Tawrāt*) that had come before him. We sent him the Gospel (*Injīl*): therein was guidance and light, and confirmation of the Law (*Tawrāt*) that had come before him, a guidance and an admonition to those who fear God.'[3]

What is not clear is whether the *Injīl* that is mentioned in the Qur'ān corresponds to the contents of the New Testament as found in the Christian tradition. In comparison with the Old Testament (which is broadly equivalent to the Hebrew Bible), Christians have seen the New Testament as the second part of the story of salvation and most have considered it to be divinely inspired.[4] The New Testament consists of twenty-seven books, but many of these books are short and might be better described as documents. They were all originally written in Greek and were composed between the years

1 Noegel and Wheeler, *The A to Z of Prophets*, p. 269.

2 Ibid., pp. 126–27.

3 Q.v.46.

4 This is the belief that the writings of the whole of New Testament were influenced by God through the Holy Spirit, which means that Christians have traditionally designated it as 'the word of God'. Many liberal Christians today are not able to accept this designation and regard the New Testament as a historical document. See, Bruce M. Metzger and Michael Coogan, *The Oxford Companion to the Bible*, New York: Oxford University Press, 1993, pp. 302–04.

50 and 150 CE. The first books in the New Testament are the four Gospels, followed by the Acts of the Apostles and then by the twenty-one documents referred to as 'epistles' or 'letters', and the final book is the Revelation of St. John.

The four Gospels—which are traditionally named after their authors Matthew, Mark, Luke and John—are writings that contain accounts about Jesus and sayings that were attributed to him. The early Christians wrote many gospels, but only four were accepted into the New Testament in the year 330 CE by the Nicaea Council; all others are now referred to as the Apocryphal Gospels. The fifth book of the New Testament, the Acts of the Apostles, continues the story of Christianity by describing the beginnings of the Church and its spread across the Roman world. The twenty-one letters that follow Acts were written by early Church leaders and addressed to various church communities and individuals in order to provide directives and exhortations. Thirteen of these letters were said to have been written by Paul, while others were attributed to some of the disciples of Jesus. The final book of the New Testament contains information about the apocalypse (the end of the world), and it is argued by many historians that there may have been other books written on the topic but that only the Revelation of St. John was included. This book is attributed either to Jesus's disciple John, who was also the author of the Gospel of John, or to John of Patmos.[1]

According to many Muslim scholars, the *Injīl* that is mentioned in the Qur'ān refers to the words of Jesus, and so could be related to parts of the Gospels in the New Testament, or to parts of any of the gospels deemed apocryphal. Others argue that the *Injīl* is no longer in existence and therefore does not relate to any of the Christian canon. In the fifth/eleventh century Ibn Ḥazm argued that the four canonical Gospels could not be considered the inspired Word of God or even count as eyewitness reports. He thus saw no true link between the

1 Delbert Royce Burkett, *An Introduction to the New Testament and the Origins of Christianity*, Cambridge: Cambridge University Press, 2002, pp. 4–6.

Injīl referred to in the Qur'ān and the Gospels of the New Testament.[1] Roughly two and a half centuries later, Ibn Taymiyya was a little more nuanced when speaking about the gospels and put forward this argument: 'What is in the *Injīl* of stories about the crucifixion of Jesus, his death, his coming to the disciples after he was "raised," are not what Jesus said. Rather they are [reports] from those who saw these things after him. What God revealed was what was heard [directly] from Jesus who is the transmitter [of God's word] from Him.'[2] An example of contemporary thinking about the *Injīl* can be found in the discussions of the late scholar Muhammad Hamidullah, who argued that it is unlikely that Jesus either compiled or dictated any specific teachings. Instead, Hamidullah proposed that it was Jesus's disciples and their successors who assembled his utterances and transmitted them in a number of recensions. Four of these recensions were finally accepted by the Church as canonical Gospels, with at least seventy others declared apocryphal. Hamidullah believed that there was enough historical evidence to suggest that the statements of Jesus were transmitted by his followers and, because of this, he thought that some of the authentic words of Jesus were likely to be found within this body of literature.[3]

Within the twentieth century, a paradigm shift has occurred in some Christian circles with regard to the theological understanding of revelation in the context of comparing the Qur'ān with the Bible. A proposed conclusion is that any comparison drawn between the Qur'ān and the New Testament is inaccurate because they are not in fact equivalent, whereas comparing the Qur'ān to the person of Jesus is more appropriate because both the Qur'ān and Jesus are acknowledged as the Word of God. The formulation of this argument is credited to Wilfred Cantwell Smith, a professor of comparative religion who was writing in the early 1950s.[4] The Christian theologian

1 Aasi, *Muslim Understanding*, p. 118.

2 Translation from Saeed, 'The Charge of Distortion', p. 430.

3 Muhammad Hamidullah, *Introduction to Islam*, London: MWH Publishers, 1979, p. 51.

4 W. C. Smith, *Islam in Modern History*, Princeton, NJ: Princeton University Press, 1957, pp. 17–18.

Kenneth Cragg expressed very similar ideas: 'God in revelation is God in Christ. Revelation is not simply recorded in a book; it is embodied in a person. Is it not more fully, more appropriately, more effectively, revelation for that reason? The question may not be readily appreciated by the Muslim accustomed to the idea of a Book as the point of revelatory impact.'[1] The formulation of these arguments in the 1950s raised the possibility in some minds that Muslims and Christians could reach some kind of consensus about the shared divine status of their revelations.

However, it soon became apparent that the proposed equivalence of Jesus and the Qur'ān is problematic since the meaning of the epithet 'Word of God', or 'His Word', is understood very differently within the two theologies. Most Christians regard 'Word of God' to literally mean 'God incarnate', especially as it is used in the Gospel of John.[2] In Islamic theology, by contrast, 'His Word' (as in the Qur'ānic verse IV.171[3]) is interpreted as meaning that God created Jesus without the agency of a human father. This is illustrated by the interpretation of this verse proposed by the scholar and exegete Shabbir Ahmad Usmani: 'There is a tremendous difference between the divinity of God and the holiness of man. The innocence and holiness of the prophets is an image or reflection of Divinity, but not Divinity itself. Jesus was the word of God and the spirit of Him. It means he was created merely by the order of God without any masculine agency from the pious body of Mary and God had breathed a spirit from Himself through the angel Gabriel into Mary. It means the body of Jesus was the reflection or image of the Divine Word and his soul was the image of the Divine Spirit while the material side worked as a mirror. But there is a great difference between the image of an object and the object itself [...].'[4]

1 K. Cragg, *The Call of the Minaret*, New York. Oxford University Press, 1956, p. 290.

2 John 1:14.

3 'O People of the Book! Commit no excesses in your religion, nor say of God aught but the truth. Christ, Jesus the son of Mary, was (no more than) a messenger of God, and His Word, which He bestowed on Mary, and a spirit proceeding from Him.'

4 Shabbir Ahmad Usmani, tr., *The Noble Qur'an: Tafseer-e-Usmani*, New Delhi: Idara Isha'at-e-Diniyat, 1992, vol. 1, p. 419.

Consequently, the Christian idea of the 'Word of God' is unacceptable for Muslim theologians. Instead, both Ibn Taymiyya and, more recently, the scholar Muhammad Hamidullah expressed the idea that Jesus's words may have been the only source for the authentic *Injīl*. Ibn Taymiyya wrote, 'What God revealed was what was heard [directly] from Jesus who is the transmitter [of God's word] from Him.'[1] Likewise, Hamidullah suggested, 'As for Jesus' life, he had not had the time to compile or dictate what he preached; it is his disciples and their successors who gleaned his utterances and transmitted them to posterity in a number of recensions.'[2] However, it is precisely due to the existence of these multiple recensions that many Muslim scholars have argued that the complete, original *Injīl* does not correspond to the four Gospels of the New Testament—not to mention the other books found within it.

THE QUR'ĀN. The final scripture that Muslims are commanded to believe in is the Qur'ān, which is their primary source for the law, doctrine, practice and ethics. For Muslims, it represents not only dogmatic doctrines and religious teachings but also a way of life. They believe that the entirety of the Qur'ān is literally the Word of God—in other words, that it is speech directly from God—and its message is believed to be universal whilst also reflecting the specific context of seventh century CE Arabia. 'For Muslims, the Quran is the Book of God. It is the uncreated, literal word of God sent down from heaven, revealed one final time to the Prophet Muḥammad as a guide for humankind.'[3]

The first verses of the Qur'ān were revealed to the Prophet Muḥammad in 610 CE through the Angel Gabriel, and these revelations continued over a period of 23 years up till his death in the year 10/632. The Prophet Muḥammad described his experience of the

1 Saeed, The Charge of Distortion', p. 430.

2 Hamidullah, *Introduction to Islam*, p. 51.

3 John L. Esposito, *Islam: The Straight Path*, New York/Oxford: Oxford University Press, 1998, p. 17.

descent of revelation as like hearing the 'ringing of a bell' or seeing Gabriel in the form of a man and hearing and comprehending his voice.[1] All the words of the Qur'ān are therefore considered to be divine and are treated separately from the sayings and teachings of Muḥammad, which are preserved in the *Ḥadīth*.

The Qur'ān is made up of 114 *sūras* (chapters) that are not arranged according to any theme, in any chronological order or according to the order they were revealed. The order of the Qur'ān was established by the Prophet Muḥammad himself. The content of the Qur'ān is vast, but the main themes are beliefs, rituals, narratives of various prophets, spiritual, ethical and legal topics and important historical events from the Prophet's lifetime.

The concept of the Qur'ān as an actual book was well established during the Prophet's lifetime. In the context of Arab oral culture, a book did not necessarily mean a written volume so, during the lifetime of the Prophet, a large number of the Prophet's Companions preserved the Qur'ān by memorising it (both the content of its verses and the arrangement of its *sūras*). In the last year of Muḥammad's life, during the month of Ramaḍān, the Prophet recited it fully to individual Companions, and many Companions recited it to each other as well. Furthermore, on the explicit order of the Prophet, verses of the Qur'ān were written down on various materials, but they were not compiled or codified during his lifetime.[2]

After the Prophet's death in 10/632, and due to the death in battles of many of the Companions who had memorised the Qur'ān, ʿUmar and other Companions advised the first caliph, Abū Bakr, to gather together all of the Qur'ānic text and combine it in one volume in order to safeguard it for posterity. At first, the Caliph Abū Bakr was reluctant and refused their request on the basis that he could not possibly issue an order relating to the Qur'ān that the Prophet had not

1 Martin Lings, *Muhammad: His Life Based on the Earliest Sources*, Cambridge: Islamic Texts Society, 1991, pp. 44–45 .

2 See Azami, *History of the Qur'anic Text,* pp. 69–78.

himself initiated in his lifetime. But in the end, ʿUmar's pragmatic argument won him over.[1] At that point, Abū Bakr set up a committee led by the Companion Zayd b. Thābit (d. 39/660) to gather the Qur'ān into a single collection, which was referred to as the *ṣuḥuf* (literally, 'leaves of parchment'[2]). Following Abū Bakr's death in 12/634, the *ṣuḥuf* were left to his successor, the Caliph ʿUmar and, eventually, they were entrusted to ʿUmar's daughter Ḥafṣa (d. 44/665), the Prophet's widow.[3]

The next significant development in the codification of the Qur'ān came during the reign of the Caliph ʿUthmān. The Islamic conquests of Syria, Egypt, Iraq and Persia expanded the caliphate well beyond Medina and resulted in disputes over the correct recitation of the Qur'ān. Thus Caliph ʿUthmān and his advisers agreed that it was imperative to produce an authoritative copy in the form of a *muṣḥaf* (a bound codex) that could easily be disseminated across the caliphate. Once again, Zayd b. Thābit and several other Companions were appointed by the caliph to compile a copy of the text based on Ḥafṣa's *ṣuḥuf*. Copies of the new *muṣḥaf* were made and distributed across the caliphate for further use and copying. ʿUthmān ordered his governors to burn any other written versions of the Qur'ān circulating in their provinces. Today, this *muṣḥaf* is the authoritative text used by all Muslims.[4]

In summary, Muslims believe in all of the scriptures sent by God to His messengers, but it is the teachings of the final book, the Qur'ān, that are central to their lives. This is because the previous

1 Saeed, *The Qur'an*, p. 43.

2 The Qur'ān was transcribed into a master copy consisting of leaves of parchment of varying size (highlighting the lack of resources in the Arabian peninsula during this period). Hence, this copy was an orderly stack of parchment sheets rather than a bound book (*muṣḥaf*) with leaves of equal size. This was the main difference between the earliest *ṣuḥuf* and the *muṣḥaf* that was later compiled at the command of the Caliph ʿUthmān in 24/645.

3 Azami, *History of the Qur'anic Text*, pp. 77–86.

4 Ibid.

scriptures are seen to have been superseded by the last scripture, the Qur'ān, which was revealed to the last messenger, Muḥammad.

The Qur'ān: The Uncreated Word

In the year 132/750, the Abbasid dynasty ruled over the entire Muslim world. The rise of the new Islamic civilisation in the ancient land of Mesopotamia resulted in a thriving intellectual atmosphere in the capital Baghdad. The earliest intellectual developments in this city and the surrounding area were witnessed in legal reasoning in the domain of *fiqh* and in the translation of scholarly works of various subjects into Arabic from Greek, Indian and Persian languages.[1] This, in turn, influenced the construction of theological arguments and debates that arose between Muslims and the followers of other religions. It was during this era that the Muʿtazilīs consolidated their theological positions and their doctrines were adopted as the caliphate's official theology under al-Ma'mūn (r. 813–833) and lasted until the coming of the reign of al-Mutawakkil in 847.

The inquisition (*miḥna*) commenced by al-Ma'mūn was a reaction to traditionalism[2] and it was one of the few examples of an inquisition in Muslim history in which the ruler enforced a specific theological position. As a supporter of the Muʿtazilīs, al-Ma'mūn tried to enforce adherence to their theological doctrines by subjecting jurists and scholars to a trial; and this despite the majority of Muslim scholars agreeing with the opinions of the traditionalists. The most controversial position that the caliphate took was insisting that the Qur'ān was 'created'.[3] The reason why the Muʿtazilīs insisted on the created nature of the Qur'ān was partly a reaction to the Christian notion of Jesus as the 'Word' (*Logos*); meaning, God incarnated as Word, Who manifested Himself in the human form of Jesus. Hence, they were arguing that the idea of an uncreated Qur'ān

1 See Hussain, *A Social History of Muslim Education*.

2 Traditionalists were *Ḥadīth* scholars who insisted on not using rationalism with regard to the attributes of God.

3 See Abdullah Saeed, *Islamic Thought: An Introduction*, London: Routledge, 2010.

infringed on the unity of God, and at the same time dangerously resembled the Christian notion of Logos. The Caliph al-Ma'mūn explicitly made this connection between the status of the Qur'ān in Islam and that of Jesus in Christianity when he wrote a letter to his judges and scholars, stating, 'Everything apart from Him is a created object from His creation and a new thing which He has brought into existence. Even though the Qur'ān itself speaks about God's creative power, sets forth its proof and decisively confutes all difference of opinion about it, these people talk just like the Christians when they claim that Jesus the son of Mary was not created, because he was the word of God.'[1]

However, for the majority of scholars at the time, the notion of the Qur'ān being created was completely unacceptable. From scholars like Aḥmad Ibn Ḥanbal to the famous historian and exegete Abū Jaʿfar al-Ṭabarī, the majority were against the caliphate's enforcement of Muʿtazilī orthodoxy, especially on the subject of the Word of God (*Kalām Allāh*). They argued that the Word of God was not created but was literally the Speech of God. If it was to be accepted as created, then its status would be equal to all other created things, which could lead to interpreting it as just another product of human contingency. Ibn Ḥanbal emerged as the main figure of resistance against the inquisition that specifically target judges and scholars rather than the wider population. The way that he responded to the theological discourse was literally through non-engagement, as he did not see theological debate to be possible. It was his courageous refusal to submit to political pressure and his steadfast support of the Qur'ān and *Ḥadīth* as the primary sources of Islam, which earned the people's admiration. This opposition, which was the first of its kind against the Muʿtazila, refused to discuss anything beyond what was in the primary sources. This practice of non-engagement in theological debate was followed by

1 Ingrid Mattson, *The Story of the Qur'an: Its History and Place in Muslim Life*, Oxford: Blackwell Publishing, 2008, pp. 138.

a number of other early scholars such as Mālik b. Anas (d. 178/795) and Muḥammad b. Ismāʿīl al-Bukhārī (d. 256/870).[1]

However, this disagreement with the Muʿtazilīs raised questions not only about the ontological nature of the Qur'ān, but also about the nature of God and how to understand the relationship between reason and revelation. A second wave of opposition to the Muʿtazilī inquisition came from those who felt the need to uphold the beliefs of Ibn Ḥanbal through dialectic arguments. This form of resistance was led by the scholars Abū al-Ḥasan al-Ashʿarī and Abū Manṣūr al-Māturīdī. Both maintained that the Qur'ān is uncreated and that this did not imply that the Qur'ān could be seen in a similar way to how Jesus is viewed within Christianity.[2] From this position, Ashʿarī and Māturīdī's contemporary Abū Jaʿfar al-Ṭaḥāwī went on to set out the Sunni creed in a concise work made up of a hundred or so articles, which were soon adopted by all Sunni scholars. In his *Creed*, Ṭaḥāwī described the Qur'ān as follows: 'The Qur'ān is the word of God that emanated from Him without modality in its expression. He sent it down to His messenger as revelation. The believers accept it as such literally. They are certain it is, in reality, the Word of God, the Sublime and the Exalted. Unlike human speech, it is eternal and uncreated. Whoever hears it and alleges it is human speech has disbelieved [...].'[3]

However, the most elaborate defence of Qur'ān as the uncreated word of God was formulated by later scholars of the Ashʿarī and Māturīdī schools. The famous Ashʿarī scholar Ghazālī wrote this about the status of the Qur'ān: 'The Koran is recited with tongues, written in books, and memorised in hearts despite being beginninglessly eternal, an attribute of the entity of Allah Most High, unsubject to disseverance and separation by conveyance to hearts and pages.'[4]

1 MacDonald, *Development of Muslim Theology*, p. 147.

2 Mattson, *Story of the Qur'an*, p. 139.

3 Ṭaḥāwī, *Creed of Imam al-Ṭahāwī*, p. 54 (Creeds 35, 36 and 37).

4 Cited in Aḥmad Ibn al-Naqīb al-Miṣrī, *Reliance of the Traveller: A Classic Manual of Islamic Sacred Law*, trans. Nuh Ha Mim Keller, Beltsville, MD: Amana Publications, 1991, p. 820.

The Māturīdī scholar Nasafī wrote something similar in what became known as the *Nasafī Creed*: 'The Qur'ān is the Word of God (*Kalām Allāh*), the Exalted, and not a creation. It is written in our copies, preserved in our hearts, recited by our tongues, heard by our ears but not in a fixed state in any of these.'[1] But perhaps the most sophisticated explanation of the Qur'ān as the uncreated Word of God came from the Ashʿarī scholar Imām Juwaynī (the teacher of Ghazālī) in his book *Kitāb al-irshād ilā qawāṭiʿ al-adilla fī uṣūl al-iʿtiqād* (A Guide to Conclusive Proofs for the Principles of Belief):

> If they maintain that speech consists of combined letters and discrete sounds, there is no way to affirm speaking that originates in the soul. To hold this on their part is to rely on what was determined previously to be false, since we have confirmed that there is a speech that arises in the soul which does not involve letters or sounds or melodies or tones. Our purpose in bringing up this topic is to be assured of exactly this. Know now, as a result, that the debate with the Muʿtazilites and other opponents on this issue is a matter involving both denial and affirmation. What they affirm and determine to be speech is actually affirmed of His Self. Their statement that it is the speech of God, the Exalted, if reduced to its particulars, brings speech back to a function of languages and nomenclature. The meaning of their declaration 'These expressions are the speech of God' is that they are His creation. For our part we do not deny that they are a

1 Najm al-Dīn Abū Ḥafṣ ʿUmar b. Muḥammad b. Aḥmad al-Nasafī, 'The Nasafī Creed', trans. Tahir Mahmood Kiani, Marifah.net, http://marifah.net/articles/matnalnasafiyya.pdf, accessed 29 March 2013.

> creation of God but we refuse to designate the Creator of the speech as the one who speaks it. We are thus of one mind as to the meaning but in disagreement, despite this accord, over how to designate it. That form of speech which the orthodox judge to be eternal is the speech that arises in the soul. Our adversaries deny it altogether and refuse to affirm it.[1]

Shahrastānī expressed the above Ashʿarī doctrine in a simpler form when he stated, 'The sentence and words which are revealed through the tongues of angels to the prophets are signs of the eternal world: the sign itself is created and originated, but what is signified[2] is eternal [uncreated].'[3] Members of the Atharī school of theology appear to have been suspicious of all discussions of the Qur'ān as the uncreated Word due to its intricacy and subtlety. They instead argued that the best description of the Qur'ān was to be found in the Qur'ān itself, and they refused to explain the Qur'ān in any other terms.

By the end of Abbasid period, this topic—however obscure it may have been for the majority of Muslims—seems to have become a point of doctrine on which all schools gave an opinion. The concept of the Qur'ān as the uncreated Word of God became a part of the creed that Sunni Muslims dogmatically learned in schools and mosques until the appearance of schools and universities in

1 Juwaynī, *Guide to Conclusive Proofs*, p. 65.

2 Signified here represents a linguistic sign that exists within a temporal (contingent) system. These linguistic signs, which consist of both signifier and signified, are found in the languages in the temporal world whose meaning is determined by context. In the traditional schools of theology in Islam the linguistic signs of the Qur'ān represent the signifier (which is temporal), while the signified is the Uncreated Word of God. See Halverson, *Theology and Creed*, p. 132

3 Muḥammad b. ʿAbd al-Karīm al-Shahrastānī, *Muslims Sects and Divisions: The Section on Muslim Sects in* Kitāb al-milal wa'l-niḥal, trans. J. G. Flynn and A. K. Kazi, London: Kegan Paul International, 1984, p. 80.

modern times.[1] Hamza Yusuf describes the differences between the three Muslim Sunni theological school on the nature of the Qur'ān as semantic: '[G]iven that Muslims accept that the Qur'ān is the uncreated word of God, the difference lies not in the statement but in its implication to the actual extant text, as the recited text is in the temporal world. While this issue was important in early Islam for political as well as theological reasons, its resolution protected Muslims from the concept of inbibliation, or God entering the world as a book, which lent an unacceptable credence to incarnation, or God entering the world as a man.'[2]

This topic seems to have resurfaced again in modern times, especially in forums on the internet. The clashes over the created or uncreated nature of the Qur'ān now appear to be between those of a neo-literalist persuasion and modern followers of the Ashᶜarī and Māturīdī schools. The latter are attempting to educate the Muslim public about what the classical scholars of their theological schools actually wrote on the topic. What is interesting is that whilst debating this issue, all of these scholars still remain in total agreement with what Ṭaḥāwī wrote about the Qur'ān, which was that it was eternal and uncreated, unlike human speech.[3]

Thus, an articulation of the uncreated nature of the Qur'ān was considered to be an essential aspect of how Muslim scripture is understood. But the significance of this viewpoint extended beyond the internal dynamics of Islam, because when Muslim theologians engaged with the Jewish and Christian scriptures, they did so within this explanatory framework as we shall now see.

Alteration or Misinterpretation?

In the Qur'ān, the names of several different religious communities are mentioned, such as in the following verse: 'Those who believe

1 Mattson, *Story of the Qur'an*, p. 140.

2 Yusuf, preface in Ṭahāwī, *Creed of Imam al-Ṭahāwī*, p. 10.

3 Ṭaḥāwī, *Creed of Imam al-Ṭahāwī*, p. 54 (Creeds 35, 36 and 37).

(in the Qur'ān), those who follow the Jewish (scriptures) and the Sabians, the Christians, the Magians and the Polytheists, God will judge between them on the Day of Judgement, for God is witness of all things.'[1] However, despite references to adherents of other religions throughout the Qur'ān, Islam is understood by Muslims to be the exclusive universal and primordial truth. As mentioned above, one of the reasons for this is that the scriptures revealed prior to Islam are believed to have been distorted by their religious communities over time. The Jewish and Christian scriptures are subject to particular attention in Muslim tradition; the Qur'ān and *Ḥadīth* speak of 'misconstrual' (*taḥrīf*), 'alteration' (*tabdīl*) and even 'confusion' or 'dissimulation' (*talbīs*) of the original revealed versions. In the Qur'ān alone, aside from *taḥrīf*,which appears four times, there is also *tabdīl* (alteration), *layy* (distorting the words of scriptures), *labs* (overlaying the truth with falsehood), and *kitmān* (suppressing and hiding the truth).[2]

In the third/ninth century, the scholar Jāḥiẓ alluded to the idea of the corruption of the text (*taḥrīf al-lafẓ*) of the New Testament in his writings, which fall within the genre known as the *milal wa'l-niḥal* (religious traditions and philosophical ideologies).[3] Later on, Ibn Ḥazm claimed that the text of the Hebrew Bible and the four Gospels of the New Testament were distorted—to the extent that he believed the original scriptures to have been totally lost. However, other scholars such as ʿAlī b. Rabban al-Ṭabarī (d. 232/847), Masʿūdī (d. 344/956), Abū Manṣūr al-Baghdādī (d. 428/1037) and Abū al-Ḥasan ʿAbd al-Jabbār (d. 415/1025) mentioned the altering of the scriptures of the People of the Book more vaguely. Their remarks implied that the scriptures contained distortion in interpretation (*taḥrīf al-maʿanā*), but that most of their contents were still similar to the original scripture.[4]

1 Q.XXII.17.
2 Q.V.13; II.75; II.59; IV.46; III.71 and II.42. Cited by Aasi, *Muslim Understanding*, p. 22.
3 Ibid., p. 38.
4 Ibid., pp. 35–41.

The famous exegetes Fakhr al-Dīn al-Rāzī and Abū Jaʿfar al-Ṭabarī proposed that, based on two particular verses of the Qur'ān (v.13 and v.41), it could be argued that there was distortion in the meaning of the text of the Jewish and Christian scriptures. However, Ṭabarī also thought it was possible that at a later point, such false interpretations had been added to the written text and attributed to God.[1] Abū ʿAbd Allāh al-Qurtubī (d. 671/1273), in his commentary on one of these verses from *Sūrat al-Mā'ida* (v.13), agreed with the opinion of Ṭabarī that the reference to *taḥrīf* (distortion) here specifically meant the changing of some of the letters of the text, and that there were therefore changes in the text itself. Ṭabarī also argued that verses LXI.6, II.147, II.159 and VII.157 were alluding to Christian and Jewish scholars' concealment of scriptural references about the coming of the Prophet Muḥammad in their own scriptures, which they did in order to deny that he was a messenger of God.[2]

In the fourteenth century, the scholar Ibn Taymiyya strongly disagreed with the position that the original revealed texts of Judaism and Christianity have been lost entirely.

> It is said that in the world there is no single copy that corresponds to what God revealed in the Torah and Gospel. All that exist are changed. As for the Torah, its transmission from a large number of people to a [subsequent] large number of people has stopped and the Gospel is taken from four [people].
>
> Then, among these people [Muslims] there are those that allege that much of what is in the Torah and Gospels [today] is false, not of God's word. Some of them said: [what is false] is not much. It is [also said]: No one changed any text of the Scriptures. Rather they [Jews

1 Saeed, *The Qur'an*, p. 149.
2 Ibid.

> and Christians] have falsified their meanings by [false] interpretations. Many Muslims have held both of these views.
>
> The correct [view] is the third view, which is that in the world there are true copies [versions], and these remained until the time of the Prophet (peace be upon him), and many copies [versions] which are corrupted. Whoever says that nothing in [these] copies [versions] was corrupted has denied what cannot be denied. Whoever says that after the Prophet [Muḥammad] (peace be upon him) all copies [versions] have been distorted, he has said what is manifestly false. The Qur'an commands them to judge with what God revealed in the Torah and Gospels. [God] informs that in both there is wisdom. There is nothing in the Qur'an to indicate that they altered all copies [versions].[1]

In other words, according to Ibn Taymiyya there were three views about the earlier scriptures: the first opinion was that they no longer exist; the second opinion varied, but the main idea was that falsification had occurred to the texts; while the third opinion, which he claimed was the correct one, contended that both authentic versions and falsified versions of the Torah and Gospel had existed up until the time of the Prophet Muḥammad. Ibn Taymiyya's student, Ibn Kathīr, later wrote about this topic in his exegesis of the Qur'ān, *Tafsīr al-Qur'ān al-ʿAẓīm*. Ibn Kathīr further developed his teacher's views and proposed that the text of the Gospel and Hebrew Bible could be divided into three categories: '1) that which we know is authentic because we have [in Islam] what testifies to its truth; 2) that which we know to be false based on what we have that contradicts it;

1 Translation from Saeed, *The Qur'an*, pp. 152–53, citing Ibn Taymiyya, *al-Tafsīr al-kabīr*, Beirut: Dār al-Kutub al-ʿIlmiyya, [no date], vol. 1, p. 209.

and 3) that which is neutral, neither from the first or second type; we neither affirm nor deny it, and we are allowed to narrate it.'[1]

Although Muslims affirm the exclusiveness of Islam as the 'Truth', this is accompanied by the strict principle of 'no compulsion in religion' and having 'good relations' with the different religious communities (*milal*).[2] Muslim knowledge about the Bible (both Hebrew and Christian) is owed in large part to the Qur'ān and the *Ḥadīth*. These references, which dated from the earliest years of Islam, motivated generations of Muslims to study the scriptures of these other faiths. The theological discussions surveyed in this section illustrate that the research conducted by Muslims on the Hebrew Bible and the New Testament are vast and also include popular stories about the earlier prophets of Israelite origin called the *Isrā'īliyyāt*.[3]

The Isrā'īliyyāt

The Qur'ān generally uses the term *Banū Isrā'īl* when it refers to the tribes of Israel or the Jews and it occurs forty-three times in the text.[4] The related term *Isrā'īliyyāt* applies to traditions from Jewish sources, but is also used to refer to literature from Zoroastrianism and early Christianity. The literature in this genre has been used to understand and expand on topics within the sciences of Qur'ānic exegesis (*tafsīr*), *Ḥadīth* and history (*ta'rīkh*). The works known as the *Qiṣaṣ al-Anbiyā'* (Stories of the Prophets) have sometimes been recognised by scholars as a subgenre of the *Isrā'īliyyāt*,[5] and were begun by Companions of the Prophet such as ʿAbd Allāh Ibn al-ʿAbbās (d. 68/687).[6]

1 Translation from Saeed, *The Qur'an*, p. 153, citing Ibn Kathīr, *Tafsīr al-Qur'ān al-ʿAẓīm*, Beirut: Dār al-Jīl, [no date], vol. 1, p. 4.

2 Q.II.256; VI.108.

3 Aasi, *Muslim Understanding*, p. 38.

4 İsmail Albayrak, 'Qur'anic Narrative and *Isra'iliyyat* in Western Scholarship and in Classical Exegesis', Ph.D. thesis, University of Leeds, 2000, p. 114.

5 İsmail Albayrak, 'Re-Evaluating the Notion of *Isra'iliyyat*', *D. E. Ü. İlahiyat Fakültesi Dergisi*, vol. XIII–XIV, 2001, pp. 69–88.

6 Camilla Adang, *Muslim Writers on Judaism and the Hebrew Bible: From Ibn Rabban to Ibn Hazm*, Leiden: E. J. Brill, 1996, pp. 11–13.

Wahb Ibn Munabbih (d. 113/732), a Yemeni of Persian descent, was the first Muslim to compose a book on the history of the Israelites and their prophets, the *Kitāb al-Isrā'īliyyāt* (Book of Israelite Traditions).[1] In a contemporary study of the Bible and Qur'ān, the scholar Uri Rubin identifies three types of Muslim representations of the Banū Isrā'īl. In terms of the larger picture, Muslims and the Banū Isrā'īl are allied through a shared history and mission, and the pious worship and asceticism of the Banū Isrā'īl is stressed. Secondly, Israelite disobedience to God and the prophets is contrasted with Muslim obedience to God and to the Prophet Muḥammad. And, thirdly, Muslims are portrayed as the people who are the inheritors of the Banū Isrā'īl and who will rectify the sins of the Banū Isrā'īl.[2]

There are a number of traditions from the Prophet that warn his followers about the literature of the People of the Book. Such *ḥadīth*s include:

> The people of the Book used to read the Torah in Hebrew and then explain it in Arabic to the Muslims. God's Messenger (peace be upon him) said (to the Muslims). 'Do not believe the people of the Book, nor disbelieve them, but say, "We believe in Allah and whatever is revealed to us, and whatever is revealed to you."'[3]
>
> Do not ask the People of the Book because they will not guide you having already led themselves astray.
>
> If the People of the Book tell you something, do not either accept it as true or reject it as

1 This title may have been a later addition; another variant is *Qiṣaṣ al-Anbiyā'*.

2 See Uri Rubin, *Between Bible and Qur'an: The Children of Israel and the Islamic Self-Image*, Princeton, NJ: Darwin Press, 1999.

3 Bukhārī, *Ṣaḥīḥ*, XCVII.167, http://sunnah.com/bukhari/97/167.

> false, for they may tell you something which is false but you may accept it as true.[1]

Because of such admonitions, there has been a great reluctance on the part of some Muslim scholars to narrate from the *Isrā'īliyyāt*.

However, other prophetic traditions are more positive about information coming from the Banū Isrā'īl. For instance, the Companion ᶜAbd Allāh b. ᶜAmr b. al-ᶜĀṣ narrated that the Prophet said, 'Convey (my teachings) to the people even if it were a single sentence, and tell others the stories of Bani Israel (which have been taught to you), for it is not sinful to do so. And whoever tells a lie on me intentionally, will surely take his place in the (Hell) Fire.'[2] In addition to this report, there are several well-known cases of Companions of the Prophet who acquired knowledge about the *Isrā'īliyyāt*, such as ᶜAbd Allāh Ibn ᶜUmar, Abū Hurayra, Ibn ᶜAbbās and ᶜAbd Allāh b. Salam.[3] Ibn Khaldūn explained what motivated these Companions to seek out information about the Banū Isrā'īl:

> When they wanted to know certain things that human beings are usually curious to know, such as the reasons for the existing things, the beginning of creation, and the secrets of existence, they consulted the earlier People of the Book and got their information from them. The People of the Book were the Jews who had the Torah, and the Christians who followed the religion of (the Jews). Now the people of the Torah who lived among the Arabs at that time were them-

1 The translations of these two *ḥadīths* come from Albayrak, 'Re-Evaluating the Notion of *Isra'iliyyat*', pp. 69–88.

2 Bukhārī, *Ṣaḥīḥ*, LX.128, http://sunnah.com/bukhari/60/128.

3 Amjad M. Hussain *A Social History of Muslim Education: From the Prophet's Period to Ottoman Times,* London: Ta-Ha Publishers, 2013, pp. 23–24 and Albayrak, 'Re-Evaluating the Notion of *Isra'iliyyat*', pp. 69–88.

selves Bedouins. They knew only as much about these matters as is known to ordinary People of the Book. The majority of those Jews were Ḥimyarites who had adopted Judaism. When they became Muslims, they retained the information they possessed, such as information about the beginning of creation and information of the type of forecasts and predictions. That information had no connection with the (Jewish or Christian) religious laws they were preserving as their own. Such men were Ka'b al-Aḥbâr, Wahb b. Munabbih, ʿAbdullâh b. Salâm, and similar people. The Qur'ān commentaries were filled with material of such tendencies transmitted on their authority; it is information that entirely depends on them. It has no relation to (religious) laws, such that one might claim for it the soundness that would make it necessary to act (in accordance with it). The Qur'ān interpreters were not very rigorous in this respect. They filled the Qur'ān commentaries with such material, which originated, as we have stated, with the people of the Torah who lived in the desert and were not capable of verifying the information they transmitted. However, they were famous and highly esteemed because they were people of rank in their religion and religious group. Therefore, their interpretation has been accepted from that time onwards.[1]

1 Ibn Khaldūn, *The Muqaddimah*, p. 445.

With the spread of Islam, an increasing number of scholars were interested to learn more about the prophets mentioned in the Qur'ān and *Ḥadīth* from Jewish and Christian sources and authorities. This contact between Muslims, Jews and Christians led to intellectual debates; and from the second/eighth century onwards, Muslim historians were producing historical works that drew directly on Jewish and Christian sources. Scholars such as Ibn Isḥāq (d. 149/767), Ibn al-Layth (d. 203/819), Ibn Qutayba (d. 276/889), Ṭabarī, Masʿūdī, Maqdisī (d. 355/966), Bāqillānī, Bīrūnī, Ibn al-Jawzī (d. 596/1200) and Ibn Khaldūn used such literature to give more details about events from the lives of the earlier prophets, or when debating theological issues.[1] For example, Ibn Qutayba cited a number of biblical verses as proof of Muḥammad's prophethood in his work, *Dalā'il al-nubuwwa* (The Proofs of Prophethood).[2]

Yet, despite this interest in the *Isrā'īliyyāt* literature, throughout the classical and post-classical period there has also been criticism of it as a trustworthy source of information, most often coming from legal scholars. However, as a source for stories of the past most scholars saw it as conventional. For example al-Ḥasan al-Baṣrī considered such story-telling to be an acceptable innovation[3] and Ibn Ḥanbal is known to have spoken of the difference between legal rulings and the narration of stories. 'When we narrate the law we are very cautious, but when we talk about *faḍā'il* (virtues) we take it easy (show compliance to it, *tasahhalnā*); we are especially flexible in telling of stories.'[4] Ibn Kathīr summarised the purpose of such

1 On Ibn Khaldūn's use of the *Isrā'īliyyat*, see Walter Joseph Fischel, *Ibn Khaldūn in Egypt*, Berkley: University of California Press, 1967, pp. 117–19, and on the other scholars listed here, see Adang, *Muslim Writers on Judaism*.

2 Cited by Saeed, *The Qur'an*, pp. 150–53.

3 Ibn al-Jawzī, *Kitāb al-quṣṣāṣ wa'l-mudhakkirīn*, ed. and trans. Merlin S. Swartz, Beirut: Dār al-Mashriq, 1986, p. 96.

4 Translation from Albayrak, 'Re-Evaluating the Notion of *Isra'iliyyat*', p. 81, citing Muḥammad Jamāl al-Dīn al-Qāsimī, *Maḥāsin al-ta'wīl*, Cairo: Dār Iḥyā' al-Kutub al-ʿArabiyya, 1957–60, vol. 1, p. 43.

sources by stating that the *Isrā'īliyyāt* are quoted for supplementary attestation (*li'l-istishhād*) and not for full support (*li'l-iʿtidād*).[1] Similarly, the Ḥanbalī scholar Najm al-Dīn al-Ṭūfī (d. 715/1316) discussed the use of *Isrā'īliyyāt* in exegesis by stating that exegetes should not be condemned as long as they used the *Isrā'īliyyāt* for the purposes of explanation and not as a source of absolute truth.[2] The only other kind of criticism against the *Isrā'īliyyāt* during the classical and post-classical period seems to have been directed against unscrupulous storytellers.

The wholesale criticism and rejection of the *Isrā'īliyyāt*, especially within the religious science of Qur'ānic exegesis, appears to be a much more recent phenomenon. Most of this criticism has come from the reformers of the nineteenth and twentieth centuries, such as Muḥammad Abduh (d. 1322/1905), Rashīd Riḍā (d. 1353/1935) and Maḥmūd Abū Rayya (d. 1380/1970). As a group, they seem to have considered the *Isrā'īliyyāt* to be external material that had no place in Islam, and they also criticised earlier scholars for including these sources in their writings. From the twentieth century onwards, this complete disregard for the *Isrā'īliyyāt* literature has become more widespread amongst Muslims and is no longer limited to the reformist movement.[3]

Islam's Theology of Religions Meets the Study of Religion

When the history of the Islamic theology of religions is studied, a charge that could easily be made against it is that it was not an objective study of religions since all other religions were evaluated in the light of Qur'ānic teachings. Yet this charge fails to take account of the way in which these religions were approached by Muslim scholars. The vast majority of Muslim scholars who studied world

1 Ibid., p. 86, citing Ibn Kathīr, *Tafsīr al-Qur'ān al-ʿAẓīm*, Cairo: Turath Publication, [no date], vol. 1, pp. 7–8.

2 Ibid., p. 86, citing ʿAbd Allāh Maḥmūd Shaḥḥāta, *al-Qur'ān wa'l-tafsīr*, Egypt: [no publisher], 1974, p. 248.

3 Albayrak, 'Qur'anic Narrative', pp. 121–25.

religions and philosophies did not look at Islam as simply one religion amongst many, but rather as the final and complete revelation of all revealed world religions. This meant that, despite viewing the other world religions through the prism of Islam, they nonetheless managed—for the first time in history—to compile a tremendous body of scholarship about them.

The extent of knowledge that they accumulated on other faiths, and the largely peaceful co-existence of multiple religious communities within the Muslim world until the eleventh/seventeenth century, should at least be considered a moderately successful example of interfaith co-existence. Most of the dialogue that took place between religions during this period indicates a peaceful co-existence between them, but polemics between the scholars of different faiths are also found.

Compared to the approach of Muslim theologians, the methods and perspectives found in the study of religion in western academia are very different. For instance, scholars such as Ninian Smart, Eric Sharpe and others have tried to define the term *religion* and have come up with different definitions. However, these scholars are united in their decision to 'bracket out' the question of actual belief. In other words, scholars of the phenomenology of religion argue that religions should be studied in sympathy with the worshipper's beliefs as a descriptive work and by avoiding individual faiths truth claim, which are rather the domain of the philosophy of religion. Although scholars of the study of religion agree that it is possible to evaluate the truth claims of religions, they choose not to, in order to describe them without reduction. Nevertheless, the Muslim theologian may argue that the study of religion is taught through such disciplines as phenomenology, sociology, history, psychology, anthropology and archaeology, which in certain ways are informed by atheism and agnosticism. Even though scholars such as Ninian Smart[1] argue that the study of religion is a multi-

1 John J. Shepherd, *Ninian Smart on World Religions*, Farnham, Surrey: Ashgate, 2009, vol. II, p. xiii.

disciplinary endeavour—meaning that it is a mistake to study it through only one approach—a Muslim theologian would respond by saying that if Smart and others truly believe it to be a multidisciplinary endeavour, then surely incorporating belief-based studies of it will only enhance our understanding.

From a Muslim theologian's perspective, the dominant view held by Western archaeologists, sociologists, anthropologists and psychologists is that religions are human constructs that were created by the earliest human communities, either through imagination or by ascribing hidden meanings to natural phenomena. This is a hypothesis that is based on an evolutionary view of religion, which is the idea that religion has evolved via belief systems such as animism, polytheism and monotheism. However, precisely how modern secular society can avoid popular contemporary truth claims indirectly becoming the dominant view in a subject such as the study of religion is a question that Muslim theologians might very well ask today.

In practice, discussions about religion often seem to make the views of the outsider (the non-believer)—through the support of the social sciences—appear to be the supposedly 'objective' view. It is interesting to note that the social scientific argument about the origins of religion can only be fully accepted if, first, one rejects or 'brackets out' God as a continuous, active creator. Secondly, for religion to have originated with primitive people—which is the popular belief in the West—one would have to believe that the earliest human communities must have been primitive. René Guénon (d. 1951) wrote firmly against this theory, which was widespread within academic circles at his time, and which he considered to be a prejudicial characterisation of primordial religion because of its portrayal as a product of human immaturity. He argued that academic definitions of primordial religion were biased because they presented it as 'a "superstition" arising in the imagination of "primitive" peoples, who, it is suggested can have been nothing but savages or men of infantile mentality, as the evolutionist theories make them out to have been.'[1]

The anthropologist Wilhelm Schmid (d. 1954) supported this statement by Guénon. Schmid's hypothesis was that non-monotheistic religions had degenerated from a monotheistic Urreligion. In his book, *The Origin and Growth of Religion*, he used his anthropological research on Native American (First Nation), Australian aborigines and other such civilisations to support his theory.[2] However, most anthropologists after the 1950s rejected this view and, in the last few decades, most sociologists, psychologists and anthropologists have also begun to abandon such evolutionary perspectives to focus instead on the effects of religion on the individual and society.

Nevertheless, the evolutionary view of religion is still very popular and the Muslim theologian's argument may be that for contemporary society to claim to study religions objectively, the disciplines mentioned above need to consciously bracket out many of the contemporary secular popular truth claims. How else can outsiders truly study Islamic theology objectively without being influenced by secular popular truth claims that go counter to the beliefs of Islam? For example, Sunni theologians insist on a belief in an active God (the first truth claim) and they do not see the first people on earth as having been primitive—in other words, they consider the first people to have been as aware of God as are contemporary believers (the second truth claim). Can Islam be studied objectively if scholars and students are unaware of their own secular truth claims according to which Islam is indirectly measured up under the guise of an objective outsider's view?

It is our view that the perspective of contemporary secular society is not that of an objective outsider; instead, it is a particular perspective like any other particular perspective and it cannot claim

1 René Guénon, *The Reigns of Quantity and the Signs of the Times*, Hillsdale NY: Sophia Perennial, 2004, p. 178.

2 See W. Schmidt, *The Origin and Growth of Religion: Facts and Theories*, New York: Cooper Square Publishers, 1972.

to be the only 'objective' perspective. For the secular view of the other to change, a few steps must be taken. Firstly, the members of secular societies must, at the very least, accept that they have their own complex frames of reference, which are themselves based on certain truth claims that legitimise them. Secondly, and just like scholars such as Smart and Sharpe have argued,[1] there needs to be an acceptance of studying religion as it is truly recognised by its adherents and according to their traditions. This means engaging with religious thought and practice without reduction, and also actively inquiring about believers' world views while knowingly bracketing out secular truth claims.

1 See Ninian Smart, *Dimensions of the Sacred: An Anatomy of the World's Beliefs*, Berkeley: University of California Press, 1999 and Eric J. Sharpe, *Understanding Religion*, London: Bloomsbury Academic, 1997.

Chapter Six

THE HEREAFTER AND ISLAMIC ESCHATOLOGY

The Origin and the Return

The word *eschatology* derives from the Greek *eschaton*, meaning 'the end', plus the anglicised suffix *logy*, meaning 'the study of'. Hence, eschatology is literally the study of the final events in the history of the world and the ultimate destiny of humanity. Even though most religions have traditionally considered eschatology to be a valid and valuable area of study, one that is based upon their sacred writings on the subject, it now seems to have been largely discredited, especially in secular countries in both East and West where belief in an Afterlife is seen as either mythic or simply fanciful.

Even within Judaism and Christianity, there is a move away from eschatology. For example, modern critiques of the Hebrew Bible by Reform and Conservative Jews has led to the conclusion that belief in the Afterlife developed late in Jewish history (specifically in the rabbinical tradition), whereas originally there was no support for such a claim in the Hebrew Bible.[1] According to numerous Jewish academics today, such as Chaim Pearl and Rueben S. Brookes, Judaism is only concerned with humankind's earthly existence. They refer to various verses in the Torah that emphasise immediate, concrete, physical rewards and punishments for believers, rather than abstract future ones. This, however, contradicts traditional rabbinical teachings, which strongly support the belief in the Olam Ha-Ba

1 Dan Cohn-Sherbok, 'Death and Immortality in the Jewish Traditions', in Paul Badham and Linda Badham, eds., *Death and Immortality in the Religions of the World*, New York: Paragon House, 1987, pp. 24–26.

(the World to Come).[1] Among the main principles in the theological tract entitled *Thirteen Principles of Faith* by Rabbi Moses Maimonides (d. 600/1204)—who is recognised as one of the most important Jewish philosophers and scholars—is the belief that God will reward the good and punish the wicked, that the Messiah will come at end of time and that the dead will be bodily resurrected.[2]

Hence, in the twenty-first century, when the belief in traditional eschatology across most religions seems to have lost its importance, it is argued by some that Muslims 'stand almost alone in retaining an interest in traditional God-given data about the end of time'.[3] Among the questions posed by the Pew Research Center survey we have mentioned earlier were about belief in paradise and hell. The survey found that 'across the six regions of the world included in the study, a median of more than seven in ten Muslims say that paradise awaits those who have lived righteous lives, whilst a median of at least two-thirds say hell is the ultimate fate of those who do not live righteously and do not repent.'[4] This means that the vast majority of Muslims around the world today believe in the reward and the punishment of the Hereafter. By contrast, surveys about belief in life after death conducted in the 1980s in the West estimated that 'between 30–40% of the respondents had no such expectations',[5] meaning that at that point in time, a significant minority of people did not believe in an Afterlife.

As opposed to the understanding of religious groups who consider that a belief in the Afterlife was slowly introduced within the text

1 Dan Cohn-Sherbok, 'The Jewish Doctrine of Hell', in Dan Cohn-Sherbok and Christopher Lewis, *Beyond Death: Theological and Philosophical Reflections on Life after Death*, Basingstoke: Palgrave Macmillan, 1995, p. 54.

2 Cohn-Sherbok, 'Death and Immortality in the Jewish Traditions', in Badham and Badham, eds., *Death and Immortality*, p. 35, n. 27.

3 Winter, preface in Ḥaddād, *The Lives of Man*, p. vii.

4 Pew Research Center report, 'The World's Muslims.'

5 David Lorimer, 'Current Western Attitudes to Death and Survival', in Badham and Badham, eds., *Death and Immortality*, p. 226.

of their scriptures over a period of time, the belief in the Afterlife is an aspect of Islam that is embedded in the Qur'ānic text. Thus, it is impossible to ignore the subject of eschatology in Islam because it is mentioned in one way or another in every page of the Qur'ān, where numerous detailed descriptions of resurrection, judgement, Paradise and Hell are to be found. As Muḥammad Abdel Haleem observes, the many references to the Afterlife in the Qur'ān 'follows from the fact that belief in it is an article of faith, which has a bearing on every aspect of the present life and occurs in the discussion of the creed, the rituals, the ethics and law of Islam. In discussing it, moreover, the Qur'ān addresses both believers and non-believers.'[1] In addition, the *Ḥadīth* literature on the topic of the Afterlife is voluminous. All of this is the reason why even in the twenty-first century, Muslims seek out the descriptions of life and death found in revelation and the prophetic traditions.

Basing themselves on the Qur'ān and *Ḥadīth*, Muslim scholars have explored the topic of eschaton for nearly fifteen centuries. The best-known classical works on the topic are *al-Tawahhum* (The Imagining) by al-Ḥārith b. Asad al-Muḥāsibī (d. 242/857); the last section of Ghazālī's *Iḥyā' ʿulūm al-dīn* (The Revival of the Religious Sciences), which is entitled *Kitāb dhikr al-mawt wa-mā baʿdahu* (Remembrance of Death and the Afterlife); *al-Tadhkira* (The Memorial) by Shams al-Dīn al-Qurtubī (d. 670/1272); *Kitāb al-rūḥ* (The Book of the Spirit) by Ibn Qayyim al-Jawziyya (d. 750/1350), *Sharḥ al-ṣudūr* (Opening of Hearts) by Jalāl al-Dīn al-Suyūṭī and *Sabīl al-iddikār* (The Lives of Man) by ʿAbd Allāh b. ʿAlawī al-Ḥaddād (d. 1131/1719).

As pointed out in the introduction of this book, the six articles of faith can be divided into three categories: *tawḥīd*, the belief that there is no deity but God and that there is no power or might except God's; *nubuwwa* or *risāla*, the belief that God has sent His prophets to

1 Muḥammad Abdel Haleem, 'Life and Beyond in the Qur'ān', in Dan Cohn-Sherbok and Christopher Lewis, eds., *Beyond Death: Theological and Philosophical Reflections of Life after Death*, Basingstoke: Palgrave Macmillan, 1995, p. 66.

all nations through time, that He has given some of them scriptures and that His angels do his bidding and that they too are recognised as messengers of God. The last category is *Ākhira*, the belief in the Last Day.

Among the terms used for the Afterlife is *Maʿād* and it literally means 'the Return' or 'the Place of Return', but it is sometimes translated as eschatology; it has generally been used in scholarly writings and discussions on eschatological realities.[1] The expression comes from the Qur'ān in verses such as, 'They say: "What! When we are reduced to bones and dust, should we really be raised up (to be) a new creation?" Say: "(Nay!) be ye stones or iron, or created matter which, in your minds, is hardest (to be raised up), (Yet shall ye be raised up)!" Then will they say: "Who will cause us to return?" Say: "He who created you first [...]"'[2] Based on the systematic study of the word *Maʿād* in verses like the one above, the term has always been paired with *Mabda'*, which means 'Origin' or 'the Place of Origin'. This term is found in Qur'ānic verses such as, 'The Day that We roll up the heavens like a scroll rolled up for books (completed), even as We originated the first creation, so shall We produce a new one. A promise We have undertaken: truly shall We fulfil it.'[3]

The whole concept of the Origin and the Return (*al-Mabda' wa'l-Maʿād*) is seen by Muslims to fit into God's overall plan for the universe, from the most extraordinary aspects of it to the most miniscule. In Islamic theology, discussions about human nature, humankind's relationship with God, the structure and the order of the universe, the course of human history, the endeavour for ultimate good and life in the Hereafter are all located within the eschatological realm. This means that nothing in life can be seen as divorced from eschatology in Islam.[4] The Qur'ān repeatedly stresses that while God's message

1 Murata and Chittick, *Vision of Islam*, p. 340.

2 Q.XVII.49–51.

3 Q.XXI.104.

4 William C. Chittick, 'Eschatology', in Seyyed Hussein Nasr, *Islamic Spirituality: Foundations*, New York: SCM Press, 1989, pp. 378–79.

to humankind has been revealed to His prophets in particular places and at specific times in history, the forms that the message took conveyed the principle of one God, of the true origin of humanity and of its final return to God. For Muslims, this makes the belief in the Afterlife not only central to the Prophet Muḥammad's message, but also pivotal to the messages of all of the prophets before him.[1]

Thus from the point of view of Islamic theology, human history is seen as moving from the moment of creation towards the eschaton, both in the lives of individuals (at a microcosmic level) and as a collective (at a macrocosmic level). The basic eschatological message of Islam that all Muslims agree upon is the belief that God created humanity for a purpose, that there is a continuation of life after death and that there is a final reckoning.[2] The origin and return of all creation means that all creatures, individually and collectively, are subject to extinction, to death and decay, to a change from one state to another and to a transition from one abode to the next. Everyday occurrence such as the passing of day into night, and the passing of night into day are seen as reflecting the perpetual change and ending of all things.[3] In comparison, God is recognised as Almighty, the Eminent, the Forgiving, He Who manages all affairs and the Maker of destinies. He alone has permanence across all of the ages, stages and lifetimes, which by necessity must wane and perish.[4]

The Microcosm and Macrocosm

The writings on Islamic eschatology by classical and contemporary scholars are generally focused on three elements. The first is the microcosmic (the individual) and the macrocosmic (the collective) journey between the origin and the return. The second is the status of realms such as Paradise (*Janna*), Hell (*Jahannam*) and the *Barzakh*

1 Abdel Haleem, 'Life and Beyond in the Qur'ān', in Cohn-Sherbok and Lewis, eds., *Beyond Death*, p. 66.

2 Smith and Haddad, *Islamic Understanding of Death*, p. ix.

3 This is an example continuously cited across the Qur'ān. For example, see Q. XXII.61.

4 Hasanayn Muhammad Makhluf, prologue in Ḥaddād, *The Lives of Man*, p. 1.

(an intermediate state between death and the resurrection). The third and final element is the apocalyptic events of the Last Days. However, the main focus of eschatology in Islam is on the twin concepts of the microcosmic and macrocosmic journey. Creation is considered to consist of both the universe and humankind as a whole, as well as each individual entity within it. Muslims believe that before the resurrection, each person will meet his death in this world at a destined time (*ajal*), as is stated in the Qur'ān, '*To every people is a term appointed: when their term is reached, not an hour can they cause delay, nor (an hour) can they advance (it in anticipation)*'.[1] And just like a person's life comes to an end, so will the life of the cosmos come to an end. The death of the cosmos is known as 'the Hour' (*Sāʿa*); this, too, will take place at a determined time which God alone knows.[2]

Thus the Qur'ānic perspective is that God created humanity for a purpose, which is to worship him, and as part of the continuation of life after death there will be an ultimate accounting whereby God's justice will be served. At the microcosmic level, each individual is destined to pass through birth, the different phases of life, death, the intermediate stage of the *Barzakh* (the Intermediate Realm) and finally, the Day of Judgement. Analogously, at the macrocosmic level, creation as a whole is destined to pass through similar stages beginning with the creation of Adam and Eve, the exile from the Garden, collective human history marked by a long line of God's prophets, the Last Days, the death of all creation and immediately following it, the Day of Judgement. It is on that day, the Day of Judgement, that the individual and the collective meet and are led to their final abode in the Hereafter.

This world view also highlights 'that behind the flow of events, both in the natural and the human orders, [there] is a divine plan, and that all of man's life from birth to death is a microcosmic part of

1 Q.VII.34.
2 See Q.VII.187 and suras LXXXI, LXXXII, LXXXIV.

that overall macrocosmic scheme.'[1] The Origin (*Mabda'*) for an individual in this world is his birth from the womb of his mother, but it is encompassed by the overall macrocosmic *Mabda'* of humanity, which started with the creation of the first human being from clay. The end of this beginning—at both microcosmic and macrocosmic levels—is the Return (*Maʿād*) to God: 'He, Who has made everything which He has created most good: He began the creation of man with (nothing more than) clay. And made his progeny from a quintessence of the nature of a fluid despised. But He fashioned him in due proportion, and breathed into him something of His spirit. And He gave you (the faculties of) hearing and sight and feeling (and understanding): little thanks do ye give! And they say: "What! When we lie, hidden and lost, in the earth, shall we indeed be in a creation renewed?" Nay, they deny the meeting with their Lord. Say: "The Angel of Death, put in charge of you, will (duly) take your souls: then shall ye be brought back to your Lord."'[2]

This whole idea of the Return is predicated on the Origin of humanity. This is when humanity had to leave its original home and was promised the possibility of return. The Qur'ān and the *Ḥadīth* tradition are rich with descriptions of the creation of Adam and Eve and their representations as the macrocosmic origin of humanity. Their origin began with their creation and their residence within the Garden:

> We said: 'O Adam! Dwell thou and thy wife in the Garden; and eat of the bountiful things therein as (where and when) ye will; but approach not this tree, or ye run into harm and transgression.' Then did Satan make them slip from the (garden), and get them out of the state (of felicity) in which they had been. We said: 'Get ye down, all (ye people), with

1 Smith and Haddad, *Islamic Understanding of Death*, p. 11.

2 Q.xxxii.7–11.

> enmity between yourselves. On earth will be your dwelling-place and your means of livelihood—for a time.' Then learnt Adam from his Lord words of inspiration, and his Lord turned towards him; for He is Oft-Returning, Most Merciful. We said: 'Get ye down all from here; and if, as is sure, there comes to you guidance from me, whosoever follows My guidance, on them shall be no fear, nor shall they grieve. But those who reject faith and belie Our signs, they shall be companions of the Fire; they shall abide therein.'[1]

The expulsion of Adam and Eve from the Garden[2] described in this verse was a result of satanic deception and was immediately forgiven when Adam acknowledged his sin and asked for forgiveness. It is important to note that in the Islamic tradition, both primordial man and woman are considered equally to blame for the Fall of Man, and Eve was never seen as a temptress. Additionally, since God forgave them immediately, there is no doctrine of Original Sin in Islamic theology. Nevertheless, they were exiled by God, and this exile applied to all of humanity for a set period of time with the promise of guidance through the prophets and eventual felicity in the Garden, but also with a warning for those who rejected His message. This forged the macrocosmic link between the lower world (*dunyā*), where Adam, Eve and their progeny were exiled, and the Hereafter (Ākhira), where they are destined to return. As we mentioned, this macrocosmic journey of the children of Adam comes to an end upon the Day of Judgement.

Life in this lower world is intricately linked with eschatology because an individual's conduct directly affects how they are judged by God after death. In connection with this, the Qur'ān offers a

1 Q.II.35–39.

2 In Arabic, the word for garden is *janna*; the same term is also used for Paradise.

comprehensive portrait of the human psyche that is both interesting and unique. Human beings are recognised as the vice-regents of God on earth and they have been given this high position due to their intelligence and to the knowledge which God has granted them. They have also been given all good things for their sustenance and have been created in the best of forms. However, the human being is also portrayed in the Qur'ān as a highly multifaceted and deeply divided personality who is in need of guidance and discipline. The human being is described as a mass of unruly and chaotic contradictions torn between illusory desires that constantly change, such as passion, anger, greed, generosity, pettiness and piety. In addition to a human being's own internal passions, there is an external enemy, Satan, who deceives the steadfast soul so that it forgets God. Thus, because the human soul can be steadfast and patient in its belief or prone to capriciousness with hypocrisy, it is described in the Qur'ān as a creature in need of the guidance sent by God through His messengers, and it is only through this guidance that a human being can return to felicity.[1]

It is now important to speak about the life stages of the microcosm or the individual. In traditional Islamic theology there is a specific reference to the pre-existence of souls, which derives from the following Qur'ānic verse: 'When thy Lord drew forth from the children of Adam—from their loins—their descendants, and made them testify concerning themselves, (saying): "Am I not your Lord (who cherishes and sustains you)?" They said: "Yea! We do testify!" (This), lest ye should say on the Day of Judgement: "Of this we were never mindful."[2] According to many theologians, this means that all human beings were created with an innate disposition and an implicit awareness of God (*fiṭra*, 'innate nature') and hence no excuse can be given on the Day of Judgement about not having known

1 For instance, see Q.IV.137, XLI.51 and XVIII.54.
2 Q.VII.172.

the truth.[1] Many contemporary Muslim scholars have stressed the ethical content of the verse; specifically, the covenant (*mīthāq*) made between God and all human beings. Classical scholarship on the subject, however, stressed not only the ethical content of the covenant but also affirmed the idea of a period spent in the Realm of the Spirits (*ᶜĀlam al-Arwāḥ*); in other words, the pre-existence of all souls. Since this existence was affirmed by classical theologians, it gave rise to an extensive literature describing an individual's microcosmic life stages before reaching the Day of Judgement.

Based on their study of the Qur'ān and *Ḥadīth* literature, classical scholars have described the stages through which a human being must pass to return to God. There is some variation in their descriptions of these stages, but many scholars, such as ᶜAbd Allāh b. ᶜAlawī al-Ḥaddād, have identified five stages.[2] The first stage of an individual's existence is the stage that is sometimes referred to as the pre-worldly Realm of the Spirits (*ᶜĀlam al-Arwāḥ*) and began with the creation of Adam and the testifying of his progeny. This means that all of the descendants of Adam entered into a covenant (*mīthāq*) with God in which they recognised God's Unity and Lordship. This is what is referred to (very briefly) in the Qur'ānic verse, '"Am I not your Lord (Who cherishes and sustains you)?" They said: "Yea! We do testify!"'[3] The second stage is recognised as being life in this world (*dunyā*), which begins in the womb and ends at the moment of death. The third stage, which is known as 'life in the grave' or the Intermediate Realm (*Barzakh*), is the stage after death when the soul is stored in the *Barzakh* awaiting the Day of Judgement. The fourth stage is when an individual is resurrected and receives God's judgement on the Day of Judgement, along with all humankind. The fifth

1 Smith and Haddad, *Islamic Understanding of Death*, p. 12.

2 For a different division see Ibn Qayyim al-Jawziyya, *Kitāb al-rūḥ* (The Soul's Journey after Death), which identified only four: the domain of the mother's womb, the domain of this world, that of the *Barzakh* and the everlasting domain of the Garden and Fire.

3 Q.VII.172.

and final stage is known as the age of the Hereafter, and is located in the realm of Paradise or Hell.[1]

Each of these stages consists of one's birth into that stage of existence and, likewise, of one's departure from that stage of existence (death). Hence, at each stage, life is relative and so is death. There is a well-known saying in Muslim literature that 'sleep is the brother of death', and many scholars have drawn an analogy between the resurrection after death and waking after dreaming. Moreover, just as dreaming can sometimes bring one closer to true reality than when one is awake, so too is death seen as an awakening to reality and a removal of the veil. Hence, another popular saying in the Muslim world is, 'People are asleep and when they die, they awaken.' Death, just like life in this world, is relative rather than absolute when compared to the Reality we know as God.[2] The contemporary theologian Ali Ünal eloquently explains the ephemeral nature of life and death in everyday terms in his book, *The Resurrection and the Afterlife*:

> Death is not extinction, but a door opening on a better, more developed, and more refined life. [In the Qur'ān, death is presented] as something created and therefore having existence (67:2). When death enters a living body, life seems to depart. In reality, however, that organism is being elevated to a higher degree. The death of a plant, the simplest level of life is a work of Divine artistry just like its life, but one even more perfect and better designed. When a tree seed 'dies' it appears to decompose into the soil. However, it actually undergoes a perfect chemical process, passes through pre-

1 Ḥaddād, *The Lives of Man*, p.xiii.

2 See Abū Ḥāmid al-Ghazālī, *Kitāb dhikr al-mawt wa-mā baʿdahu*, trans. T. J. Winter as *The Remembrance of Death and the Afterlife: Book XL of The Revival of the Religious Sciences*, Cambridge: Islamic Texts Society, 1989, pp. 124 and 153–54.

> determined states of reformation, and grows into an elaborate, new tree. A dead seed represents the beginning of new tree, and shows that death is something created (like life) and, accordingly, is as perfect as life.[1]

However, this does not mean that Muslims do not feel the pain and sorrow when someone close to them dies. The best illustration of this is how the Prophet Muḥammad grieved when his own son Ibrāhīm died at sixteen months of age. He is reported to have said, 'O Ibrāhīm, were the truth not certain that the last of us will join the first, we would have mourned you even more than we do now [...] The eyes send their tears and the heart is saddened, but we do not say anything except that which pleases our Lord. Indeed, O Ibrāhīm, we are bereaved by your departure from us.'[2] When faced with death, it is common for Muslims to recite the Qur'ānic verse, 'To God We belong, and to Him is our return.'[3]

The Lower World

The second stage of an individual's existence is the life of this lower world (*dunyā*), which begins when the soul enters the embryo in the womb during the gestation period. *Dunyā* literally means 'closer' or 'lower', and it refers to the universe we inhabit as well as the period of time that each individual spends in this life. The universe is also recognised by theologians to have a determined time limit (*ajal*), just as an individual has a determined time span within it.

As noted in the previous section, most theologians have agreed that an individual's life begins before conception. At this stage, all the souls of Adam's lineage entered into a covenant (*mīthāq*) with God in which they recognised God's Unity and Lordship. Most classical

1 Ali Ünal, *The Resurrection and the Afterlife*, Istanbul: Tughra Books, 2000, p. 38.

2 Translation from Muhammad Husayn Haykal, *The Life of Muḥammad*, Kuala Lumpur: Islamic Book Trust, 1994, p. 488.

3 Q.II.156.

theologians have argued that this event should be understood to have taken place in a realm of existence other than that of the lower world (*dunyā*). Furthermore, this verse indicates that Adam's descendants possessed the ability to hear and speak in that realm of existence, which was needed to affirm and testify to God's oneness (*tawḥīd*).[1]

From its stage of proximity to the Divine Presence, the soul descends into the womb of the mother. The Qur'ān describes this first stage in the human being's existence in the world in these terms: 'He [God] began the creation of man with (nothing more than) clay, and made his progeny from a quintessence of the nature of a fluid despised. But He fashioned him in due proportion, and breathed into him something of His spirit. And He gave you (the faculties of) hearing and sight and feeling (and understanding).'[2] A common belief in Islam is that the soul only enters the womb one hundred and twenty days after conception; before then, the new life is considered to be biological but not spiritual. During the whole period of gestation, the pregnant woman is held fully responsible for the embryo's nourishment and well-being.

The Yemeni scholar ʿAbd Allāh b. ʿAlawī al-Ḥaddād (d. 1132/1720) further elaborated on this stage of life: 'This life begins with a prologue which resembles the Intermediary World [*Barzakh*] of the life-to-come [...] This "prologue" is the period of gestation, for it sees the appearance of some of the worldly influences which will apply to a person after his leaving his mother's womb, just as he retains something of the essences of the special existences within loins and wombs[3] in which he had lived before he appeared in his mother's womb.'[4] Thus, the separation that occurs at the moment when the soul enters the womb is recognised as a separation from the Realm of the Spirits (*ʿĀlam al-Arwāḥ*), and life in the womb is said to

1 Ḥaddād, *The Lives of Man*, p. 7.

2 Q.xxxii.7–11.

3 Here the translator means a place of sanctuary for the soul.

4 Ḥaddād, *The Lives of Man*, pp. 15–16.

resemble life in the Intermediate Realm (*Barzakh*), which in a sense is a place of gestation for the next life.

Understanding the Qur'ānic view of the stages a soul goes through before and after it is born into this lower world is a prerequisite for understanding Islamic eschatology as a whole, because life in this world is intricately linked with the abode of the Hereafter. Indeed, as Abdel Haleem stresses, 'The plan of two worlds and the relationship between them has been, from the beginning, part of the divine scheme.'[1] He also notes that the term *Ākhira* (the Hereafter) appears 115 times in the Qur'ān, which is exactly the same number of times that *dunyā* (the lower world) is mentioned. This equivalence elegantly illustrates the importance of both realms within Islamic eschatology. Moreover, because the two realms are so deeply connected, much of Islamic literature is devoted to encouraging Muslims to live their lives in this world by following the paths sanctioned by God in order to attain perpetual life in the Hereafter. These paths—in other words, the way that a person ought to live his life in the lower world—are prescribed by the divine scriptures and the prophets. And because every person is assessed in the Hereafter as well as the lower world, Muslim theologians attach great importance to the *Sharīʿa* and adherence to it.

The medieval Atharī scholar Abū al-Faraj Ibn al-Jawzī divided human life in the lower world into five phases: childhood, youth, maturity, old age and, finally, decrepitude and death.[2] It is also made clear in the Qur'ān that some individuals have a longer predetermined lifespan than others:

> O mankind! If ye have a doubt about the Resurrection, (consider) that We created you out of dust, then out of sperm, then out of a leech-like clot, then out of a morsel of flesh,

1 Abdel Haleem, 'Life and Beyond in the Qur'ān', in Cohn-Sherbok and Lewis, eds., *Beyond Death*, p. 66.

2 Cited in Ḥaddād, *The Lives of Man*, p. 22.

> partly formed and partly unformed, in order that We may manifest (our power) to you; and We cause whom We will to rest in the wombs for an appointed term, then do We bring you out as babes, then (foster you) that ye may reach your age of full strength. And some of you are called to die, and some are sent back to the feeblest old age, so that they know nothing after having known (much).[1]
>
> It is He Who has created you from dust then from a sperm-drop, then from a leech-like clot; then does he get you out (into the light) as a child; then lets you (grow and) reach your age of full strength; then lets you become old—though of you there are some who die before; and lets you reach a term appointed; in order that ye may learn wisdom.[2]

At the birth of a child, and following the example of the Prophet Muḥammad, the call to prayer is recited in the right ear of the child. This is so that the infant will be reminded of the covenant made with God (*mīthāq*) and its innate nature (*fiṭra*). The Prophet Muḥammad is reported to have said, 'Every newborn baby has, when born, his *fiṭra*; it is his parents who make of him a Jew, a Christian, or a Zoroastrian.'[3] This innate awareness of Reality is deeply imbedded in our human nature and some have argued that it is part of all living things, although in a manner incomprehensible to us. It is in line with this belief that the majority of Muslim scholars consider every child prior to puberty to be in conformity with their innate nature (*fiṭra*). According to the *Sharīʿa*, this means that such a child is not accountable in the eyes of the law and is therefore not required to perform

1 Q.XXII.5.

2 Q.XL.67.

3 Cited in Ḥaddād, *The Lives of Man*, p. 18.

any obligatory religious duties (such as praying and fasting) until he or she reaches puberty. At puberty, if the child is considered to be sane, then he or she becomes legally accountable (*mukallaf*) through all the following phases of his or her life until death.[1]

A vast body of Islamic literature has grown up around the subject of how a Muslim should behave within each distinct phase of life and how to respect others who are at a different stage in theirs. This kind of guidance was set up by the Prophet Muḥammad, who, in a famous *ḥadīth*, is reported to have said, 'Someone who does not show respect for our elders and compassion for our youngsters, and does not enjoin good and forbid evil, is not of us.' He also said, 'Whenever a young man honours an older person, God sends him someone who will respect him when he reaches that age.'[2]

Scholars like Ghazālī, in his *Revival of the Religious Sciences*, have also written about how individual phases of life can be beneficial for the Afterlife. This has always been an important subject for Muslims because the promise of Paradise is specifically linked to their faith and good deeds in the lower world: 'Blessed be He in Whose hands is Dominion: and He over all things hath Power. He Who created Death and Life, that He may try which of you is best in deed: and He is the Exalted in Might, Oft-Forgiving.'[3] Life in this lower world is seen as a rehearsal stage for the Hour and a place where all individuals are tried and tested. This is why it is essential to live wisely with what God has bestowed upon humankind.

But while the believer is striving to attain Paradise, the Qur'ān contains a reminder to not forget the present world: 'But seek, with the (wealth) which God has bestowed on thee, the Home of the Hereafter, [and do not] forget thy portion in this world, but do thou good, as God has been good to thee, and seek not (occasions for) mis-

1 Ibid., p. 19.
2 Both *ḥadīth*s are cited in ibid., p. 27.
3 Q.LXVII.1–2.

chief in the land; for God loves not those who do mischief.'[1] Similarly, believers are encouraged to recite the prayer: 'Our Lord, give us good in this world (*dunyā*) and good in the Hereafter (*Ākhira*).'[2] The reason given for why one should not forget about this lower world and only focus on the Hereafter is that it is a goodness from God which deserves to be paid forward in this world through faith and good deeds. This life is therefore of great consequence—all actions and deeds matter and nothing in life is trivial.

An individual Muslim's responsibility for his faith and deeds in this world is very much coupled to his responsibilities as a member of the larger community (the Muslim *Umma*), so the idea of a righteous society and its relationship to the Hereafter is also emphasised in Islam.[3] Human beings are recognised as social creatures and, accordingly, all of the laws of the *Sharīʿa*, as well as the moral and ethical guidance contained in the Qur'ān and the teachings of the Prophet, stress the importance of the believer's relationships within this world. For example, there is a famous tradition of the Prophet in which Muslims are informed that the obligatory ritual prayer (*ṣalāt*) is more greatly rewarded when prayed as a community than when it is fulfilled individually.[4] The implications of the believer's fulfilment of social responsibilities are immense since the way in which one behaves and acts towards one's fellow human beings and other creatures is not only rewarded or punished in this lower world, but ultimately plays a major role in where one is sent in the Hereafter.

As an illustration of how the Muslim view of life in this lower world encompasses all of these aspects—individual and communal worship, life within society, how to avoid perdition, how to achieve salvation and so on—the subjects covered by Ghazālī's famous

1 Q.XXVIII.77.

2 Q.II.201.

3 Sulayman S. Nyang, 'The Teaching of the Qur'ān Concerning Life after Death', in Badham and Badham, eds., *Death and Immortality*, pp. 76–77.

4 Bukhārī, *Ṣaḥīḥ*, x.43, http://sunnah.com/bukhari/10/43.

work, *The Revival of the Religious Sciences*, serve as an excellent example. Ghazālī divided his *Revival* into four parts each consisting of ten chapters. In the first part, he put down the requirements of faith and rites, like the ritual prayer, the fasting, pilgrimage, etc., which are deemed obligatory for every adult of good health and sane mind. In the second part, he elaborated on life within society at large, focusing on such aspects as eating, marriage, earning a living, friendship, travel, music and forbidding wrong and enjoining right. This second part demonstrates that classical theologians also wrote about Muslim social life and portrayed it as a major part of faith that relates to the Hereafter. In the third part, Ghazālī discussed how to overcome the vices within one and, in the fourth part, the virtues that an individual must strive to achieve. The latter include repentance, patience and thankfulness, facing hope and fear, self-examination, meditation and finally the remembrance of death and the Afterlife.[1]

The final phase of life in the lower world ends with death, which is the function of the Angel of Death known as ʿIzrāʾīl. In Islamic literature, giving up one's soul to death is recognised as being very difficult since it is a separation from all that one holds dear. However, it is also recognised that this separation can be made easier if one understands that this lower world is a barrier to Reality.[2] The human being's ultimate quest in this world is not his material and physical growth through childhood, adulthood and old age but the spiritual growth of his soul in achieving what is known in Arabic as *taqwa* (God consciousness). Hence, in Islamic theology—specifically, in Islamic eschatology—death plays a major role as a reminder and a warning for the living. Indeed, the Prophet Muḥammad famously called death 'the only preacher you need.'[3]

1 Most of the chapters in this important book are available in English translation. See, for example, the translations by The Islamic Texts Society.

2 Chittick, 'Eschatology', in Nasr, ed., *Islamic Spirituality: Foundations*, p. 380.

3 Ibid., p. 379.

Thus, in Islam it is understood that there is a strong relationship between the dead and the living. In the *Ḥadīth* literature, it is made clear that praying for the dead, asking God's forgiveness for them and giving charity on their behalf are some of the deeds that can benefit those who have passed on from the lower world. Another element of social conduct in Islam that is related to this is visiting the graves of the deceased. The Prophet Muḥammad is well known for recommending this by stating, 'So visit the graves, for they will remind you of death.'[1] Once at a grave, it is recommended practice to recite the Qur'ān and seek God's forgiveness and mercy for the deceased. Many scholars have argued that visiting graves can be instructive; for instance, ʿAbd Allāh b. ʿAlawī al-Ḥaddād wrote, 'He should remember that soon he will go to the same end, and learn the lessons to be drawn from their condition.'[2]

This practice of respecting death—not trivialising it and not living in denial that it is the fate of each and every one of us—is something that today's society needs urgently to re-familiarise itself with because death is part of life. Although it brings grief and sadness to those left behind, there is still much that can be learnt from death. It is the most humbling part of our existence and therefore deserves to be given its due respect. What is increasingly a worry in the twenty-first century is that people have become divorced from this reality because of the trivialisation of death through mediums like films and computer games. In the world view of Islam, death needs to be recognised, spoken of, seen and, finally, appreciated as a gateway to the next world.

The Intermediate Realm

The stage of existence known as the *Barzakh* is also known as the life in the grave. It is an intermediate stage through which every individual passes after their life in the lower world (*dunyā*) and

1 Ibn Māja, *Sunan*, VI.1572, http://sunnah.com/urn/1289220.
2 Ḥaddād, *The Lives of Man*, p. 47.

before their raising on the Day of Resurrection. *Barzakh* literally means 'isthmus', a narrow strip of land that forms a barrier between two seas. The word is found with this meaning in two verses of the Qur'ān: 'It is He Who has let free the two bodies of flowing water: one palatable and sweet, and the other salt and bitter; yet has He made a barrier (*barzakh*) between them, a partition that is forbidden to be passed',[1] and, 'He has let free the two bodies of flowing water, meeting together. Between them is a barrier (*barzakh*) which they do not transgress.'[2]

However, the word *barzakh* is also used in the Qur'ān to refer to the intermediate stage of life which forms a barrier or partition for those who have died: 'Before them is a partition (*barzakh*) till the Day they are raised up.'[3] Just as an isthmus separates two seas in the lower world, in the context of this verse the *Barzakh* separates two entities which cannot mix: life in the lower world (*dunyā*) and life in the Hereafter (*Ākhira*). This separation between the realm of the living and the realm of the dead has always been stressed in Islamic eschatology; hence, Muslims do not believe that anyone can return to the world once they have tasted death.

The Prophet Muḥammad described life in the Intermediate Realm in the following terms: 'The grave is either one of the chasms of Hell or one of the gardens of Paradise', and 'When one of you dies his [future] seat is displayed before him morning and evening: should he be of the people of Paradise, then it is situated among them, while should he be of the people of Hell, then it is situated among them.'[4] Muslim scholars have written extensively about the *Barzakh* (also called *qabr*, 'the grave'). For example, ʿAbd Allāh b. ʿAlawī al-Ḥaddād described it as follows: 'The Intermediate Realm is the abode which lies between the world and the life to come. It

1 Q.xxv.53.

2 Q.lv.19–20.

3 Q.xxiii.100.

4 Ghazālī, *Remembrance of Death and the Afterlife*, p. 127.

has more affinity with the latter, and is in fact a part of it. It is a place where spirits and spiritual things are predominant, while physical bodies are secondary but share with the spirits in their experience, whether felicity and joy, or torment and grief.'[1]

Ghazālī in turn explained the status of the body and soul in the grave as analogous (though not identical) to when the limb of a living person is immobilised due to a health issue. After death, the soul (*ruḥ*)[2] continues to apprehend and perceive sorrow or joy, while the body is no longer capable of anything.[3] By means of another analogy, Suyūṭī described the link between spirit and body after death in this way: 'The spirit is connected to its body in a way not like the connection of earthly life, but resembling the condition of sleep.'[4] Ibn Qayyim al-Jawziyya also compared the state of the *Barzakh* to sleep:

> In the sleeping state, the soul does not completely leave the body as it does in the case of death, but remains inside the body not leaving it to move freely through the heavens. We can liken it to a ray or a thread whose end remains connected to the body. The ray of this soul stretches out to the heavens and then returns again to the body when the sleeper wakes up. It is like the rays of the sun. The orb of the sun is in the heaven but its rays are on the earth. The two cases are not exactly the same, but it is a way of making the meaning clearer. In the case of death, the body remains in the ground

1 Ḥaddād, *The Lives of Man*, pp. 41–42.

2 Ghazālī explained the spirit or soul as the abstraction through which human beings apprehend the sciences and through which they feel the pain of sorrow and the pleasures of felicity.

3 Ghazālī, *Remembrance of Death and the Afterlife*, pp. 122–23.

4 Quotation from Jalāl al-Dīn al-Suyūṭī, *Bushrā al-ka'īb bi-liqā' al-ḥabīb*, Cairo: Maktabat wa-Maṭbaʿat Muṣṭafā al-Bābī al-Ḥalabī wa-Awlādihi, 1969, p. 72, cited by Smith and Haddad, *Islamic Understanding of Death*, p. 49.

> while the soul is in the interspace between the two worlds. An 'interspace' [*Barzakh*] is something which separates two things: heaven and earth, or this world and the Next World. In other words, it is the period between death and resurrection. The bliss or punishment of the interspace is not the same as the bliss and punishment of the Next World. It is something that happens between this world and the Next World. Despite the fact that the soul is in the interspace between the two worlds and the body is inside the earth, the two are still connected.[1]

There was agreement amongst the majority of Muslim scholars that the body and soul would share in the torment and bliss of the grave,[2] and that a person who has died is said to remain aware of his body after death.

There are verses in the Qur'ān that suggest that there is some kind of reward and punishment in this Intermediate Realm for deeds carried out in the lower world, and there are also many *ḥadīth*s to this effect.[3] Consequently, this is an important topic in Islamic eschatological literature and it is often presented as a reminder to the living of the impermanence of life and as the reason for meeting religious obligations and following righteousness. In addition to this, the literature on the subject has traditionally included advice on how the living can help the dead through their prayers and by visiting their graves.[4]

1 Ibn al-Qayyim al-Jawziyya, *Kitāb al-rūḥ*, ed. and trans. Layla Mabrouk as *The Soul's Journey after Death*, http://ia600409.us.archive.org/6/items/KitabAlRuhSummary-IbnAlQayyim/23713846-The-Souls-Journey-After-Death.pdf.

2 Smith and Haddad, *Islamic Understanding of Death*, p. 57.

3 See verses such as Q.III.169–71, VI.93, VIII.52, XIV.32, XVI.32, XXV.21, lx.11, XL.45–46, XL.49, LII.47 and LXII.25.

4 Smith and Haddad, *Islamic Understanding of Death*, pp. 36–40.

But although the vast majority of Muslim scholars upheld the belief in the *Barzakh* as a part of their creed and have attested to the reward and punishment of the body and soul there (as was the case with the Ashᶜariyya and the Māturīdiyya), not all theologians agreed. For instance, the Khārijiyya, the Jahmiyya and even some of the Muᶜtazila rejected this description of the *Barzakh*. Instead, they argued that human beings become nothingness for the duration of their sojourn in the grave and hence neither suffer punishment nor feel the delights of reward in the Intermediate Realm until after they are resurrected.[1]

Another opinion held by some Muslim scholars was that only souls experience reward and punishment; not bodies. But the most divergent theory about the Intermediate Realm came from the philosophers Fārābī and Ibn Sīnā. They suggested that the soul was a simple and incorruptible substance that received its individualisation from the human body. Hence, according to Fārābī, once the body died, it then perished, and the soul returned to God because there no longer remained an individual substance. Ibn Sīnā argued along similar lines by suggesting that the rewards and punishment of the grave were metaphorical symbols which only served to motivate the masses in their belief. These views have been regarded by the majority of Muslim scholars as irreconcilable with the textual sources of Islam, the Qur'ān and *Ḥadīth*.[2]

The most complete description of the events within the *Barzakh* is found in the *Ḥadīth* literature, which states that the beginning of the *Barzakh* is the arrival of two interrogating angels named Munkar and Nakīr. All traditions agree that the two angels have been commanded by God to ask the deceased three questions in the grave: Who is your Lord? What is your religion? Who is your prophet? The correct answers to these are said to be God, Islam and Muḥammad, and

1 Marcia Hermansen, 'Eschatology', in T. J. Winter, ed., *The Cambridge Companion to Classical Islamic Theology*, Cambridge: Cambridge Press, 2008, p. 313.

2 Ghazālī, *Remembrance of Death and the Afterlife*, footnote on p. 122.

the righteous answer without hesitation. After hearing the answers of the deceased to these questions, the angels open a window either to Paradise (*Janna*), whereupon the righteous may gaze and feel the atmosphere of felicity, or the angels may open one to the Fire (*Nār*). However, the literature also raises the possibility of people being punished in the grave—despite their faith—due to their actions in the lower world (*dunyā*). There are repeated warnings in the Qur'ān and *Ḥadīth* that even though people may believe in the One God, if they continue to commit evil deeds and reject His commandments, they may be punished. Nonetheless, in Islamic theology there is also a continuous reminder that it is God who makes the final decision.[1]

A number of new theories about the *Barzakh* have been proposed by Muslim scholars in modern times and interestingly, some of them echo Christian doctrines about life after death. For instance, there is now a trend amongst many contemporary Muslim writers to describe all of the souls in the *Barzakh* (and even those in Hell) as being purified within a quasi-spiritual hospital so that they may become one with God.[2] This concept of *Barzakh* as a 'spiritual hospital' in which the soul resides after death to be rehabilitated (rather than simply waiting there in bliss or torment) is new to Islam, but is found within Christian tradition. Traditional Catholic theologians refer to a similar place known as Purgatory. This is believed to be a temporary place for those who have died in a state of grace,[3] but who need to expiate their lesser sins by undergoing punishment before being admitted to the vision of God.

Furthermore, some modern Muslim scholars believe that the *Barzakh* is psychological or metaphorical. Writers such as the Egyptian Sayyid Quṭb have argued that suffering in the grave may be best

1 Smith and Haddad, *Islamic Understanding of Death*, pp. 41–55.

2 Salih Tug, 'Death and Immortality in Islamic Thought', in Badham and Badham, eds., *Death and Immortality*, p. 88.

3 Meaning, those who had been baptised by the Church.

understood as a psychological condition,[1] whereas the contemporary Turkish scholar M. Sadeddin Evrin has proposed a metaphorical interpretation of Qur'ānic references to 'those in the grave' as referring to those who live their lives immorally in this world and who are self-absorbed.[2] This opinion is very similar to the views of many contemporary Catholics and Orthodox Christians, who believe that punishment in Purgatory and/or Hell is a state of mind, or an allegory, rather than a literal place. In fact, a belief in Purgatory was rejected by Eastern Orthodox churches in favour of a belief in the final theosis. This, again, is a place or state for those who have died, but here they become one with the Trinity.

Many modern Muslim thinkers have also begun to de-emphasise the intermediate state of the *Barzakh* by focusing instead on the deeds of an individual's life and on the Day of Judgement. This position shares some resemblance with that of Protestant Christians, who have generally rejected the idea of any intermediate state between this life and the Afterlife.[3] They have traditionally seen death as the moment of full entry into the next life.[4]

The other eschatological stage that is commonly compared with the *Barzakh* in the West is the state of Limbo. This is a speculative theological opinion found mostly amongst Catholics and in popular western writings, but it is important to note that the Catholic Church has never pronounced it as a creed. According to scholarly opinions, Limbo was a response to the question of what happened to righteous people who died prior to the coming of Christ; would they be sent to Heaven, Purgatory or Hell? To reach Heaven or Purgatory, one would have to be baptised according to Catholic creed, so instead

1 See the discussion about Sayyid Quṭb's *Mashāhid al-qiyāma fī al-Qur'ān* in Smith and Haddad, *Islamic Understanding of Death*, p. 109.

2 Ibid.

3 John L. Esposito, *The Oxford Dictionary of Islam*, Oxford: Oxford University Press, 2003, p. 38.

4 Ronald J. Allen, *A Faith of Your Own: Naming What You Really Believe*, London: Westminster John Knox Press, 2010, pp. 73–76.

some Catholic theologians proposed that those who had been righteous before the coming of Christ and un-baptised children who never accrued actual sins (but were nonetheless born with Original Sin) would be sent to the Limbo of the Patriarchs and the Limbo of the Infants.[1] In Islamic eschatology, this concept of limbo is entirely missing; however, there is no doubt that the Christian ideas about Purgatory, the final theosis and Limbo all share some similarities with the *Barzakh*, given that they are recognised as a stage after death. But, as can be seen from the above descriptions of each, there are still significant differences in the understanding of each tradition of this intermediate stage after death.

The Intermediate Realm of the *Barzakh* draws to a close for all individuals with the macrocosmic end of the universe, which is known in the Qur'ān as 'the Hour' (*Sāʿa*). Only God knows when the Hour will occur, as is stated in the Qur'ān, 'They ask thee about the (final) Hour, when will be its appointed time? Say: "The knowledge thereof is with my Lord (alone). None but He can reveal as to when it will occur. Heavy were its burden through the heavens and the earth. Only, all of a sudden will it come to you." They ask thee as if thou were eager in search thereof. Say: "The knowledge thereof is with God (alone), but most men know not."'[2] Another verse explains why this is so: ' Verily the hour is coming, My design is to keep it hidden, so that every soul be rewarded by its endeavour.'[3] Here the message is that the Hour will come, but the exact day and time is hidden from humankind so that all human beings will receive their reward equally for that which they have strived in their earthly life.

While from the Islamic perspective there is uncertainty about when the Hour will occur, there is no such uncertainty about what will occur at the end of the universe, during the Resurrection and on

1 For more information on limbo and purgatory please see Gavin D'Costa, *Christianity and World Religions: Disputed Questions in the Theology of Religions*, Chichester: John Wiley and Sons, 2009.

2 Q.VII.187.

3 Q.XX.15.

Judgement Day because there are explicit descriptions of them in the Qur'ān and *Ḥadīth*. These are described as the events of the eschaton, which is understood as the end of time or as the end of days.

The Signs of the Last Day

Whereas death in the lower world and existence in the *Barzakh* are experiences specific to each individual, the events of the eschaton apply to all of creation. If the reader surveys writings on the subject of the eschaton in Islamic literature, they will discover a consistent set of events that are said to take place on the Last Day, although the sources differ on the order in which they occur. The subject is generally divided into events that will occur before the Hour (which are known as the 'Signs of the Hour') and those that come afterwards. After the arrival of the Hour, the approximate sequence of events is said to begin with the sounding of a trumpet followed by the destruction of the cosmos, Resurrection and the final reckoning. Though there are verses about the terrestrial signs of the Hour in the Qur'ān, most of the verses referring to the eschaton are concerned with God's cosmic undoing of the world before the Last Judgement. The details of the actual destruction of the cosmos, the Resurrection, the Last Judgement and the fact that every individual being will be assigned for eternity to Paradise or Hell are fully developed in the Qur'ān, and expanded accounts of these events are to be found in the *Ḥadīth* literature and exegetical writings.

The coming of the Last Days before the arrival of the Hour (which is marked by the sounding of a trumpet) is said to be marked by the *ishrāṭ al-Sāʿa* or *āyāt al-Sāʿa* (signs of the Hour). These signs are further divided into the minor signs, which list the decay of society's moral order, and the greater signs, which are cataclysmic events that occur when the Hour is imminent. The eight major signs or tribulations (*fitan*) are: the appearance of the Smoke, the *Dajjāl* (Antichrist), the Beast, the sun rising in the west, the descent of Jesus, Gog and

Magog, three major earthquakes[1] and fire.[2] These cataclysmic events are dramatically and graphically described either in the Qur'ān or in the *Ḥadīth* literature as the devastation of creation and as a complete reversal of the natural order.[3] These events are foreshadowed, it seems, by widespread moral decay, whose description is found within the traditions of the Prophet Muḥammad, and are recognised by most Muslim scholars as signs indicating the onset of the cataclysmic events. Traditionally, the minor signs of the Last Days are believed to have begun upon the birth of the Prophet Muḥammad and are said to continue until the appearance of his descendant, named the *Mahdī* (the Rightly-Guided One). Because of this, Norman O. Brown observes, 'In the Islamic sense of time, we are always in the last days.'[4]

More detailed accounts of the minor signs of the Hour are to be found in the *Ḥadīth* literature. They describe a morally decadent society in which piety gives way to pride, truth gives way to lies, ignorance increases, alcohol and music prevail, usury or interest is the norm, adultery is prevalent and peoples' hearts become as hard as stone. In addition to the *ḥadīth*s on the topic, Muslim scholars have written about the signs of the end of time. They describe how in this morally decadent world the major tribulations will arise.[5] Ṭaḥāwī gives a concise description of these major signs in his book on the creed in these words: 'We believe in the signs of the End of Time, including the appearance of the Antichrist and the descent of Jesus, the son of Mary (peace be upon them both), from the celestial realm. We also believe in the sun's rising from the west and the appearance of the Beast of the Earth from its appointed place.'[6]

1 In some sources 'three lunar eclipses'.

2 The Qur'ān mentions three of these: smoke (XLIV.10–2), the beast (XXVII.82) and Gog and Magog (XVIII.94, XXI.96).

3 For example, see Q. XI.73, XVIII.99, XX.102, XXIII.101, XXVII.87, XXXVI.51, XXXIX.68, L.20, LXXIV.8 and LXXVIII.18.

4 Norman O. Brown, 'The Apocalypse of Islam', *Social Text*, vol. VIII, Winter 1983–84, p. 165.

5 Smith and Haddad, *Islamic Understanding of Death*, pp. 63–67.

6 Ṭaḥāwī, *Creed of Imam al-Ṭaḥāwī*, p. 78 (Creed 125).

Another eschatological event that was not mentioned by Ṭaḥāwī, but which is found in both in the *Ḥadīth* literature and later sources, is the coming of the *Mahdī*. By the time Ibn Khaldūn wrote his famous *Muqaddima* at the beginning of the ninth/fifteenth century, it appears that this belief in the coming of the *Mahdī* was universally accepted by Muslims:

> It has been accepted by all Muslims in every epoch, that at the end of time a man from the family of the prophet will without fail make his appearance, one who will strengthen Islam and make justice triumph. Muslims will follow him and he will gain domination over the Muslim realm. He will be called the Mahdî. Following him, the Antichrist will appear together with all the subsequent signs of the Day of Judgement. After the Mahdî, Jesus will descend and kill the Antichrist. Or Jesus will descend together with the Mahdî and help him kill the Antichrist. Such statements have been found in the traditions that religious leaders have published. They have been (critically) discussed by those who disapprove of them and have often been refuted by means of certain traditions.[1]

Ibn Khaldūn further described how some of his contemporaries were fond of relating the idea of the coming of the *Mahdī* to contemporary political affairs, and was very critical of them: 'They firmly imagine that the Mahdî will appear there, since these regions are not under the control of dynasties and out of the reach of law and force. Many weak-minded people go to those places in order to support a deceptive cause that the human soul in its delusion

1 Ibn Khaldūn, *The Muqaddimah*, pp. 257–58.

and stupidity leads them to believe capable of succeeding. Many of them have been killed.'[1]

The concept of the *Mahdī* is not an example of millenarianism (a notion found in some Christian apocalyptic movements, which believe that in the imminent future there will arise a thousand-year age of bliss and peace brought about by radical change). In actual fact, centennialism is what is more commonly found in the history of Sunni Islam, because based upon statements in the *Ḥadīth* literature, it is believed that every hundred years a Renewer (*Mujaddid*) will appear amongst the Muslims. Various lists of Renewers exist—not all agreed upon—and include only saintly and scholarly figures. Although the coming of the *Mahdī* is not a millenarian concept for most Muslims, it has certainly been utilised throughout Muslim history as a means to launch politically driven movements with apocalyptic and millenarian overtones at times of crisis.[2] The first historical reference to a political movement using the name of the *Mahdī* was the rebellion of al-Mukhtār b. Abī ʿUbayd (d. 67/687) against the Umayyad dynasty in 66/686. When Mukhtār launched his rebellion, he declared that he was doing so in the name of Muḥammad Ibn al-Ḥanafiyya (d. 81/700; the third son of the Caliph ʿAlī), who Mukhtār claimed was the *Mahdī*.[3] In modern times, the Sudanese Sufi Muḥammad Aḥmad b. ʿAbd Allāh (d. 1302/1885) declared himself the *Mahdī* in 1299/1882 and then defeated the occupying Ottoman-Egyptian forces. Afterwards, he formed an independent state and even defeated the British two years later. While his successor continued to fight the British occupying forces in Sudan, they eventually defeated the Mahdist regime

1 Ibid., p. 259.

2 Hermansen, 'Eschatology', in Winter, ed., *Cambridge Companion to Classical Islamic Theology*, p. 315.

3 Interestingly enough, Ibn al-Ḥanafiyya was not himself involved at all in the rebellion, and was left alone by the Umayyads throughout.

in 1306/1899.[1] Another person to have claimed to be the *Mahdī* was the Indian theologian Mīrzā Ghulām Aḥmad (d. 295/1908), who founded the Aḥmadiyya movement.[2]

Although the idea of the *Mahdī* is a theological doctrine common to both Sunnis and Shiᶜis, it is understood quite differently by each. The majority Sunni view of the *Mahdī* is that, at the end of time, a man born from within the family of the prophet will make his appearance and fight against injustice. By contrast, Twelver Shiᶜis believe that their twelfth Imam Abū al-Qāsim Muḥammad b. Ḥasan al-ᶜAskarī (b. 255/869), who went into occultation in the year 260/874,[3] is the *Mahdī* and will return during the apocalypse as the *Qā'im* (The One Who Rises Up) and the *Ṣāḥib al-Zamān* (The Lord of the Age).[4]

Because the *Mahdī* is a figure who features widely in theology, politics and even fiction,[5] many contemporary academics have argued that it is difficult to separate eschatological predictions from political circumstances, and some critics have gone further by stating that the whole concept of the *Mahdī* is a product of various Muslim political events and positions held in early Islamic history. It is also argued

1 For more details, see Haim Shaked, *The Life of the Sudanese Mahdi*, London: Transaction Publishers, 2008.

2 The majority of Sunni Muslims consider the Aḥmadiyya to be outside of Islam. For further information, see Yehoiakin Ben Ya'ocov, *Concepts of Messiah: A Study of the Messianic Concepts of Islam, Judaism, Messianic Judaism and Christianity*, Bloomington, IN: WestBow Press, 2012, pp. 18–19.

3 The Imam was believed to have been hidden by God during his minor occultation between the years 260/874 and 894, and he is said to have communicated with his deputies during that period. His second, major occultation began in 941 and he is believed by the Twelvers to have been hidden by God until he returns as *Mahdī* at the end of times (other Shiᶜi sects do not accept him as the Mahdī).

4 For more details, see Abdulaziz Abdulhussein Sachedina, *Islamic Messianism: The Idea of Mahdi in Twelver Shiᶜism*, Albany: State University of New York Press, 1981.

5 The figure of the *Mahdī* has also appeared in several western works of fiction in recent years, such as Frank Herbert's science-fiction book *Dune* (1965), in which the main character Paul Atreides is seen as the predicted saviour *Mahdī* of the planet Arrakis, a desert world, and in A. J. Quinnell's *The Mahdi* (1981).

by these contemporary academics that the wide number of sources describing these eschatological events makes their sequence difficult to determine. This is not helped by the fact that many of these sources blur the lines between a literal and symbolic interpretation of the *ḥadīth*s about these events.[1]

But despite the wide range of opinions about the *Mahdī* as a symbolic or metaphorical character, the majority of Muslim scholars have recognised the *Mahdī* as a saviour figure who is a prophetic descendant and is a sign of the End of Times. As mentioned earlier, most sources describe the major signs of the Hour as occurring after the onset of a morally corrupted society, and it is into this context that the *Mahdī* is believed to appear. He will come as a reformer (but not as a prophet) to rescue society from its moral decay. During the same period, another figure is also said to appear: the Antichrist, who in Arabic is known as the *Dajjāl*.[2] The *Dajjāl*, who is only mentioned in the *Ḥadīth* literature, is a false messiah and is variously portrayed in the sources as a beast, a monster and also as a human being.[3] These events precipitate the descent of Jesus (*nuzūl ʿĪsā*), which is commonly known as the Second Coming in Christianity. His descent is described as a sign of the Hour in the Qur'ān[4] and is referred to in the *Ḥadīth*. 'It is important to recognize that the emphasis on Jesus as a [ascetic] figure of the first century CE is complemented in Islam with the eschatological Christ who is believed to return at the end of time. In these last days he will, it seems, very much live out the other side of the equation. It is argued that he will descend to earth, fight against the Antichrist, marry and have children. He will live and deal with everyday life as a prophet of God and even die a natural death.'[5] Jesus is largely credited for defeating the *Dajjāl*, but the

1 Smith and Haddad, *Islamic Understanding of Death*, pp. 67–70.

2 See further description in Ṭaḥāwī, *Creed of Imam al-Ṭaḥāwī*, p. 122, n. 65.

3 These terms are not necessarily exclusive since in discussions on the topic these have been taken literally, symbolically and metaphorically.

4 Q.XLIII.61.

5 Hussain, 'Jesus in Islam', in Barker and Gregg, eds., *Jesus beyond Christianity*, p. 141.

Mahdī is also said to have a hand in this. With the fall of the *Dajjāl*, society will be restored, for a period of time, from its decayed state to one of righteousness.

The peaceful era that is brought about by the victory of Jesus and the *Mahdī* over the *Dajjāl* will eventually come to an end, and the sources go on to describe the sudden appearance of the people of *Yājūj* (Gog) and *Mājūj* (Magog). The story of Gog and Magog is referred to in the Qur'ān in connection with the righteous king, Dhū al-Qarnayn. The king was petitioned for help by some people who were plagued by Gog and Magog and sought a form of defence against their incursions. The king succeeded in containing them by erecting a barrier to keep them out, and there is a promise in the Qur'ān that this barrier will only break when the trumpet is blown to signal the arrival of the Hour.[1] In addition to these verses, there are also traditions of the Prophet which provide graphic descriptions of how the people of Gog and Magog will break free from their enclosure during the last days and go on to destroy all that is in their path. However, these *ḥadīth*s also indicate that God will ultimately destroy them.

After the destruction of Gog and Magog, the remaining major signs and tribulations, such as the 'sun rising from the west' and 'the Beast from the Earth',[2] follow in quick succession until a complete reversal of the natural order takes place.[3] The blowing of the trumpet—mentioned eleven times in the Qur'ān—will announce the beginning of the end of the universe. One such verse states, 'Then, when one blast is sounded on the trumpet, and the earth is moved, and its mountains, and they are crushed to powder at one stroke, on

1 See Q.xviii.83–99 and xxi. 96–97. Gog and Magog are also mentioned in the Hebrew Bible (Genesis 10:2; Ezekiel 38:2 and 39:6) and in the New Testament (Revelations 20:8).

2 'When the word is fulfilled against them, We shall produce from the earth a beast to speak to them, because people did not believe with assurance in our signs.' Q.xxvii.82.

3 Smith and Haddad, *Islamic Understanding of Death*, pp. 68–70.

that Day shall the (Great) Event come to pass. And the sky will be rent asunder, for it will that Day be flimsy, and the angels will be on its sides, and eight will, that Day, bear the Throne of thy Lord above them. That Day shall ye be brought to judgement: not an act of yours that ye hide will be hidden.'[1]

The cataclysmic events that are described so dramatically in the Qur'ān signal the end through this cosmic disintegration and lead finally to the Day of Judgement. In the Qur'ān it is said:

> When the sun (with its spacious light) is folded up; when the stars fall, losing their lustre; when the mountains vanish (like a mirage); when the she-camels, ten months with young, are left untended; when the wild beasts are herded together (in the human habitations); when the oceans boil over with a swell; when the souls are sorted out, (being joined, like with like); when the female (infant), buried alive, is questioned for what crime she was killed; when the scrolls are laid open; when the sky is unveiled; when the Blazing Fire is kindled to fierce heat; and when the Garden is brought near—then, shall each soul know what it has put forward.[2]

Judgement Day is referred to by various terms in the Qur'ān, including the Day of Resurrection (*Yawm al-Qiyāma*), the Day of Judgement (*Yawm al-Dīn*), the Hour (*al-Sāʿa*), the Last Day (*al-Yawm al-Ākhir*), the Day of Decision (*Yawm al-Faṣl*) and the Day of Reckoning (*Yawm al-Ḥisāb*). The call of the trumpet brings forth the total annihilation of everything created and another call of the trumpet brings forth the Day of Resurrection. On that day, the trumpet shall be blown by the Angel Izrāfīl, destruction will commence and,

1 Q.LXIX.13–18.
2 Q.LXXXI.1–14.

when the trumpet is blown the second time, all will be resurrected from their graves and enter an enormous plain. There is no mention of the timeline of events between the calls of the trumpet because, by all accounts, time and space are created entities and so will cease to exist at this point. Consequently, the events of the Day of Judgement should not be understood as occurring within the space of this terrestrial twenty-four hour day, but instead, as William C. Chittick states, 'The Day of Resurrection is itself a major stage of becoming. Some sayings of the Prophet speak of its length in terms of thousands of years.'[1] In the Qur'ān it is said:

> On the Day of Judgement the whole of the earth will be but His handful, and the heavens will be rolled up in His right hand. Glory to Him! High is He above the partners they attribute to Him! The trumpet will (just) be sounded, when all that are in the heavens and on earth will swoon, except such as it will please God (to exempt). Then will a second one be sounded, when, behold, they will be standing and looking on! And the earth will shine with the glory of its Lord: the record (of deeds) will be placed (open); the prophets and the witnesses will be brought forward and a just decision pronounced between them; and they will not be wronged (in the least). And to every soul will be paid in full (the fruit) of its deeds; and (God) knoweth best all that they do.[2]

1 William C. Chittick, 'Your Sight Today is Piercing: The Muslim Understanding of Death and Afterlife', in Hiroshi Obayashi, ed., *Death and Afterlife: Perspectives of World Religions*, New York: Greenwood Press, 1992, p. 137.

2 Q.xxxix.65–70.

According to ᶜAbd Allāh b. ᶜAlawī al-Ḥaddād, the call of the trumpet commences the fourth life of the human being.[1] This life extends from the point when a person leaves his or her *Barzakh* for the Resurrection and Judgement until when it is time for each to enter Paradise or Hell. He warned, 'Know that the Day of Rising is a formidable Day [...] Its hardships are protracted and its terrors great.'[2] This stage of life is recognised to be both a macrocosmic and a microcosmic event. It is a macrocosmic event because all will be going through it at the same time collectively and it is also a microcosmic event since each individual will be resurrected and judged for their individual merit.[3]

After the trumpet blast, some of the perilous events that follow are described by Ghazālī as 'the Resurrection on the Day of Arising, the Presentation before the Almighty, the Inquisition regarding matters both important and minor, the Erection of the scales in order that men's destinies might be known and the passage over the Traverse despite the fineness and sharpness of its edge. These things will be followed by the awaiting of the Summons to final judgement, either bliss or misery.'[4]

Throughout the history of Islam, there has been considerable debate over the question of the resurrection of the body: firstly, between the Muᶜtazilīs and the Atharīs, and later between theologians and philosophers. It is evident from the historical sources that this question was not entertained by the early Muslims, and the possibility of the physical resurrection of the body has never truly been denied by the majority of Muslims at any time. However, the matter has raised a number of questions. An important one is whether the resurrection will be physical, spiritual or both. As already indicated, the vast majority of theologians believed that the resurrection is both

1 Ḥaddād, *The Lives of Man*, p. 52.

2 Ibid., p. 66.

3 Ibid., pp. 52–69.

4 Ghazālī, *Remembrance of Death and the Afterlife*, p. 173.

physical and spiritual, but a small minority (who are amongst the philosophers) held that it was only spiritual.[1]. The proponents of a purely spiritual resurrection, such as the philosophers Ibn Sīnā and Fārābī, denied the physical resurrection by arguing that all of the Qur'ānic statements about a physical resurrection are only figures of speech intended for the understanding of the masses, because the common people would not be able to understand the imaginal sphere. What is interesting is that their philosophical predecessor, Yaʿqūb b. Isḥāq al-Kindī, instead explicitly upheld the doctrine of the bodily resurrection. This meant that the earliest Muslim philosopher fully agreed with the majority of the theologians on this issue.[2]

In response to the position of scholars like Ibn Sīnā, Ghazālī devoted part of his famous book, *Tahāfut al-Falāsifa* (The Incoherence of the Philosophers), to refuting Ibn Sīnā's denial of the bodily resurrection. Ghazālī affirmed the truth of the bodily resurrection and the resurrection of the soul.[3] The vast majority of scholars have since agreed with Ghazālī's views and so there has been little further debate on the subject. However, another question that has more recently been debated is the nature of the resurrected body. Some have argued that the resurrected body will be identical to the earthly body, whereas others argue that the resurrected body necessarily has to be different from the physical body. Most scholars accept that there are several possible interpretations of the matter.[4]

The Qur'ān and *Ḥadīth* indicate that, after the Resurrection, a number of further events will take place. Ṭaḥāwī lists these as 'the recompense of deeds on the Day of Judgement, the review [of one's entire life], the reckoning, the recital of [one's own] book [of actions], the reward and punishments, the Bridge over the Fire, and the Scales

1 Smith and Haddad, *Islamic Understanding of Death*, p. 73.

2 John Inglis, *Medieval Philosophy and the Classical Tradition: In Islam, Judaism and Christianity*, London: Routledge Curzon, 2005, p. 20.

3 Cited in Smith and Haddad, *Islamic Understanding of Death*, pp. 131–34.

4 Ibid.

[upon which one's actions are weighed].'[1] After the Resurrection, the Gathering (*Ḥashr*) where all living beings will stand before God will be followed by the Reckoning (*Ḥisāb*) and the Weighing (*Mīzān*), which will be a just evaluation of the deeds of every individual. Muslims believe that their deeds are recorded in a book over their lifetime and that, after death, this book is presented to them; this event is known as the Reckoning (*Ḥisāb*). In the Qur'ān it is stated, 'We shall set up scales of justice for the Day of Judgment, so that not a soul will be dealt with unjustly in the least, and if there be (no more than) the weight of a mustard seed, We will bring it (to account): and enough are We to take account.'[2] The Qur'ān also specifies that those whose good deeds outweigh their bad deeds will be triumphant, and those whose scales are light with good deeds will have lost out.[3] It also states, 'Then he that will be given his record in his right hand will say: "Ah here! Read ye my record! I did really understand that my account would (one day) reach me!" And he will be in a life of bliss.'[4] By contrast, the one who is given his record in his left hand will lament knowing his reckoning, which leads to Hell.

The descriptions of Judgement Day also state that everyone will be ordered to cross the Path or Bridge (*Ṣirāṭ*) over Hell. It is interesting to note that Muslims recite the verse, 'Guide us on the straight path (*ṣirāṭ*)',[5] in each of the five daily prayers, and although *ṣirāṭ* here is commonly understood to mean the metaphorical straight path of Islam, numerous scholars have argued that this prayer is also meant for seeking guidance for walking over the actual Bridge found in the Afterlife. In the *Ḥadīth* literature, some people are said to fall off the bridge due to their lack of faith, while others successfully pass over it by the grace of God.

In Muslim manuals on creed, it is also common to come across

1 Ṭaḥāwī, *Creed of Imam al-Ṭaḥāwī*, p. 72 (Creed 101).

2 Q.XXI.47.

3 Q.XXIII.103–03.

4 Q.LXIX.19–21.

5 Q.I.6.

the belief in the Pond or Basin (*Ḥawḍ*) of the Prophet, mentioned in the Qur'ān by the name *Kawthar*,[1] where the triumphant will meet with the Prophet Muḥammad. It is at this pond that most manuals mention the intercession of the prophets taking place, with the Prophet Muḥammad being the first to intercede for his *Umma*. This is where God's mercy is shown to be greater than His wrath, and yet, His mercy is shown not to diminish His divine justice.

It is made clear that in all of these events, each individual is responsible for their own actions and no one else can be asked to carry another's burden. There is also mercy to be found in the way that God rewards good and requites evil. In the Qur'ān it is stated, 'If any does good, the reward to him is better than his deed; but if any does evil, the doers of evil are only punished (to the extent) of their deeds',[2] and, 'He that doeth good shall have ten times as much to his credit. He that doeth evil shall only be recompensed according to his evil. No wrong shall be done unto (any of) them.'[3] The Prophet Muḥammad explained the reality of deeds in the lower world (*dunyā*) as follows: 'God says, "If My slave intends to do a bad deed then (O Angels) do not write it unless he does it; if he does it, then write it as it is, but if he refrains from doing it for My Sake, then write it as a good deed (in his account). (On the other hand) if he intends to do a good deed, but does not do it, then write a good deed (in his account), and if he does it, then write it for him (in his account) as ten good deeds up to seven-hundred times."'[4] Thus it is believed that even the smallest number of good deeds registered to one's credit may, in the long run, bring a person to felicity.

The Hereafter: Paradise and Hell

Today, Islam may be one of the few religions that still places great emphasis on the Hereafter or the Afterlife (*Ākhira*). While it is cer-

1 Q.cviii.1.

2 Q.xxviii.84.

3 Q.vi.160.

4 Bukhārī, *Ṣaḥīḥ*, xcvii.126, http://sunnah.com/bukhari/97/126.

tainly true that in Islam importance is given to the present life, the central focus is always on the life to come. The Hereafter is considered by Muslims to be incommensurate with the lower world (*dunyā*). The Qur'ān and the *Ḥadīth* repeatedly state that life in this world is temporary whereas the real and lasting life is that of the Hereafter.[1] The realms of Hell and Paradise are considered real and part of the *ʿĀlam al-Ghayb* (Unseen Realm); their location is known only to God.

According to many mythologies and religions, Hell, or the underworld, is beneath the terrestrial world; and Heaven, or Paradise, is thought to be located in a high earthly place, or even in a future world. The Muslim understanding of the earth, sky and the heavenly bodies that are mentioned in the Qur'ān is that they are observable by means of the senses and are considered as reminders and signs of their Creator: 'Behold! In the creation of the heavens and the earth, and the alternation of night and day, there are indeed signs for men of understanding.'[2] Thus the earth and heavens that are described in the Qur'ān are not to be confused with the sphere of the Hereafter which is beyond the physical senses.

The primary sources of Islam feature a very graphic visualisation of both Paradise and Hell that is not paralleled in any other faith. In general, most Muslim scholars agreed that Paradise and Hell have already been created and are in existence now, so the Muʿtazilīs were in the minority in their belief that God would create these two realms on the Day of Resurrection. However, there have been differences of opinion amongst theologians from the main Sunni theological schools concerning how long Hell would continue to exist. Most scholars shared Ṭaḥāwī's view that 'Paradise and the Fire are both created; however, they neither perish nor terminate.'[3] But a handful of eminent scholars presented a coherent argument that Hell would at some point cease to exist, based on what is recorded

1 See for example, Q.LVII.20.

2 Q.III.190.

3 Ṭaḥāwī, *Creed of Imam al-Ṭaḥāwī*, p. 72 (Creed 102).

in the Qur'ān and in the *Ḥadīth* literature. They included scholars with surprisingly diverse perspectives, such as the Sufi Ibn ʿArabī, Ibn Taymiyya and his student Ibn Qayyim al-Jawziyya, and the Shiʿi philosopher Mullā Ṣadrā (d. 1049/1647).[1] What they all agreed upon was that the two realms existed, and that even though similitudes have been drawn between them and aspects of the present world, their true form cannot ever be grasped. About Paradise, it is said in the Qur'ān: 'Now no person knows what delights of the eye are kept hidden (in reserve) for them as a reward for their (good) deeds.'[2] As for Hell, there are many descriptions of it in the Qur'ān, where it is variously referred to there as *al-Nār* (the Fire), *Jahannam* (Gēhinnōm),[3] and *al-Jaḥīm* (the Blazing Fire). As stated earlier, no location for Hell is mentioned in the Qur'ān or the *Ḥadīth*, but it is said to be a place of punishment with seven gates: 'And verily, Hell is the promised abode for them all! To it are seven gates: for each of those gates is a (special) class (of sinners) assigned.'[4] It is a place of crackling and roaring flames, of fierce boiling waters, scorching wind and black smoke. In keeping with this, the punishments of Hell are physical; the people of the Fire are said to be wretched, sighing, wailing and bound by chains. There is also no doubt about why someone would be sent there: it is made clear in the Qur'ān that if a person is sent to Hell it is because of their own wrongdoing—be it a lack of faith, the denial of God and the Hereafter, wrongful deeds in the lower world and so on. During the classical Islamic era, a number of theologians debated over whether Hell existed as an unending place for punishment for sinners, or if it was more like a temporary purgatory. Despite the range of opinions on the matter, the view that came to be accepted by all Sunni schools of theology was that for sinning believers, Hell was like a temporary Purgatory.

1 Mohammed Rustom, *The Triumph of Mercy: Philosophy and Scripture in Mulla Sadra*, Albany: State University of New York Press, 2012, p. 85.

2 Q.xxxii.17.

3 A Hebrew metonym for Hell.

4 Q.xv.43–44.

In contrast to the fires of Hell that awaited sinners, those who believed, refrained from evil, performed good deeds, had God consciousness (*taqwa*) and were truthful, penitent and heedful were promised the rewards of Paradise. Most frequently referred to as *al-Janna* (the Garden), Paradise is vividly described in the *Ḥadīth* and, especially, the Qur'ān: '(Here is) a parable of the Garden which the righteous are promised: in it are rivers of water incorruptible; rivers of milk of which the taste never changes; rivers of wine, a joy to those who drink; and rivers of honey pure and clear. In it there are for them all kinds of fruits; and Grace from their Lord.'[1] Other similar names for it are *Jannāt al-Firdaws* (the Gardens of Paradise), *Jannāt ʿAdn* (the Gardens of Perpetual Bliss), *Jannāt al-Naʿīm* (the Gardens of Bliss), *Dār al-Maqāma* (the Home that Will Last), *Dār al-Salām* (the Home of Peace), *Dār al-Ākhira* (the Home of the Hereafter) and *Maqʿad Ṣidq* (an Assembly of Truth).[2] It is understood to be a place of rewards with eight gates leading to it. The Hereafter is depicted as having both physical and spiritual delights and as a place where the faithful are contented, satisfied, secure and at peace. Here they will not hear any evil, they will not experience death, but rather feel true peace, hear gentle speech and, most of all, abide in the presence of God. Beyond spiritual contentment, the believing men and women of Paradise are said to live with spouses in gardens with rivers flowing beneath, in pleasant shade, reclining on couches consuming the plentiful fruits, food and drink, clothed in the finest silk, embroidery, gold and pearls, waited upon by servants and have the companionship of houris (*ḥūr*).[3]

The majority of Muslims today generally agree on these descriptions of Hell and Paradise.[4] However, as the case with the question of whether the resurrection will be physical or spiritual, there are similar disagreements amongst scholars over whether the descrip-

1 Q.XLVII.15.

2 Q.XVIII.107; XIII.23; X.9; XXXV.35; X.25; XXIX.64; LIV.55.

3 See Q.LV.46–78.

4 Smith and Haddad, *Islamic Understanding of Death*, p. 135.

tions of Paradise and Hell were meant to be understood literally or not. Marcia Hermansen notes, 'More than any other key postulate, the nature of heaven [Paradise][1] and hell has been subjected to a range of interpretations stretching from the purely literal to the utterly allegorical.'[2] While the majority of Islamic scholars have understood accounts of the physical and spiritual rewards and punishments of Paradise and Hell literally, a minority has argued that they should only be understood as being spiritual or psychological.[3]

It is important here to reiterate the idea of salvation in Islamic eschatology. For those people who lived before the time of Prophet Muḥammad, it is generally accepted that their monotheism and affirmation of the messages of previous prophets will be their salvation—the ultimate decision being, of course, God's. Concerning the salvation of those people who came before or after the time of the Prophet Muḥammad, but who did not come across his or another prophet's teachings in their lifetime, three opinions arose amongst the theologians. Māturīdī argued that reason alone should lead a person to monotheism even if no revelation via a prophet had reached him. This meant that the adherents of the Māturīdī school of theology argued that belief in the unity of God based upon reason was incumbent upon all people for their salvation[4] —with or without a prophet and before or after Muḥammad.

On the other hand, Ashᶜarī held that prophets (in other words, external revelation), were necessary for salvation. Therefore for him, belief in God was not a requirement for those who had not been reached by God's messengers (either directly or indirectly) in order to attain salvation.[5] It was on the basis of this school's doctrine that

1 This author prefers the term Paradise, rather than Heaven, which is reminiscent of Christian theological writings and is not a good translation for *Janna*.

2 Hermansen, 'Eschatology', in Winter, ed., *Cambridge Companion to Classical Islamic Theology*, p. 319.

3 For further information, see ibid., pp. 134–40.

4 Unless they are not of sound mind.

5 Rippin, *Muslims*, p. 71.

Ghazālī formulated the argument that non-Muslims could attain salvation on the condition that they had either not heard the message of the Prophet Muḥammad, or that Islam had not been accurately presented to them and they had not wilfully rejected it after learning about it.

The Atharī position on the possibility of salvation for non-Muslims was even more nuanced than that of the Ashʿarīs or Māturīdīs. The view of the Atharī scholar Ibn Taymiyya was that the intellect should be capable of discerning between what is right and what is wrong, and because of this the rational being should be able to arrive at a belief in God, Who alone is worthy of being worshipped. However, Ibn Taymiyya also argued that those who were never exposed to a prophetic message might not be punished by God, out of His infinite mercy and justice.[1]

Let us end this section by turning to what is known as the 'Vision of God' or the 'Beatific Vision' (*Ru'yā*). According to the Qur'ān and *Ḥadīth* literature, the men and women at the highest level of Paradise will be spiritually rewarded with a vision of God—a reward that has no equal. The Muʿtazilīs and the majority of Shiʿis have argued that because sight is corporeal, and given that God is neither an accident or a body, a vision of God cannot be possible, even in the Hereafter. However, the Atharīs, Ashʿarīs and Māturīdīs all agreed that this vision is real (although they differed in their precise interpretations[2]) and they concurred that this was the highest spiritual reward that any believer could attain in the *Dār al-Maqāma* (the Home That Will Last).[3] One *ḥadīth* describes this spiritual reward as follows: 'The

1 Cited by Yasir Qadhi, 'The Path of Allah or the Paths of Allah', in Mohammad Hassan Khalil, ed., *Between Heaven and Hell: Islam, Salvation, and the Fate of Others*, Oxford: Oxford University Press, 2013, p. 110.

2 The only difference between the Ashʿarīs and Māturīdīs was that Māturīdī said that people would see God, but not with eyesight, whereas Ashʿarī said that people would see their Lord with actual sight. For further information, see Elder, ed. and tr., *Commentary on the Creed of Islam*, pp. 72–79.

3 Hermansen, 'Eschatology', in Winter, ed., *Cambridge Companion to Classical Islamic Theology*, p. 319.

Messenger of God, may blessing and peace be upon him said: "After the people of paradise have entered paradise, He Who is Blessed and Exalted shall ask: 'Do you wish Me to give you anything more?' And they will reply: 'Have you not made us enter paradise and saved us from the fire?' He will then remove the veil, and nothing they were ever given will have been dearer to them than the vision of their Lord, the High, the Majestic.'"[1]

1 Ḥaddād, *The Lives of Man*, p. 80.

Chapter Seven

THE DIVINE DECREE

God's Secret within Creation

A Pew Research Center report published in 2012 indicated that, based on its surveys involving more than 38,000 face-to-face interviews with Muslims worldwide, Muslims overwhelmingly share a strong belief in fate or predestination. Regarding this specific belief, the report concludes, 'The expression "Inshallah" ("If God wills") is a common figure of speech among Muslims and reflects the Islamic tradition that the destiny of individuals, and the world, is in the hands of God. And indeed, the survey finds that the concept of predestination, or fate, is widely accepted among Muslims in most parts of the world. In four of the five regions where the question was asked, medians of about nine-in-ten (88% to 93%) say they believe in fate, while a median of 57% express this view in Southern and Eastern Europe.'[1]

However, this survey obscures the sixth article of faith—the belief in the divine decree (*qadar*)—as it translates this Arabic term as 'fate' or 'predestination'. This translation fails to even come close to what the Arabic term means with the result that understanding this topic (which is perhaps the most complex matter within all of Islamic theology), and understanding Muslims' perceptions of it, becomes even more convoluted. The most appropriate translation of *qadar* is 'divine decree', which is used by many scholars writing on this topic. This is very different to the meaning of the English terms 'fate' and 'predestination' found in the Pew report, both of

1 Pew Research Center report, 'The World's Muslims.'

which imply the idea of fatalism. Other Arabic terms used to refer to the divine decree are *taqdīr* (determination of measurement) and *al-qaḍā' wa'l-qadar* (divine will and divine decree). Correspondingly, references to a human being's free will or power of choice are given within the matrix of *al-qaḍā' wa'l-qadar* by means of terms like *ikhtiyār* (choice), *ṭalab* (desire), *kasb* (acquisition), or *irāda juz'iyya* (limited power of choice).

The difficulty of understanding the true meaning of *qadar* arises when the human intellect considers any of the components of the divine decree within a timeline. 'Predestination' and 'fate' are inappropriate terms in this context because, as we saw in Chapter Three, God is recognised as being the Creator of space and time and yet is not bound by them. Consequently, God's divine decree is not bound by these limited conceptions. Furthermore, the concept of fate makes one believe that the human being is totally devoid of free will, and that a person's actions are determined in advance by an impersonal force. Thus, terms such as predestination and fate are not suitable for the present discussion.

Even if we move the discussion away from the idea of fatalism, obstacles to fully understanding this article of faith remain. Perhaps the greatest obstacles comes from a number of the preoccupations of contemporary secular thought, particularly those related to the issue of free will. This issue is still a source of controversy in contemporary western thought, especially in the fields of philosophy and psychology. However, these debates are largely non-metaphysical discussions of whether human beings are genuinely free in their actions despite there being a mass of evidence pointing towards human actions being determined by biological and social factors beyond an individual's power.

Three main positions on free will are found within modern secular thought.[1] Firstly, advocates of contemporary libertarian theory

1 For an overview of these positions, see Joseph Keim Campbell, Michael O'Rourke, David Shier, eds., *Free Will and Determinism*, Cambridge, MA: MIT Press, 2004.

argue that human beings have genuine free will in their acts and are responsible for all of their actions. This is because, even though it may be that an individual has played an extremely minimal role in a given incident, when compared with other internal and external determining factors, that person is still free to make a morally undetermined decision. On the other hand, proponents of the theory of hard determinism—the second main position on the issue—argue that there really is no genuinely free will. This, consequently, leads one to the supposition that human beings cannot be held accountable for their actions, since their actions are in one way or another shaped by internal and external determining factors. The third theory is soft determinism, whose supporters contend that human behaviour and actions are wholly determined by causal events, with the caveat that human free will does exist when defined as the capacity to act according to one's own nature. This theory holds that human freedom and moral responsibility are far from being incompatible with determinism; rather, determinism is incomprehensible without them. The misconception that these two are incompatible, it is argued, is due to confusion over the concept of freedom, which itself is incompatible with fatalism but not with determinism.

In modern thought it is argued that all actions are wholly governed by causes, but there are two different types of causes. There are internal causes, such as motives and desires, which lead to voluntary actions of free will, and then there are external causes, which lead to involuntary actions of compulsion. Soft determinists therefore define freedom as the liberty of spontaneity—the freedom to act according to one's nature, which is determined by external factors such as heredity, education and background.[1] However, this theory has been criticised (in fact, as early as the sixth/twelfth century by Fakhr al-Dīn al-Rāzī) on the basis that any delineation of what constitutes an internal or external cause is inevitably highly simplistic

1 B. R. Hergenhahn, *An Introduction to the History of Psychology*, London: Cengage Learning, 2009, p. 16.

because the study of an individual's wishes and desires demonstrates that not only internal, but also external, causes figure prominently in the making of their so-called voluntary actions.[1]

This topic of free will and determinism is further complicated when it is approached from within metaphysical studies, which is how it is considered within Islam. The reason why the subject becomes a much more complicated issue is because we are dealing with an absolute divide between all things that are created and the Creator. In so many ways, this topic—by its very nature—defies complete conceptualisation, since *tawḥīd* means that there is nothing like God. Hence, any decision or determination by God with regards to creation can never be effortlessly articulated or wholly or adequately conceptualised by human experience and understanding.

Ṭaḥāwī wrote in his *Creed*, 'The essence of the divine decree is God's secret within creation. No intimate angel or prophetic emissary has ever been privy to it.'[2] What he meant by this was that there has to be a degree of theological sensitivity when approaching the topic. To delve into the topic of God's power is seen by most Sunni Muslims as claiming knowledge of the workings of the unseen when such knowledge, some argue, was not even given to the angels or the prophets. Despite this objection, it is clear that both the Qur'ān and various *ḥadīths* provide ample evidence of God's role as the ultimate creator and having power over everything that exists in creation, whether it be good or evil; so it is still possible to describe the divine decree and speculate about the relationship between divine and human agency.

Evidence of this kind comes from Qur'ānic verses such as VI.125, XIII.6, XXXVII.96 and XLV.23. As Yasin Ceylan has observed, these verses suggest that 'God is the Creator of man and his actions, that it is He who facilitates belief for the believers and unbelief for the

1 See further below for Fakhr al-Dīn al-Rāzī's thoughts about the divine decree and free will.

2 Ṭaḥāwī, *Creed of Imam al-Ṭaḥāwī*, p. 60 (Creed 57).

unbelievers and that the ultimate decision has already been taken for future events'[1] and so on. Yet, at the same time, the scriptural sources also speak frequently of human beings having free will. Many verses of the Qur'ān, such as II.79, II.225, XII.18, XIII.11, XX.15, XXVII.90, LV.60 and LXXXVI.29, support the idea that human beings are responsible for their own actions.[2] There are also many *ḥadīth*s in which the Prophet informed his Companions about the reality of the divine decree and there are many other *ḥadīth*s that deal with human responsibility for human actions.[3] It is very clear from the earliest historical sources that these two apparently contradictory notions were understood side by side without any major challenge from the earliest Muslims.[4] In connection with this, it is interesting to note that while the Prophet spoke about belief in the divine decree in many *ḥadīths*,[5] when a few of the Companions began to discuss the contradictory nature of the topic, he reprimanded them and told not to engage in such a discussion.[6]

Perhaps this is why scholars such as Yaḥyā b. Sharaf al-Nawawī (d. 676/1277)—whose description of the divine decree remains one of the clearest in the classical theological literature—did not write about the more complex aspects of the divine decree and human free will. Nawawī wrote in his famous *ḥadīth* compilation and commentary, *Kitāb al-arbaᶜīn* (Forty Ḥadīths), that the meaning of the divine decree 'is that God has decreed things from eternity', which means beyond the limits of space and time. He then continued, 'And He knows they

1 Yasin Ceylan, *Theology and Tafsīr in the Major Works of Fakhr al-Dīn al-Rāzī*, Kuala Lumpur: International Institute of Islamic Thought and Civilization, 1996, p. 164.

2 Ibid.

3 For example, see Tirmidhī, '*Kitāb al-Qadar*', in *Jāmiᶜ al-Tirmidhī*, XXXII, http://sunnah.com/tirmidhi/32, 22 February 2016.

4 See Yusuf, introduction to Ṭaḥāwī, *Creed of Imam al-Ṭaḥāwī*, p. 19.

5 Such as the *ḥadīth*s in book 32 of Tirmidhī's *Jāmiᶜ al-Tirmidhī* cited above.

6 Abdur Rashid Bhat, 'Free Will and Determinism: An Overview of Muslim Scholars' Perspective', *Journal of Islamic Philosophy*, volume II, no. 1, 2006, pp. 7–24. See also Sulaymān Nadvī, *Sirat ul Nabi*, trans. Mohammad Saeed Siddiqui, New Delhi: Kitab Bhavan India, 2004, vol. III, p. 152.

will happen at times and places known to Him. Also they will happen in accord with His decree [will].'[1]

Nawawī described four kinds of divine decrees. The first kind, he wrote, is that which subsists in divine knowledge; in other words, God has knowledge of everything. Secondly, there is the decree that is inscribed on the Preserved Tablet (*Lawḥ Maḥfūẓ*). Decrees of this kind are susceptible to change only if God wills it, based upon the verse in the Qur'ān that says, 'God erases whatever He desires and He affirms. The Mother of the Book is His.'[2] The third kind of decree is that in the womb, where 'the angel is commanded to write down for a foetus its provision, its lifespan, and its miserable or prosperous end'.[3] Finally, there is the fourth decree, which is that God is the Creator of everything, both good and evil, and all is willed (decreed) by Him. On this, Nawawī wrote, 'This category of decree may be averted from man before the time of its arrival, if divine grace supervenes', and then he proceeded to cite the following *ḥadīth*: 'Between heaven and earth, prayer and misfortune struggle, and prayer may cancel misfortune before it occurs.'[4]

Though Nawawī's overview of the divine decree is very helpful, it gives no hint of the heated theological disputes over the divine decree and human free will that had taken place several centuries earlier. These disputes proved to be critical to the development of Muslim theological doctrine and it is to them that we turn next.

Between Free Will and Determinism

Nearly half a century after the death of the Prophet, this tenet of the Muslim creed was very aggressively brought into dispute in connection with the contentious events which gave rise to the *kalām* tradition. During this politically charged period (which commenced

1 Norman Calder, Jawid Mojaddedi and Andrew Rippin, eds., *Classical Islam: A Sourcebook of Religious Literature*, London: Routledge, 2012, p. 145.

2 Q.XIII.39.

3 Calder, Mojaddedi and Rippin, eds., *Classical Islam*, p. 145.

4 Ibid.

during the late first/seventh century), a major theological controversy arose between various factions concerning whether they believed in *jabr* (literally, 'compulsion', but used as a technical term to indicate 'determination' or 'fate') or *ikhtiyār* (literally, 'choice', but used as a technical term for 'free will'). The controversy over these two positions arose alongside the wider political debate about the legitimacy of the Umayyad leadership, and it prompted many theologians from the Athariyya, Ashʿariyya and Māturīdiyya schools to write treatises defending the belief in the divine decree while at the same time stressing human responsibility. Nonetheless, most theologians recognised that there was a limit to how much human beings could understand about the divine decree.

The tension between free will and determinism led to the first theological dispute in Islamic intellectual history. However, it is important to appreciate that it arose against the backdrop of political challenges to the Umayyad dynasty's authority. In fact, many of the individuals who argued for absolute free will were embroiled in politics and used their free will argument to challenge what they believed to be the unjust rule of the Umayyad dynasty. The case put forth for free will was that rulers should not be able to relinquish responsibility for their own unjust actions on the basis of a belief in an inevitable divine decree. The first recorded advocate of this opinion was Maʿbad al-Juhanī (d. 80/699), founder of the Qadariyya school of thought. He asserted that human beings determined their own actions; not the divine decree. In time, this view came to be refined by the later school of theology, the Muʿtazila. Eventually, Juhanī and his follower Ghaylān al-Dimashqī (d. c. 100/719) were executed by order of the Umayyad Caliphs ʿAbd al-Malik (r. 65–86/685–705) and Hishām (r. 105–125/724–743), on the grounds that they were a threat to the stability of political order.[1]

Some evidence seems to point towards the notion of fatalism or unqualified predestination being utilised in some form to defend the

1 Ibid., pp.47–49.

Umayyad dynasty. The proponents of such a theological view were known as the Jabariyya, due to their belief in an unqualified doctrine of fatalism (*jabr*). The Jabariyya denied that there was human free will or choice, and they argued that human beings were under the control of God just like inanimate beings. They further held that attributing actions to human beings should only be done figuratively, not literally. Hence, they described human actions in the same way as saying that plants grow or the sun rises. This meant that human beings were not responsible for their own actions.[1]

It is important to recognise that this perspective was not accepted by the majority of Muslims at the time, and today there are no representatives of either the Qadariyya or the Jabariyya. Yet it is worth noting that during the nineteenth and early twentieth centuries, Orientalist scholars charged Muslims with adhering to a creed of fatalism similar to that of the Jabariyya. Although there were some Orientalist scholars who argued that the Muslim faith was not fatalistic, they still believed that, in practice, Muslims had become fatalistic. Such an Orientalist scholar was the Reverend W. Gardner, who in 1916 wrote in his treatise, *The Qur'anic Doctrine of God*, that his research had demonstrated that the Islamic sources did in fact support a free will doctrine and not predestination. He wrote, 'The development of the orthodox Muḥammadan doctrine of Predestination which, if it is not itself fatalistic, has, in practice, at least, led to fatalism, appears to be a wrong interpretation of the Qur'anic teachings.'[2]

By contrast, in 1945, another Orientalist scholar, J. Windrow Sweetman, proposed an opposing argument to Reverend W. Gardner, concluding that the sources themselves taught predestination and that therefore orthodox Muslim belief was highly fatalistic. He explained, '[T]hough they were possessed of free will, there is overwhelming evidence for the Qur'anic teaching of predestination, and therefore the

1 Ṭaḥāwī, *Creed of Imam al-Ṭaḥāwī*, p. 124.

2 W. R. W. Gardner, *The Qur'anic Doctrine of God*, Colombo: Christian Literature Society of India, 1916, p. 95.

orthodox Muslim teaching on this point is really rooted in the Islamic scripture.'[1] Sweetman admitted that he found the views of the Jabariyya and what he referred to as 'the orthodox Muslim' difficult to differentiate: 'It is sometimes hard to differentiate between this orthodox view and that heretical theory which is supposed to be at the furthest extreme from the Qadarite position, namely, the Jabarite heresy, which holds that a man is absolutely compelled in all his actions.'[2] It seems that most Orientalist scholars of the time were unable to distinguish between the nuanced differences that existed amongst Muslims with regard to the belief in predestination and the divine decree.

One of the main reasons for this misunderstanding amongst Orientalist writers was that they never seemed to have recognised that the historical sources also reveal a third majority opinion amongst Muslims, according to which the divine decree and free will were seen as existing side by side, as understood by the Prophet and his followers. One of the main proponents of this position during the turbulent early period of Islam was the traditionist scholar al-Ḥasan al-Baṣrī.[3] According to Hamza Yusuf, al-Ḥasan al-Baṣrī held that free will and the divine decree should only be 'understood within the conceptual space of antinomies, i.e. propositions, which in formal logic, are mutually exclusive without being irrational'.[4] This view would be formulated and systematised in more detail two centuries later by the two towering theologians Abū al-Ḥasan al-Ashʿarī and Abū Manṣūr al-Māturīdī.

The Muʿtazilī Position on the Divine Decree

Even though the Qadariyya school of theology did not survive very long, the majority of their views were taken up by the Muʿtazila, including the notion that human beings were the creators of their

1 J. Windrow Sweetman, *Islam and Christian Theology*, London: Lutterworth Press, 1945, vol. II, pp. 162–63.

2 Ibid., p. 169.

3 Fakhry, *History of Islamic Philosophy*, pp. 43–48.

4 Yusuf, introduction to *Creed of Imam al-Ṭaḥāwī*, p. 19.

own actions. Interestingly, the founder of the Muʿtazila, Wāṣil b. ʿAṭāʾ, had originally been a student of al-Ḥasan al-Baṣrī, but during a disagreement with his teacher about a matter of creed, Wāṣil b. ʿAṭāʾ withdrew from the gathering and created his own circle. It is reported that al-Ḥasan al-Baṣrī said, 'He has withdrawn (*iʿtazala*) from us', and this is how this group was given the name *Muʿtazila*.[1]

Over the next two centuries, the Muʿtazilīs created a complex theology heavily influenced by Hellenistic thinking, in which they fine-tuned the idea of man as the creator of his own actions. It is argued by Fakhry that it was their insistence on demonstrating the all-pervasive justice of God that led their thinkers to try to resolve what they saw as problems raised by the idea of God's unlimited sovereignty. In addition, their thought developed in response to the Jabariyya. For instance, Wāṣil b. ʿAṭāʾ was a contemporary of Jahm Ibn Ṣafwān, whose position on fatalism must have provoked an intense reaction from Wāṣil and his followers because they would have felt the need to repudiate what they saw as unfairness to the idea of God's justice and wisdom. This evoked within the Muʿtazila a strong urge to emphasise the concept of human responsibility.[2] They argued that God cannot command what is contrary to reason or act with complete indifference to the welfare of His creation. This led the Muʿtazilīs to propose that human beings have the capacity to act freely in this world, and they developed a number of theories to elaborate on this thesis.

The Muʿtazilī scholar Bishr b. al-Muʿtamir (d. 210/825) argued that all deeds were 'engendered' (this idea was referred to as *tawallud*) through a causal relationship between the agent (the human being) and the act, and that all ensuing acts generated by that first act were also attributable to the agent. However, his fellow scholar Abū al-Hudhayl al-ʿAllāf (d. 226/841) thought that the generation of an act by a human being could be divided into two aspects:

1 Ibid.

2 Fakhry, *History of Islamic Philosophy*, p. 51.

those acts whose modality (*kayfiyya*) is known and those acts whose modality is unknown. By this, he meant that acts whose modality was known, such as the flight of an arrow or the impact of two solid objects, should be attributed to humans, whereas acts such as pleasure, hunger, knowledge or smell, whose modality was unknown, must be attributed to God. Although these two Muʿtazilī scholars disagreed on how to define a human act, they both agreed that it was down to the individual to inwardly will and choose, and that an individual was able to outwardly accomplish or cause acts through his will alone.[1] As Khalid Blankinship has put it, the Muʿtazilīs believed that 'God only creates in humans the power or ability to act, not the acts themselves'.[2] This meant that the fate of human beings lay entirely in their own hands.

Furthermore, Muʿtazilī theology inadvertently led to a belief in an impersonal God, a force whose justice was mechanistic. This was because they argued that God had to systematically judge every person on the basis of their deeds, and that an unrepentant person could not escape this mechanistic justice. Consequently, they believed that no concept of a personal deity could exist, that there was no unlimited mercy by God and no intercession by the Prophet.[3]

Other scholars from the Muʿtazilī school of theology, such as Ibrāhīm al-Naẓẓām (d. 220/835), Muʿammar b. ʿAbbād (d. 215/830) and Thumāma b. Ashras (d. 213/828), all proposed their own theories in support of the idea of free will. It could be argued that by positing the theory of *kumūn* (latency), Naẓẓām may have been the first to come close to what would later become known as Enlightenment Deism in seventeenth-century Europe. According to this theory, God is only seen as being indirectly involved in each act in the world, whereas each act is directly linked to secondary

1 Ibid., pp. 44–49.

2 Khalid Blankinship, 'The Early Creed', in T. J. Winter, ed., *The Cambridge Companion to Classical Islamic Theology*, Cambridge: Cambridge Press, 2008, p. 50.

3 Ibid., pp. 49–50.

natural agents. This means that God does not intervene directly. In third-/ninth-century Iraq, this view was heavily criticised from within and from without Muʿtazilī circles. One such critic was the later Muʿtazilī scholar Abū ʿAlī al-Jubbāʾī (d. 302/915), who instead advanced the idea that God could grant unmerited grace (*tafaḍḍul*) to whomever He wanted, which was an attempt to soften this mechanistic understanding of God.[1]

There is ample evidence that there was great diversity in the theories of Muʿtazilī thinkers; nevertheless, they all agreed upon the fundamental idea of absolute free will, which they connected to the concept of justice. Hamza Yusuf explains this as follows: 'They fixed upon heaven the mandates of earth, arguing that earthly justice must, by necessity, be true of heaven. They felt it would be unjust of God to determine the lives of men and then punish them for their predetermined actions. They believed that a person's final destiny was a result of his own actions; he was justly punished if immoral or justly rewarded if upright. And because justice necessitated that God does what is best for man, they believed that sending messengers was God's obligation to man.'[2]

A reaction to the ideas of the Muʿtazila came from the Atharī, who completely rejected the Muʿtazilī concept of free will on the grounds that it compromised God's majesty, power and sovereignty. Blankinship describes the traditionalist response to this Muʿtazilī vision of God's justice in the following terms: 'The mechanistic image of a deity constrained by His own laws and incapable of true mercy because of the demand for absolute mathematical requital of deeds appalled them…'[3] The traditionalists were in total agreement that God could not be constrained by anything and that He had ultimate power. However, and as had been the case with other

1 Ibid., p. 51.

2 Yusuf, introduction to *Creed of Imam al-Ṭaḥāwī*, p. 20.

3 Blankinship, 'The Early Creed', in Winter, ed., *Cambridge Companion to Classical Islamic Theology*, p. 52.

contentious issues, the decisive formulation within Sunnism of how the divine decree and free will could be understood side by side was presented by Abū al-Ḥasan al-Ashʿarī and Abū Manṣūr al-Māturīdī.

The Middle Ground

Abū al-Ḥasan al-Ashʿarī was originally a Muʿtazilī student of Abū ʿAlī al-Jubbā'ī, who, as seen above, had himself moved significantly away from some of the major Muʿtazilī positions. Ashʿarī eventually broke away from his teacher and the Muʿtazilīs, and began to advocate Atharī theological positions on various issues. However, he did so with highly developed methods of argumentation based on those used by the Muʿtazila, and on account of this methodology the new Ashʿariyya school of theology arose.[1] Ashʿarī's role was to attempt to reconcile divine sovereignty with human responsibility by denying any limitations on the divine. Thus, according to Ashʿarī, God was not obligated to anyone nor was He constrained by anything. Moreover, God was the sole and absolute Creator of all human actions, as well as the Creator of the power (*qudra*) and choice (*ikhtiyār*) that are acquired and exercised by human beings. Hence, all actions, be they recognised as good or evil, were the creation of God; but although action, power and choice are created by God, it is the human being who acquires the act, and for that they are held responsible. Nazif Muhtaroglu observes that 'if we examine Ashʿarī's view of human actions, we see that he divides them into two groups: voluntary and involuntary human actions. Involuntary actions are performed under compulsion, which we intuitively feel, such as trembling, for instance. God creates these actions and people have no effect on them. However, regarding voluntary human actions, Ashʿarī makes a distinction: the creation of them by God and the acquisition of them by humans. Humans freely acquire the actions created by God.'[2]

1 Ibid., p. 53.

2 Nazif Muhtaroglu, 'An Occasionalist Defence of Free Will', in Anna-Teresa Tymieniecka and Nazif Muhtaroglu, eds., *Classic Issues in Islamic Philosophy and Theology Today*, London: Springer, 2010, p. 48.

This theory of acquisition (*kasb*) was inferred from the Qur'ān; according to it, human beings only *perform* an action, whereas the action is in fact created by God. Thus, God alone is recognised as the Creator or Agent (*Fāʿil*) Who determines, through a created power (*qudra*), the individual existence of each act in all its particulars. Yet this act is created in order to be acquired and performed by a creature, so it cannot be seen as God's own act. Hence, Abū al-Ḥasan al-Ashʿarī was arguing that any action created by God could not be predicated on God. In other words, one could not say that God did it, but rather that the person who performed the act did it.

According to the Ashʿarīs, power could either be classified as eternal (*qadīm*) or originated (*muḥdath*). God's power is eternal and it is only through His power that anything can be created, whereas originated power cannot create. It is this power that is given to human beings, and as such is derived or originated. God creates the power and ability for the human being to perform an act; He also makes it possible for each to choose freely, and this is simultaneously acquired.[1] The later Ashʿarī scholar Bāqillānī modified this view by stating that all actions, whether good or bad, were created by God, but that what made these actions good or bad was a human being's own initiative.[2]

During the same period as Abū al-Ḥasan al-Ashʿarī, Abū Manṣūr al-Māturīdī also developed a theory of acquisition (*kasb*). However, due to his location in Samarqand, far removed from the Islamic intellectual centres of the time, his ideas about human agency did not become widely known in the Muslim world until nearly two centuries later.[3] He wrote about *kasb* in his book, *Kitāb al-tawḥīd* (The Book of Divine Unity); in fact, his discussion of human acts covers about a quarter of the entire text, which demonstrates the

1 See Abū al-Ḥasan al-Ashʿarī, *Kitāb al-lumaʿ fi al-radd ʿalā Ahl al-Zaygh wa'l-Bidaʿ*, ed. and trans. Richard Joseph McCarthy, Beirut: al-Maktaba al-Kāthūlīkiyya, 1952.

2 Ceylan, *Theology and Tafsīr*, p. 157.

3 Rippin, *Muslims*, p. 86.

importance of this topic at the time. He argued that, according to the Qur'ān, there is no doubt that God is the Creator of everything and, as actions exist, they too are considered 'things'. In other words, Māturīdī considered all actions to be God's creation and therefore all human acts to fall under the creative power of God. He described the created nature of the act and its relationship to the human being through *kasb*. The second principle that Māturīdī proposed on this issue—clearly inferred from the Qur'ān as well—was that every individual instinctively knew within their own mind that they were free (*mukhtār*) in what they did. He argued that this did not need any proof since this simply was the case.[1]

According to Māturīdī, human beings have been created with a natural disposition (*fiṭra*), an intellect, the capacity to will, think, judge and choose, along with the power to distinguish between what is right and wrong. He placed due emphasis on the first capacity of human beings, which he said was the power or 'aptness for action' (*qudra*); that is, the means to act that exists within a person prior to any action. The second capacity of human beings was freedom of choice (*ikhtiyār*), which has been granted by God and exists specifically for an act, and comes to be simultaneously with it. His argument was that freedom of choice alone was where rewards or punishments for human actions could be attached, whereas the necessary power to perform the act (*iktisāb*) was not emphasised. He wrote—with regards to reconciling human freedom with the Qur'ānic conception of divine will, infinite power and eternal decree—that when an individual exercises his reason, chooses and intends to perform an action, it is God Who creates that action, making the individual an agent and a performer of this action, whilst the individual should also recognise that the same action is created by God. In this sense, a human being acquires and performs a created action with his own will (*irāda*).[2]

1 J. Meric Pessagno, '*Irāda, Ikhtiyār, Qudra, Kasb*: The View of Abū Manṣūr al-Māturīdī', *Journal of the American Oriental Society*, vol. CIV, no. 1, January–March 1984, pp. 177–91.

2 Ibid.

In this theology, an emphasis is also placed on the argument that God's willing or creating an evil action cannot be seen as repugnant in His wisdom, because He wills it in accordance with an individual's exercise of free choice. There are clear demarcations of evil deeds that are prohibited in Islam, but it is recognised that individuals have the autonomy to commit a sin. Hence, even though sins are in accordance with what is willed by the divine, this does not indicate that these actions are in any way in accordance with divine guidance or pleasure. These actions are recognised as breaching the *Sharīʿa* and so an individual is held accountable for his acquisition and performance of the act in question through his free will. From this conclusion, Māturīdī held that the basis of man's obligation (*taklīf*) to God lay in his freedom of choice and acquisition, and not in relation to the issue of whether he possessed the power to create his own actions.[1]

The general theory of *kasb* was not only embraced by the Ashʿarīs and the Māturīdīs but, thanks to the efforts of Ṭaḥāwī, it was also embraced by the Atharī school of theology, whose adherents generally censured much of the speculative thinking produced by the other two schools. Ṭaḥāwī wrote in his *Creed*:

> All will act in accordance with their design and are moving inexorably toward the purpose for which they were created. Welfare and affliction, good and evil are determined for everyone. The [divine enablement] that an act requires—for example, an act of obedience—which cannot be attributed to a creature, occurs concurrent with the act. As for the [material] enablement that results from health, capacity, poise and sound means, it precedes the act. In sacred law, it is upon the latter that

1 See Abū Manṣūr al-Māturīdī, *Kitāb al-tawḥīd*, ed. Fatḥ Allāh Khulayf, Beirut: Dār al-Mashriq, 1970, p. 256.

> legal and moral obligation hinge, just as God, the Sublime and Exalted, states 'God obliges no soul with more than its capacity' (Qur'ān 2:228). Human actions are God's creations but humanity's acquisitions [*kasb*].[1]

However, even when writing the above, Ṭaḥāwī also included in his book (as mentioned earlier), 'The essence of the divine decree is God's secret within creation. No intimate angel or prophetic emissary has ever been privy to it.'[2]

This secret, or rather the inability of humanity to explain the manner of 'determining' by the divine decree, led Ghazālī to argue that any scheme or attempt to explain it was, in the end, only a metaphor, since the divine ordering could not be truly comprehended in any human scheme.[3] In his *Kitāb al-tawḥīd wa'l-tawakkul* (Faith in Divine Unity and Trust in Divine Providence), Ghazālī asked his readers how there could be any common ground between divine unity and the sacred law.[4] What he was implying was that, according to the accepted understanding of *tāwḥīd* (divine unity), there is no power but God and He is the only agent; but in the *Sharīʿa*, the individual human being is recognised as an agent and therefore considered responsible for his actions. Hence, how could the same term—namely, 'agent' (*fāʿil*)—be used for the Creator and the created?

Ghazālī answered this question by explaining that the term 'agent' had two meanings; on the one hand, God is the agent as the Originator and on the other, the human being is seen as an

1 Ṭaḥāwī, *Creed of Imam al-Ṭaḥāwī*, pp. 72–73 (Creed 104–07).

2 Ibid., p. 60 (Creed 57).

3 David B. Burrell, 'Creation', in T. J. Winter, ed., *The Cambridge Companion to Classical Islamic Theology*, Cambridge: Cambridge Press, 2008, p. 155.

4 See Ghazālī, *Kitāb al-tawḥīd wa'l-tawakkul*, trans. David B. Burrell as *Faith in Divine Unity and Trust in Divine Providence, The Revival of the Religious Sciences*, Book xxxv, Louisville, KY: Fons Vitae, 2001, p. 43.

agent in the sense of being the locus (*maḥal*) in which power is created. It is clear from this distinction that Ghazālī was repeating the scheme developed by Ashʿarī. He then went on to say that the true and correct understanding of Reality was to know that all acting relates to God, whereas statements which attribute it to anything other than God (such as, 'This person threw the stone') are in fact figurative expressions. The practice of using figurative expressions and metaphors in this way, Ghazālī said, was in fact the legacy of linguists, who had misappropriated the term 'agent' by applying it to created beings. However, he reiterated, the term 'agent' can truly only belong to God, although metaphorically it may be applied to anyone else.

In order to clarify these two meanings of the word 'agent', Ghazālī cited the following verses from the Qur'ān: 'It is not ye who slew them; it was God. When thou threwest (a handful of dust), it was not thy act, but God's in order that He might test the believers by a gracious trial from Himself, for God is He Who heareth and knoweth (all things).'[1] Ghazālī then asked, 'Does this verse then not lead to a belief in *jabr* (coercion) and what is to be said about human responsibility?'[2] He responded by stating that a firmly held conviction in divine unity brings about the realisation that everything happens according to a wise and ordained order. But he warned that this truth was like an immensely deep sea with vast dangers and chaotic swells, which could bring about confusion to any mind. Due to this complex reality, Ghazālī informed his readers that even though one can state the various creeds about the divine decree, and the place of human responsibility, the only true unveiling of it comes from living with trust in divine providence (*tawakkul*), which will enlighten the believer in such a way that he recognises that there is no power (agent) but God.[3]

1 Q.VIII.17.
2 Ghazālī, *Faith in Divine Unity*, p. 43.
3 Ibid.

Occasionalism and the Divine Decree

At the same time as the debate about determinism and free will was going on, another directly related controversy over causation had arisen within the branch of theology known as *daqīq al-kalām*. The Ashʿarīs, and later the Māturīdīs (with some modifications), advanced a theological doctrine called occasionalism or atomism, by means of which they attempted to explain all phenomena in terms of the divine decree. By the middle of the third/ninth century atomism was firmly established as the main theory of the theologians. The philosophers, including Ibn Sīnā and, later, Ibn Rushd, had argued that there were two kinds of causes: immediate and secondary. But the Ashʿarī and the Māturīdī theologians rejected this idea of secondary causality and instead argued that there was no real causation in the world. They argued that creation—meaning everything other than God—consisted of transitory elements, atoms and accidents, created and recreated from one instant to another. Despite the universe being an inseparable whole with all its parts connected to one another, there was no real causality. Consequently, no causes could exist in isolation and instead all had to be understood in a holistic manner.[1]

Ghazālī went on to oppose the philosophers' idea that there were two kinds of causes, and instead argued that God causes all things to exist and continually recreates them if He wishes them to remain in existence. Since a cause and its effect exist for too short a time for a significant connection to take place between them, one can only say that the effect occurs with the cause (*maʿahu*) rather than by it (*bihi*). Hence, it is important to recognise that there is no such thing as a natural causality; although it could be said that one act or event may predictably give rise to another act or event, but only because it is recognised that God's actions in creation are consistent. However, Ghazālī further argued that there was no reason to assume, for instance, that the next time a person sees a fire he will necessar-

1 Mohammad Hashim Kamali, 'Causality and Divine Action: The Islamic Perspective', http://www.ghazali.org/articles/kamali.htm, accessed 10 July 2013.

ily also observe burning along with it because it is only God Who consistently associates fire with burning, but it is within His power to uncouple this association at any time.[1]

However, the philosophers disagreed with Ghazālī's line of reasoning and argued instead for real causality. Ibn Rushd stated that to deny the logical status of causality was to deny knowledge. His argument was that even though God was the ultimate cause of everything, He had still established a secondary cause for every phenomenon. Ibn Rushd argued that even though God could bring anything into being at any time, He did not normally do so, and when He did, it was known as a miracle and was beyond the reach of the human intellect.[2]

Even though Ashʿarī's theory of occasionalism was the first widely disseminated theory of its type in the Muslim world, it was Maturīdī's idea of the reality and purposefulness of harmful substances in the divine scheme, and the wisdom behind them, that became uniquely utilised to explain the doctrine of divine decree. In his writings, Maturīdī was unparalleled in giving the raison d'être for the existence of harmful things in the universe. He argued:

> Even though human understanding is incapable of comprehending the nature of the wisdom of Lordship, the wisdom of God regarding the creation of good things and harmful substances is known from the aspects of trial (*al-miḥna*) by what is harmful and the

1 In light of modern physics, it appears that the classical Islamic theory of atomism needs to be revisited. See Walter J. Schultz and Lisanne D'Andrea Winslow, 'Divine Compositionalism: A Form of Occasionalism or a Preferable Alternative View of Divine Action?', paper presented at the Occasionalism East and West conference, Harvard University, May 4–5, 2013, available online, http://occasionalism.org/wp-content/uploads/2012/11/SCHULTZ-WINSLOW-PAPER.pdf, accessed 20 February 2016.

2 Mohammad Hashim Kamali, 'Causality and Divine Action: The Islamic Perspective', http://www.ghazali.org/articles/kamali.htm, accessed 10 July 2013.

> benefits to be derived from present realities so that by both one may know the pleasure of the reward for obedience and the pains of punishment for disobedience. This is in accord with the preceding statement about each thing, as God created it, being necessarily an act of wisdom, even if its quiddity is not known. Since creatures were created to face the consequence of their actions, God made from what can be seen an exemplar for these consequences so that what was promised could be pictured in man's imaginations and the way to Paradise thereby made easy for him.[1]

Maturīdī thus dealt with the question of theodicy by arguing that evil or harmful things were a function of wisdom. Perceived injustices were attributed to either a lack of full understanding of a situation or simply to moral evil, which was always committed in violation of the divine command. This violation was attributed to a human being's ability to acquire and perform these actions as his own. According to this theological view, creation was a testing ground, and so harmful things had a purpose as a means to knowledge about, and justification for, the Hereafter. Maturīdī further commented: 'Someone may say: it is evil to command acts of disobedience why is it not equally evil to will their existence? One should say in response: it is not evil to do this for several reasons. First, to command disobedience would be a contradiction, but that is not the case in willing its simple existence because action is sometimes done according to command and sometimes against it. But to command disobedience would be absurd because that action done by order would then become an act of obedience. So the idea of disobedience would be non-existent since it would be done in

1 Translation from J. Meric Pessagno, 'The Uses of Evil in Māturīdīan Thought', *Studia Islamica,* vol. LX, 1984, p. 76, citing Māturīdī, *Kitāb al-tawḥīd.*

accord with the command to be disobedient. That is not the case with willing something's existence.'[1]

The celebrated theologian Fakhr al-Dīn al-Rāzī followed in the footsteps of his predecessor Ghazālī a century later by insisting that accepting the divine decree meant believing that God created all of the actions of humanity. In his later years, Rāzī argued that after rationally considering all of the verses of the Qur'ān relating to free will and the divine decree, he thought that there was conclusive rational proof to support a literal interpretation of the following verse from *Sūrat al-Anᶜām*: 'That is God, your Lord! There is no god but He, the Creator of all things; then worship ye Him. And He hath power to dispose of all affairs.'[2] This verse, he wrote in his famous exegesis of the Qur'ān, *al-Tafsīr al-kabīr*, denotes the belief that God not only creates the actions of humanity, but also the motivation behind their acts. At the moment when power and motivation are joined, the action occurs, which proves that God is the absolute Creator of all creatures' acts.[3] Furthermore, he challenged the views of Ashᶜarī on the theory of *kasb/iktisāb* by stating that the concept of acquisition was ambiguous and without true meaning.

Rāzī also disapproved of Bāqillānī's theory of human will, motive or initiative being the characteristic quality of human actions. In other words, since a human being has no power to create or avert causal factor(s) which leads to the action, so by logical implication it must be argued that he cannot be seen as the sole initiator of any act. Hence, Rāzī argued that motives arise from the agent's own mental states, which are determined by both internal and external factors.[4] He supported his argument by citing environ-

1 Ibid.

2 Q.vi.102. See also Fakhr al-Dīn al-Rāzi, *Tafsīr mafātiḥ al-ghayb / al-Tafsīr al-kabīr*, http://www.altafsir.com/Tafasir.asp?tMadhNo=0&tTafsirNo=4&tSoraNo=6&tAyahNo=102&tDisplay=yes&UserProfile=0&LanguageId=1, accessed 1 July 2013.

3 Burrell, 'Creation', in Winter, ed., *Cambridge Companion to Classical Islamic Theology*, pp. 155–56, citing Rāzī, *al-Tafsīr al-kabīr*.

4 Ceylan, *Theology and Tafsīr*, pp. 161–62.

mental and hereditary factors, such as one's human characteristics (based upon the variance in human souls), physiognomic variation, temperament, habit and mental ability, arguing that these factors determined much of a human being's motivations and actions. He contended that all of these various factors determined a person's character, whereas unintentional external conditions, perceived through the senses, served more as a direct factor in the making of individual motives. As a result of this, it was clear to him that a human being's own will has no control over these factors. He further maintained that even if a person were able to change their own behaviour in spite of all the above factors, and was even able to abandon a particular enforced causal decision, he would in fact be acting not from his own free will, but due to some other introduced determinants that he would be powerless to overcome. What this meant was that if a factor was challenged or neutralised, then this was itself an outcome of another factor or set of factors, not of one's own free will.[1]

It is nevertheless important not to mistake Rāzī's opinions with those of the Jabariyya school of theology, since the Jabariyya persistently claimed not only that God determined all things, but also that human beings could not be held at all responsible for their actions because, rationally, their actions were not carried out due to their will. Moreover, Rāzī criticised this kind of deterministic notion proposed by Jahm Ibn Ṣafwān and other scholars amongst the Jabariyya. Rāzī argued that he was not one of the Jabariyya because he recognised that human beings act in accordance with their will, notwithstanding the fact that a person's will was ultimately determined by divine decree.[2] Here lies the crux of Rāzī's argument (which was not that dissimilar to Ghazālī's): the acceptance of human responsibility can only be understood within the wider spectrum of the divine decree, which is a paradox. He states:

1 Shihadeh, *Teleological Ethics*, p. 31.
2 Ibid., p. 38.

There is a mystery (*sirr*) in [this issue]; viz. that proving the existence of God compels one to uphold determinism (*jabr*), ... while proving prophecy compels one to uphold [human] autonomy (*qudra*). For if man does not act autonomously, what use is there in sending prophets and in revealing scriptures?

Indeed there is even yet another mystery here, which surpasses all; viz. that if we return to sound primordial nature and primary intellect (*al-ʿaql al-awwal*), we will find that when existence and non-existence are on a par in relation to something, neither will preponderate over the other without a preponderator—which leads to determinism. Yet we also find a self-evident distinction between voluntary movements and movements by compulsion, and a self-evident certitude in the goodness of praise and the badness of blame, and in command and prohibition; and this leads to the doctrine of the Muʿtazila.

It is as though this question falls in the sphere of contradiction (*fī ḥayyiz al-taʿārruḍ*), in relation to both immediate and discursive knowledge, in relation to proclaiming the greatness (*taʿẓīm*) of God, with reference to His power and wisdom, in relation to upholding divine unity and de-anthropomorphism (*tanzīh*), and in relation to scriptural proofs... The question is thus difficult and obscure. We pray God guide us to truth![1]

1 Fakhr al-Dīn al-Rāzi, *Tafsīr Mafātiḥ al-Ghayb al-Tafsīr al-Kabīr*, cited by Shihadeh, *The Teleological Ethics*, pp. 38–39.

It should be clear from this historical survey of early theological debates on the divine decree that defending the idea of divine power—and that of human free will and responsibility—became a central focus after various sects took up extremely polarised positions. For example, the Muʿtazila rejected God's unlimited sovereignty and defended human free will or responsibility instead; while the theologians Abū Manṣūr al-Māturīdī and Abū al-Ḥasan al-Ashʿarī were the first to propose theories that tried to balance these two concepts. They did so by stating that God created everything, including human actions, but at the same time they were able to theorise about how human beings could still be responsible for their actions. The mainstream theological consensus on the issue shifted during the early post-classical era, when Ghazālī and Fakhr al-Dīn al-Rāzī demonstrated the complexity of what qualified as human choice and action in comparison with the vast and immeasurable divine decree. They came to a similar conclusion as had Ashʿarī and Māturīdī that the belief in the divine decree is an antinomy; namely, that there was a seeming contradiction between the divine decree and human autonomy despite each being perfectly reasonable to believe in. They resolved this contradiction by explaining that, due to the inadequacy of human rational abilities in the field of metaphysics, the two conclusions might appear to contradict one another, but that in reality no real paradox existed. According to Ghazālī, this creed could only be understood intuitively by living a life of trust in divine providence; according to Rāzī, all rigorous reasoning leads one to conclude that enlightenment on the issue may only be reached through the divine. Many later scholars such as Saʿd al-Dīn al-Taftāzānī (d. 792/1390), Abū ʿAbd Allāh Muḥammad al-Sanūsī (d. 895/1489), Muḥammad b. Pīr ʿAlī—better known as Imam Birgivī (d. 981/1573), ʿAbd al-Ḥakīm b. Shams al-Dīn al-Siyalkūtī (d. 1067/1657) and Shāh Walī Allāh (d. 1176/1762) followed in the footsteps of Ghazālī and Rāzī in their attempts to explain the doctrinal belief in the divine decree. However, it was not until the modern era that the pendulum once more swung back towards an emphasis on free will.

Interpretations of the Divine Decree in the Modern Era

By the nineteenth century, most of the Muslim world had been colonised by European powers. It was in this context that Muslim scholars began once more to confront the topic of free will and determinism. Jamāl al-Dīn al-Afghānī (d. 1314/1897) was one of the first in the modern era to write about this topic. He had the opportunity to travel widely both in the East and the West and in so doing came to the conclusion that there was a need to emancipate all Muslim peoples from colonialism and from the ignorance and backwardness that he believed had overtaken the Muslims of his time. In his autobiography, he wrote that his travels to the West had shown him just how far behind the Muslim world had fallen. At the same time, his main work, *al-Radd ʿalā al-dahriyyīn* (Refutations of the Materialists), indicated that he believed there still was a need for religion within society, and he was highly critical of the nihilists and Marxists in Europe who were antagonistic to religion. His main argument for the superiority of Islam over other world faiths was that its fundamental creeds could be rationalised and were free from any kind of mystery.[1] This excessively rationalistic interpretation of Islam coupled with the disregard for its spiritual dimensions was to have a significant influence on Muslim modernist thinkers of the twentieth and twenty-first centuries.

It is interesting to consider whether this emphasis on rationalism was wholly Afghānī's or if his views were shaped by external factors, particularly the prevailing rationalism and empiricism found within Europe. Afghānī's interest in the divine decree did not stem from a scholastic, theological curiosity but arose from a desire for reform. Hence, many of his and later reformers' descriptions of the divine decree lacked the detailed rigorous study that scholars before them had afforded the subject. The divine decree as an article of faith was instead looked at through the prism of reform and its definition seems to have been mainly a defence against the charge of the Orientalists

1 Fakhry, *History of Islamic Philosophy*, pp. 346–50.

that it was equivalent to fatalism. Afghānī stressed that none of his fellow scholars—be they Sunni or Shiʿi—believed in pure determinism like the Jabariyya, whose belief had not left a lasting impression on Muslim thought. He held that Muslims subscribed to the belief that human beings were partially free within the parameters set by the concept of acquisition (*kasb*). His main concern was therefore to correct the prevailing Orientalist interpretations of the divine decree by distancing the understanding of *qadar* from the ideas of the Jabariyya.

Afghānī went further by arguing that all things in the universe happen through a sequence of causes and effects, and human will was a necessary part of that sequence. This view was actually closer to Ibn Rushd's theory than that of the Ashʿarīs or Māturīdīs, who had rejected it because it restricted God omnipotence. It is important to clarify that the the Sunni orthodox view of the Ashʿarīs and the Māturīdīs did not entail the rejection of cause and effect per se; they only considered that according to the criteria of logic the link was tenuous. This meant that 'there is no logical, deductive necessity between cause and effect but only the consistent, inductive association of cause and effect in our past experiences'.[1]

Hume had come to the same conclusion during the eighteenth century (albeit without any mention of the divine); namely, that we understand these causes and effects through simple accumulations of empirical events. This resembles Ghazālī's view, in fact, that by using these simple accumulations of sequential empirical events, we may be able to anticipate and explain predictable causes and effects, and even, perhaps, a holistic system. However, it should be evident that we cannot use this to explain the reality of the divine decree because causality, due to its empirical nature, is too tenuous to explain an overarching power beyond causality. Hence, it may be argued that our experience in the world (*dunyā*) gives us the appearance of a closed and self-sufficient system filled with cause and effect bounded

1 Aminah Beverly McCloud, Scott W. Hibbard and Laith Saud, *An Introduction to Islam in the 21st Century*, Oxford: Blackwell Publishing, 2013, p. 72.

by worldly categories, but in reality, God alone is the cause of each event. Gai Eaton eloquently explained this occasionalism by stating:

> Until the present century this [occasionalism] must have been a difficult theory to grasp. Today any child could understand it. We have, in cinematography, an exact illustration of what the Ashᶜarites were saying. The audience watching a movie sees a smooth sequence of cause-and-effect operating in time, but in fact the successive frames on the film passing through the projector do not have any such relationship. A single frame is flashed on the screen; there is then a moment of darkness, imperceptible to the human eye, after which another frame appears. The film editor controls the order in which these frames are shown. The audience sees a stone strike a window whereupon the glass shatters, but the frame which shows the stone being thrown did not 'cause' those which show the breakage. The editor could have removed the latter and inserted others in their place, or he could have reversed the order in which they were projected. The editor can do as he pleases in the cutting-room, just as God 'does as He pleases,' and since—for the Muslims—it is unthinkable that God could be under any compulsion whatsoever, it follows that He is not obliged to allow a particular effect to follow a particular cause.[1]

Modern science and rationalism attributes all effects to earthly causes and, by extension, excludes God from the chain of causality.

1 Eaton, *Islam and the Destiny of Man*, pp. 242–43.

Eaton argues that the theory of occasionalism laid down by the two Sunni classical schools of theology seems to have pre-empted this kind of exclusion by denying such causality.[1] Nevertheless, by the nineteenth century, both Afghānī and his student in Egypt, Muḥammad Abduh, had begun to deny this kind of occasionalism and instead proposed the argument of causality, which became the main idea espoused by the modernist school of thought in Islam.

Abduh's writings on the divine decree were actually theological rather than simply being rooted in the twentieth-century reform movement. He wrote with regard to free will that, just as a human being knows of his own existence and needs no evidence for this, so too does he know of the existence of his voluntary acts. It is interesting to note that this argument is the same as the one posited by Māturīdī in his *Kitāb al-tawḥīd.* Abduh went on to say that human beings are invested with free will, and through this an individual 'weighs the consequences of his acts in his mind, measures them by his will and then performs the acts by a power existing in himself'.[2] Abduh argued that there are only two ways that human beings are limited in their freedom: the first is that by miscalculating the consequences of their actions, they are unable to proceed as they wished, and the second is that external sources (such as unforeseen natural circumstances) prevent the person from carrying out their planned act. From this, it is clear that Abduh saw the will of God controlling events and actions only through natural events, which he called the *Sunan Allāh* (the Divine Way).

Through this concept of the *Sunan Allāh*, Abduh also seemed to imply that God has Himself limited His Own powers. In his *Tafsīr al-manār* (The Commentary [reprinted from the periodical entitled] *The Lighthouse*), he elaborated on it by stating that the *Sunan* of God are fixed trends according to which events and effects come into

1 Ibid.

2 Harun Nasution, 'The Place of Reason in ʿAbduh's Theology Its Impact on His Theological System and Views', Ph.D. thesis, McGill University, 1968, p. 146, quoting Muḥammad Abduh, *Risālat al-tawḥīd.*

being, and it is through them that God relates cause to effect. There is a different variation of *Sunna* for each creature; hence, Abduh seems to equate it with natural law. Thus, the idea is that God does not deviate from these laws and human beings are free to choose which *Sunna* to follow. Here, it is clear that Abduh argued for man's power to be similar to the one advocated by the Muʿtazilīs and also for real causality, which was espoused by Ibn Rushd but rejected by both the Ashʿarīs and Māturīdīs. However, Abduh still accepted the notion of free will through acquisition (*kasb*) and choice (*ikhtiyār*), which was posited by both the Ashʿarīs and Māturīdīs, albeit with some degree of difference.[1] For him, *kasb* had two meanings: firstly, it meant man's power, which he acquires from God by virtue of his own nature; and secondly, the power he freely uses according to his own choice.[2] He went on to accuse the Ashʿarīs (and, by extension, the Māturīdīs) along with the Ḥanbalīs (meaning, the Atharīs) of folly for reducing God to a capricious despot who acted arbitrarily and irresponsibly. Moreover, he criticised the Muʿtazilīs for their impertinence in reducing God to the status of a servant who is subject to the dictates of his master.[3]

By Abduh's time, what some perceived as the decadence and backwardness of Muslims began to be attributed to a misunderstanding of the concept of *qaḍā'* and *qadar*. Abduh argued that *qadar* had degenerated to fatalism due to the infiltration of Islam by foreign elements and because of the Sufi orders who convinced the masses that fatalism was the essence of the faith.[4] Abduh shared this opinion with Afghānī and with most of the later modernists, such as Rashīd Riḍā (d. 1354/1935), Sir Sayyid Aḥmad Khān (d. 1315/1898) and Amīr ʿAlī (d. 1346/1928).[5]

1 Ibid., pp. 145–89.

2 Ibid., p. 151.

3 Fakhry, *History of Islamic Philosophy*, p. 355, citing Muḥammad Abduh, *Risālat al-tawḥīd*.

4 Ibid., p. 357, citing Muḥammad Abduh, *al-Islām dīn al-ʿilm wa'l-madaniyya*.

5 Kamali, 'Causality and Divine Action'.

On the other hand, the traditional understanding of the divine decree has continued to be explored by a variety of scholars. During the nineteenth century, the *mujāhid* and scholar ʿAbd al-Qādir al-Jazā'irī (d. 1300/1883) wrote a very interesting treatise on the divine decree and its relationship to the game of chess in his book, *Dhikrā al-ʿāqil wa-tanbīh al-ghāfil* (A Reminder to the Wise and a Caution to the Heedless). He wrote:

> Whoever ponders the game of chess, and reflects deeply upon the nature of its pieces and the fixity of its patterns will realize that a profound secret concerning the nature of destiny has been disclosed to him by the simplest of methods. [...]
>
> Indeed, both players, despite being entirely free to choose their actions, to deliberate their possibilities, to utilize their strategies, and to exert all of their personal efforts in their moves are nonetheless entirely circumscribed in their possibilities, due to the very limitations predetermined by the inventor himself. They cannot break the laws set, nor exempt themselves from the limited possibilities given. In this way, they are fated yet appear free and, equally, they are free yet appear fated!
>
> The inventor caught a glimpse of a sacred secret among the paradoxes of providence and realized that all human beings are freely accruing their actions and either gaining the rewards of their right moves or suffering the consequences of their wrong ones. Furthermore, he realized that God, the Exalted, does not oppress His servants, but that they themselves are the oppressors. Human beings are fulfill-

> ing their destiny without being forced against their will in the paths they pursue. Indeed, God left the creation free to err or act appropriately. Analogously, the inventor of chess has decreed certain things for those who play his game, and while they are held to those limitations, they are nonetheless free to choose their moves while not being stripped entirely of their own volition.
>
> Hence, if one plays his game well, it is to his advantage, and if poorly, it is to his detriment. Neither of the two players can escape the limits of the squares, the pieces, their numbers, and their prescribed movements. Had its inventor allowed other possibilities, the players would have been constrained by them as well.[1]

The Turkish theologian Saʿīd Nursī (d. 1379/1960), known in modern Turkey as Bediüzzaman Said Nursi, is perhaps one of the most recent Sunni scholars to develop ideas about the divine decree in the tradition of the Māturīdī school of theology. He wrote, 'Yes, divine determining and the power of choice are at the final degrees of belief and Islam; the former has been included among the matters of belief to save the soul from pride, and the latter, to make it admit to its responsibility. [...] We do not know many of the numerous aspects of the All-Just and Wise One's wisdom; our not knowing how the power of choice is compatible with divine determining does not prove that it is not so.'[2] In his book, *Risāle-yi*

1 For the complete text, see ʿAbd al-Qādir Al-Jazāʾirī, 'Chess and the Divine Decree', trans. Hamza Yusuf, *Seasons: The Journal of the Zaytuna Institute*, vol. III, no. 1, spring 2006, pp. 16–17, http://www.scribd.com/doc/24300197/Chess-and-the-Divine-Decree-Jaza-Iri, 1 August 2013.

2 Bediüzzaman Said Nursi, *The Words: Risale-i Nur*, Ankara: İhlâs Nur Neşriyat, 2001, p. 482.

Nūr, Nursi presented seven rational theological arguments for the existence of the divine decree and free will that were based upon the earlier writings of Taftāzānī and Ṣadr al-Sharīʿa ʿUbayd Allāh (d. 744/1344).[1]

Even though the modernist views on the divine decree and free will differ somewhat from the traditional positions of the Ashʿariyya and the Māturīdiyya, it is evident in contemporary Muslim societies across the world that the majority of Muslims continue to believe in the notions of free will and determinism side by side. The following extract from the book, *What Everyone Should Know about Islam and Muslims*, illustrates how belief in free will and determinism are understood within the every day life of a contemporary Muslim:

> Islam teaches, the task of a human being is to make a sincere effort, to strive, to do his best—not as is so often incorrectly stated, simply to sit back and let things take their course in blind resignation to some supposed 'fate' or 'destiny'; for a human being does not know and cannot know wherein his destiny lies, and until he has exhausted all possible means and what is inevitable occurs, he cannot be said to have encountered that destiny. But then whatever comes to one after all his efforts have been made, should be received with patient and trusting acceptance of what He in His Infinite Wisdom has seen fit to send, and with the expectation that it may prove to be a source of good and ultimate blessing in the broader perspective of the life to come. Belief in the

1 Ahmed Akgunduz, 'Bediuzzaman's View of Divine Determination (*al-Qadar*) and Free Will (*al-Irâdah al-Juz'iyyah*)', Nursi Studies Database, İstanbul İlim ve Kültür Vakfı, http://www.iikv.org/academy/index.php/articles/article/view/1716/3387, accessed 30 July 2013.

> divine decree is thus a statement of belief in the meaningfulness and purposefulness of all that it is, an essential part of the Muslim's sense of total trust, dependence and submission in relation to his Creator.[1]

Several of these statements are very reminiscent of what Ghazālī wrote about how the divine decree can only be understood by living with trust in God, and of what Māturīdī wrote about the greater purpose of harmful substances in life.

Muslim theologians have explored the subject of the divine decree over the last fifteen centuries and many theologians have conducted rational and mystical explorations of it. Their readers have been given glimpses of the sacred secret amongst the paradoxes of divine providence, but it is clear from the majority of their writings that the divine decrees remains God's secret.

1 Haneef, *What Everyone Should Know*, p. 40.

PART III
THE FUTURE OF ISLAMIC THEOLOGY

Chapter Eight

ISLAMIC THEOLOGY TODAY AND TOMORROW

The Rise and Fall of ʿIlm al-Kalām

Ṭaḥāwī described Islam as lying 'between the extremes of excess and neglect, between immanence and transcendence, between determinism and free will, and between assurance of salvation and despair of God's grace.'[1] As the previous chapters have shown, the development of Islamic theology was shaped by internal political disputes and debates that emerged very soon after the time of the Prophet. The rise of the three Sunni schools of theology[2]—the Athariyya, Ashʿariyya and the Māturīdiyya—and their stance on matters of faith were a defence against the numerous sects that arose, and their teachings were intended to elucidate how faith had been conceptualised by the Companions and their followers. These three schools maintained the established creed and defended it successfully over the next millennium. The above description of Islam by Ṭaḥāwī can only be truly comprehended by appreciating Islamic theology's history and the processes that brought it about.

Following the civil wars and sectarian strife that took place during the early history of Islam, Islamic theology has been remarkably successful at bringing about consensus amongst Sunnis on the fundamental tenets of faith. Despite lacking any single centralised religious institution, like the Catholic papacy, the judgements and

1 Ṭaḥāwī, *Creed of Imam al-Ṭaḥāwī*, p. 80 (Creed 129).

2 As mentioned above, this study focuses on the Sunni schools of theology. The Ithnā ʿAsharī share the same basic creed with Sunni Muslims and the main differences have been mentioned in Chapter One.

recommendations of the *Ahl al-Sunna wa'l-Jamāʿa* have always been reached, in the case of practice, according to the methodology of at least one school of law (for issues relating to religious practice) and in accordance with the schools of theology (for issues relating to belief). Consequently, there has been great continuity in traditional Sunni orthopraxy and orthodoxy.

As the present study has shown, the two main schools of Islamic theology—the Ashʿariyya and the Māturīdiyya—were able to preserve Muslim orthodoxy and consensus on matters of creed for more than a millennium. The theological scholarship produced by these schools helped Muslims to define the content of their faith, it demonstrated that their creeds were coherent and proved that the rational mind could accept and be convinced by them. This science of *kalām* was able to create a tolerant intra-faith Muslim society in which the community agreed on the essentials, even if there were differences on the specifics, and in which any disagreements could be settled in an intellectual arena rather than on a physical battleground.

However, it appears that the very success of Islamic theology in forging consensus amongst Sunni Muslims has contributed to its own demise as a branch of religious science. This is because the fundamentals of the Muslim creed have become so widely known and their arguments so normalised within Sunni tradition that the science of *kalām* has all but ceased to exist. Indeed, very few Muslims today even know about the classical Ashʿarī and Māturīdī schools of thought.[1] Similarly, the broader science of *kalām* and its history is little known amongst the majority of contemporary Muslims, even those from intellectual circles.

There is still a debate amongst scholars as to how long the Ashʿarīs and the Māturīdīs remained active as a source of theological discourse and when, if at all, there was a demise of the science of *kalām*. Some contemporary historians pinpoint the ninth/fifteenth

1 See Halverson, *Theology and Creed*, p. 6.

or the tenth/sixteenth centuries as the point when Islamic theology entered its terminal decline. Regardless of the details of these arguments, it is clear that when an extreme puritanical literalism, one the one hand, and a modern mode of thought (which ultimately derived from the European Enlightenment), on the other, entered the Muslim world in the late eighteenth and early nineteenth centuries, there was no active school of Islamic theology to counter them. Since then, it appears as if most Muslim communities have continued to worship without any connection with active theological discourse of the kind described in this book. But despite all of this, it is undeniable that the axiomatic creeds produced during the heyday of Islamic theology continue to be central to Islamic thought. Moreover, given the difficulties that modernity presents to Islam in the forms of atheism, agnosticism, positivism and postmodernism, it appears that Muslims today are again in need of a vigorous Islamic theology.

The Crisis of Religions Today

Islam is not alone in facing the challenges of a modern world. Most religions have already faced, or are currently facing, these challenges. The case of Christianity is particularly germane to the present discussion. In pre-modern and early modern Europe, Christianity was the first religion to be confronted by major social transformations in all aspects of life and thought. It was also in Christendom that all of these transformations began. Commencing with the Renaissance, and then continuing through the Reformation, the Enlightenment, the French Revolution, followed by the rise of nation states and the industrial revolution, the emergence of modern secular society undermined traditional Christian theology.

From all of these scientific, cultural, social and political developments in Europe, there emerged the notion that human beings had the ability to reason and did not need the strictures of faith and revelation. The belief that human beings are autonomous and able to change their surroundings without the restraint of customs or traditions became widespread, as did the idea that science was the arbiter of truth. Utopia was therefore considered to be attainable through a natural world order. 'The machine, gigantic industrial projects, steel, iron and electricity—all were thought to be at the disposal of humanity to achieve this objectivity. This drive towards industrialisation and reliance on the physical created an ideology which emphasised materialism as a way of life.'[1] All of these shifts in the Christian world view brought about what has been called the 'crisis of theology' in Christianity.[2]

Whereas traditional Christian theology had largely operated within a social and cultural context that reinforced the truth of its dogmas, the secularisation of society compelled it to change its methods, broaden its spheres of operation and embrace a more ecumenical and liberal outlook. The result was what is now known as 'modern theology'. This modern theology has attempted to reinterpret Christian dogmas and to provide meaning for Christians in the modern world. Traditional dogmas relating to God, revelation, sin and evil were redefined by different schools of modern theology, such as those of systematic theology, dogmatic theology and constructive theology. Other practitioners of modern Christian theology have placed greater stress on integration with modernity, and have done so by concentrating on formulating theological methods that are comparable to those of modern disciplines. This, for example, is very noticeable in practical theology, which emphasises how to put these ideas into practice in everyday life, and also in ecumenical

1 Akbar S. Ahmed, *Postmodernism and Islam: Predicament and Promise*, London: Routledge, 1992, pp. 6–8.

2 Theology of crisis is an approach to theology developed by the Protestant theologian Karl Barth (d. 1968). It has been seen as a reaction against nineteenth-century liberal theology and it initiated a trend towards neo-orthodoxy in Protestant theology. For further details, see Angela Dienhart Hancock, *Karl Barth's Emergency Homiletic, 1932–1933: A Summons to Prophetic Witness at the Dawn of the Third Reich*, Cambridge: Wm. B. Eerdmans Publishing, 2013.

theology, which takes secular notions and the theologies of other Christian denominations into account and incorporates them into its own theological system.[1]

However, tensions have arisen between the proponents of modern thought and the defenders of Christian authority because of their scepticism about each other's methods and assertions. Liberation theology has attempted to recover the status of Christianity from the complete dismissal of its importance in the modern world. It has given rise to other theologies dealing with specific social issues, such as feminist theology, Marxist theology and Black theology. Finally, there is postmodern theology, which has its roots in the thought of Friedrich Nietzsche (d. 1318/1900), and which has become a central part of modern theological discourse on Christianity.

Modern Challenges to Islamic Theology

Externally, Islam has been facing similar challenges to those that the Judeo-Christian theological tradition confronted during the early modern period. These external obstacles concern the unique problems emerging from life in the modern world, primarily the attitudes and world view associated with modernity. The end of the nineteenth century saw most Muslim countries either fully colonised or heavily influenced by modern Europe. One consequence of this was that the ideas of the Enlightenment became ubiquitous within the Muslim world. There, as in Europe, the modern age was that of a post-traditional, post-medieval society marked by a move away from agrarianism and feudalism towards industrialisation, capitalism, secularisation, positivist rationalisation and the creation of nation states. After gaining independence, most Muslim nations embraced the Romantic notion of nationalism and the secularism of 'modernity', albeit (as in Europe before

1 For more about the rise of modern theology in Christianity, see Kelly M. Kapic and Bruce L. Mccormack, *Mapping Modern Theology: A Thematic and Historical Introduction*, Grand Rapids, MI: Baker Books, 2012.

it) to varying degrees. It was in this new atmosphere and context that traditional Islam began to be challenged by the absolute commitment of modernity to reason and science and by the ideas of deism, secularisation and atheism that these gave rise to. However, since Islamic theology had long been dormant by that point, most of these challenges from modernity persisted, and continue to exist, in the Muslim world today.

In recent decades, Islam has been confronted with another external challenge: postmodernism. Postmodernism argues that the extolment of reason and natural science by modernity cannot be a reliable source of knowledge. Thus, the movement is seen as a reaction to the certainty and claims of objectivity of modernity. Postmodernism believes that human understanding skews objectivity, and it calls for universal scepticism, which acknowledges that no truth claim can be valid for all human beings due to their variation in terms of culture, race, traditions and history. Instead, postmodernism focuses on the truth of the individual and thus makes all truth relative; it emphasises that ultimate truth is impossible to attain because everyone has their own truth. Thus, postmodernism makes all truth claims—be they from revelation, reason or science—relative, in contrast to modernism, which held reason and science as absolute.

Whereas modernity's grand narrative was science and reason, postmodernism is distinguished by nihilism and a loss of spiritual centre, allowing society to be inherently pluralistic in nature but at the same time inherently agnostic. This is to say that there is no one unitary point of reference for truth and multiple perspectives are equally valid. Thus, postmodernism directly challenges the Islamic faith as an exclusive revealed religion from God because its proponents consider everything to be relative, and because absolute meaning has been deconstructed and reinterpreted as merely specific to a local, tribal or national sphere. As a result, scepticism becomes the mediator for all truth claims and Islam is seen as only one of many truths. This exaltation of relativism and scepticism has led some contemporary thinkers to challenge postmodernism and accuse it of being a commercial paganism that turns religion into playthings.[1]

Both modernity and postmodernism are challenges to Sunni Islamic theology in themselves and in their promotion of materialism, secularism, scepticism, relativism, etc. However, it must be remembered that the challenge of justifying the unique truth of Islam is an old one because that is what many medieval theologians wrote about in response to attacks from other religions and philosophies in the past. Therefore, an Islamic theology based on the traditional Ashʿarī and Māturīdī schools is perfectly capable to respond to such challenges.

In addition to these external challenges to Islamic theology, there are also internal ones that have arisen from within the tradition of Islam and Muslim societies. Foremost amongst these has been the move away—since the second half of the nineteenth century—from religious education, and the now almost universal adoption in Muslim countries of secular education. The loss of the experience of a religious education with all its different facets, methodologies and training is a real tragedy for the Islamic world. The breadth of vision and the strict disciplines of traditional religious education ensured that those who graduated were fully qualified and had the background to speak for Islam. The move away from religious education has gone hand in hand with the marginalisation by secular governments of the remaining Islamic institutions, such as the Azhar in Egypt.[2]

It is difficult to overestimate the corrective and balancing contribution of proficient and experienced Islamic scholars to Muslim

1 Aslam Farouk Ali, 'Islamic Discourse after Modernity and Post-Modernity', in Ibrahim M. Abu-Rabiʿ, ed., *The Blackwell Companion to Islamic Contemporary Thought*, Oxford: Blackwell Publishing, 2006, pp. 290–99.

2 For more information on the subject of Islamic education, see Amjad. M Hussain, *A Social History of Education in the Muslim World: From the Prophetic Era to Ottoman Times*, London: Ta-Ha Publishers, 2013.

societies. Their exposure to all the different disciplines of the Islamic curriculum, coupled with their rigorous training, granted them the ability to build on past scholarship to offer solutions to present situations. The loss of experience of a religious education and of competent scholars is detrimental in numerous ways to Islamic societies. Above all, it opens the door to unqualified persons or movements and allows them to have a disproportionate impact on Muslim societies. For example, there is the descent into superstition, popular religion and 'pseudo-Sufism' (which has nothing to do with authentic Sufism), which are linked to a lack of basic, as well as, religious education or knowledge. 'Popular religion' is a term that has been used by historians such as Jonathan P. Berkey and Boaz Shoshan,[1] but it is challenging to define folk religion in a Muslim context since Islam has had a very inclusive attitude to different devotional practices. As laid out in the *Sharīʿa*, Islamic practice is a combination of formal Islamic law mixed with a range of acceptable cultural norms, resulting in one united religion manifested in a diversity of cultural forms across the Muslim world. In addition, Sufism has traditionally been accepted by Muslims (with the exception of contemporary Salafis) as a legitimate path as long as it adheres to the *Sharīʿa*, although there are a number of Sufi practices whose legitimacy is debated amongst jurists, such as the practice of celebrating the Prophet's birthday. Still, much of the controversy relates to the legitimate legal question of whether those practices should be considered to be within the wide range of orthopraxy or not.

However, the greater threat to Islamic theology does not come from popular religion, it comes from movements who believe that they can exist outside of traditional Islamic theology and who have no regard for any of the historical developments within Islamic thought. This can clearly be seen in the tremendous upheavals tak-

1 See Boaz Shoshan, *Popular Culture in Medieval Cairo*, Cambridge: Cambridge University Press, 1993 and Jonathan P. Berkey, *Popular Preaching and Religious Authority in the Medieval Islamic Near East*, Seattle: University of Washington Press, 2001.

ing place in the heartlands of Islam, in the appearance of movements that speak in the name of Islam but that do not base themselves on anything that traditional Islam would recognise.

From the above, it will be amply clear that there is a great need for an engaged and thriving discipline of Islamic theology to respond to these internal and external challenges to Islam in the modern age. However, Islamic theology in its present form is not equipped to respond to these challenges because it has almost died out as a discipline and there are vocal objections to reviving it, as we shall see in the next section.

Impediments to the Reintroduction of Islamic Theology

Despite the obvious need to reintroduce the religious science of Islamic theology, there are a number of major obstacles to this. As already noted, there is today widespread ignorance of Muslim intellectual history—including the history of the theological schools. This is a barrier to the development of theological discourse even in parts of the Muslim world with high rates of literacy. But the obstacles go far beyond this. For instance, some have suggested translating classical theological works from Arabic, televising contemporary theological debates and organising theological debates online in order to reintroduce the science of *kalām* to the Muslim world. However, the complexity of theology poses certain problems to this, the main one being the general lack of any intellectual training of the kind necessary to comprehend the material found in classical texts and their authors' methodologies. The subtleties and sophistication of both Māturīdī and Ashʿarī thought seem to be beyond many Muslims at the present moment due to both a lack of qualified teachers and educational institutions teaching theology, and the low level of literacy in many parts of the Muslim world. Furthermore, there is also a need to intellectually comprehend and critically analyse both modernity and postmodernity in order to make theology applicable to the contemporary world.

An added impediment is widespread active opposition to reviving the two classical Sunni theological schools in contemporary Muslim society. This opposition comes from both ends of the spectrum: from modernists and from Salafis. These two movements have done much to limit the discourse within modern Islamic thought to either excessive empirical rationalism or to puritanical Salafism.

Since the nineteenth century, Muslim modernists have denounced Ashʿarī thought (and by association, Māturīdī) as being the source of fatalism, decadence and decline in Islam.[1] As Jeffry Halverson has observed, these modernists—including more contemporary thinkers such as Amina Wadud, Fazlur Rahman, Muḥammad Arkoun, Fatima Mernissi, Muḥammad Saʿīd al-ʿAshmāwī, Ḥasan Ḥanafī and Farid Esack—seem to occupy positions close to those of the Muʿtazilīs or philosophers at an earlier period of Islamic history. Consequently, they have been referred to as Neo-Muʿtazilīs by Halverson and others.[2] In fact, most research on theology by liberal Muslims and academics has solely focused on historical Muʿtazilism, which was long ago deemed heretical and beyond the boundaries of the *Ahl al-Sunna wa'l-Jamāʿa*. Halverson further argues that this exclusive pursuit of philosophy and Neo-Muʿtazilism by many contemporary modernists has brought no major advantages to the wider Muslim populace.[3]

Among the above mentioned scholars, ʿAshmāwī, Fazlur Rahman and Ḥasan Ḥanafī have repeatedly denounced Ashʿarī thought in their writings. But it seems that many of these thinkers have also confused Ashʿarī with Atharī thought. For example, ʿAshmāwī writes that in order to revive the 'Islamic mind', Muslims need to abandon the thought of Ashʿarī and of Ghazālī as it promotes literalism and is the reason for the stagnation in rational thinking in the

1 Halverson, *Theology and Creed,* pp. 143–44
2 Ibid., pp. 50, 130, 144 and 145.
3 Ibid., p. 129.

Muslim world.[1] This is an instance of a modern scholar confusing Atharī and Ashᶜarī doctrines. This is clearly incorrect as demonstrated by all of the evidence presented in this book. More broadly, Halverson notes that this kind of contemporary modernist writing seems to make no distinction at all between the three Sunni theological schools, and he argues that 'such heterodox tendencies bring with them serious vulnerabilities to reform efforts'.[2] Indeed, in conflating the three very distinct Sunni theological schools and characterising them as identical to Atharī thought, these modernists create a false and deceptive view of Muslim intellectual history. Furthermore, based on this mistaken view, modernists conclude that the only theological school suitable for adapting to the purposes of reform in the contemporary Muslim world is that of the historically discredited Muᶜtazila. However, any real reform or revival of theology in Islam would have to recognise the standing of the three theological schools in Muslim intellectual history.

At the opposite end of the spectrum to Neo-Muᶜtazilism is the widespread Wahhābī/Salafi movement, which is anti-theological. The Wahhābī movement emerged in eighteenth-century central Arabia and its name derived from that of the Muslim preacher Muḥammad Ibn ᶜAbd al-Wahhāb (d. 1205/1791). He preached a return to the pristine purity of Islam by going back to the study of the primary sources of Islam. In this pursuit, he rejected *taqlīd* (literally, 'imitation' or 'emulation'), which means following one of the four schools of Islamic jurisprudence and instead he introduced new interpretations, albeit along very strict literal and puritanical lines. Historically, those who adhered to the Wahhābī movement called themselves *Muwaḥiddūn* (Unitarians), but later on, when the movement encountered influences from outside the Arabian

1 Ibid., p. 146.
2 Ibid., p. 148.

Peninsula, Salafi became the preferred name for its adherents.[1] Today, this movement continues to be very influential amongst Muslims across the world.

The Ashʿarī and Māturīdī theological schools are perceived by the Salafi movement as being antithetical to true Islam because of their use of rational discourse, and they have dismissed theologians who were from these schools as mere 'philosophers'—a derogatory label in this context. This is the unfortunate outcome of a misreading of the historical landscape of Islamic intellectual history, because historically (as demonstrated in the preceding chapters of this book) the Ashʿarīs and Māturīdīs held very different positions to the Muʿtazilīs and philosophers. In addition, the Salafis' notion that a rational approach to doctrinal questions was only the domain of the Muʿtazilīs or the philosophers is quite mistaken given that the historical evidence clearly shows that all schools used reason, albeit in different ways and to different degrees.

Comparisons have been made between contemporary Salafis and Atharīs. However, this is to miss the nuanced differences between the classical traditional group and modern-day literal and puritanical thought. It could be argued that there are similarities between the two, such as their sole reliance on the Qur'ān and *Ḥadīth* for interpreting these primary sources and not relying on reason to do so. But the differences between the two groups are many. The Salafi movement goes much further in its puritanical form, as can be seen in its reinterpretation of orthopraxy today.[2] Furthermore, the Atharī school encompassed a far broader range of theological viewpoints in the past than the Salafi movement does today. For example, Aḥmad Ibn Ḥanbal—who is recognised as the being the founder of Atharī theology—refused to enter into any rational discussions on theology,[3]

1 For further information, see Roel Meijer, *Global Salafism: Islam's New Religious Movement*, Oxford: Oxford University Press, 2009.

2 For example, prohibiting women from driving.

3 This was also true for Imam Mālik.

while Ibn Taymiyya—a later adherent to the Atharī school—wrote a refutation of Ibn Sīnā's treatise on resurrection in which he engaged in complex rational arguments proposed by both theologians and philosophers. Also, if we compare the two Atharī theologians Ibn Ḥazm and Ibn Taymiyya, the former belonged to the Ẓāhirī school of law, whereas the latter belonged to the Ḥanbalī school of law. By contrast, and as demonstrated by their writings, Salafi preachers share a very limited range of legal opinions. Moreover, Atharī scholars all accepted the legal schools, Sufism[1] and the status of the *Ahl al-Sunna wa'l-Jamāʿa*; while Muḥammad b. ʿAbd al-Wahhāb, as is clear from his writings, opposed all of this, rejecting the diversity of schools of law and Sufism. Thus, while it is true that the Salafi movement has similarities with Atharī thought, particularly the thought of the Ḥanbalī legal school, it would be a grave error to conflate these two very different schools.

Salafism presents an especially strong impediment to reintroducing Islamic theology because its particular combination of puritanism and literalism is not only found within the movement itself, but has also become widespread among Muslims. Although the historical circumstances that led to this state of affairs is beyond the remit of this book, the widespread popularity of the Salafi way of thinking in the Muslim world means that traditional Islamic theology is often rejected alongside heterodoxies such as Muʿtazilism, and is tainted by similarly negative connotations.

It is interesting to note the parallels between currents in the contemporary Muslim world and those in earlier Islamic history that have been discussed in this book. In fact, in many ways, it appears that the doctrinal disputes that formed the backdrop to the development of *ʿilm al-kalām* during the first two centuries of Islam are in some

1 Both Ibn Taymiyya and Ibn Qayyim al-Jawziyya were members of the Qadariyya Sufi order, and the staunch Atharī scholar ʿAbd Allāh Anṣāri al-Harawī (d. 481/1089) was a well-known Sufi. It seems that many scholars from the Atharī tradition were sympathetic to Sufism in general but were nonetheless strongly critical of certain Sufi excesses.

way repeating themselves. Certain theological challenges that were laid to rest long ago by the *Ahl al-Sunna wa'l-Jamāʿa* have resurfaced, such as the 'epidemic' of accusations of apostasy (*takfīr*) and support for deism. Today, the puritanical beliefs of the Salafis echo older challenges like the fatalism of the Jabariyya, the Khārijī interpretation of faith that promotes sectarian violence, and the anthropomorphists who promoted anthropomorphism. On the other hand, modernist positions claiming that the universe is an autonomous machine come close to the kind of deism once proposed by the Qadariyya and, later, by the Muʿtazila. Furthermore, the excessive empiricism concerning cause and effect that is evident in some modern Muslim thought is reminiscent of the causation theory advanced by philosophers such as Ibn Rushd during the sixth/twelfth century.[1] But, whereas these disputes in early Islam were eventually resolved through vigorous theological debate, the challenges that have arisen since the end of European imperialism in the Muslim world have not been met by any active theological discourse.

Towards a Modern Islamic Theology Based on the Traditional Schools

Sophisticated methodologies of thought are needed to confront the recent challenges to the Muslim faith from new atheism, agnosticism, universal scepticism, postmodernism, relativism and religious pluralism, and this is not possible without first understanding the place of reason and faith in Islam, or the relationship between them in past Islamic history. Although all three of the main Sunni schools of theology had a role to play in the past, today there is a need for theological schools that can provide Muslims with the tools to engage in intellectual discourse. It is our opinion that of the three theological approaches, the Ashʿariyya and Māturīdiyya are best suited for revival in the modern world. However, as noted above, over the last two centuries the Māturīdiyya and, especially, the Ashʿariyya have been erroneously characterised in some circles as

1 See Chapter Six on the divine decree.

major sources of anti-rational literalism and are accused of causing the resulting intellectual stagnation in the Muslim world. In order to counter this misinterpretation of the Ashʿarī and Māturīdī schools, their history, doctrines and methodologies need to be studied anew and brought forward.

Firstly, there has to be much more support for the editing and translation of Māturīdī and Ashʿarī scholarship. At present, Muslim thinkers simply lack the resources to further develop the thought of classical theologians because a large number of manuscripts remain uncatalogued and are therefore inaccessible, and many of those that are accessible have not been edited or published, nor have they been translated into any of the main world languages. Secondly, a larger community of scholars is required to work on theology than do so at the moment.

Some scholars, such as Halverson, have called for a return to classical theology based solely on the Ashʿarī school of theology. The reasoning here is that Māturīdī thought is believed to be irrelevant for the Muslim world today because it is restricted to Ḥanafī circles and is considered to have made a limited contribution to Muslim intellectual history.[1] This position unfortunately lacks any appreciation for the nuanced methodologies of each of the two main Sunni schools with regard to the use of reason (*ʿaql*) and scripture (*naql*). There has always been a certain amount of diversity in Muslim schools of thought, and this is of paramount importance because diversity promotes intellectual discourse, and intellectual discourse is essential for the development of any successful theology. Thus, any revival of Islamic theology should extend to more than one school of theology.

Even though the science of *kalām* is recognised as focusing mainly on scholastic theology, we believe that today it needs to encompass much more than what is traditionally understood as theology. In fact, the remit of *ʿilm al-kalām* has always been to provide the context for

1 On Halverson's thoughts along these lines, see Halverson, *Theology and Creed*, pp. 143–44.

all of Muslim thought. It is a theologically-oriented form of thinking which encompasses not only God's unity and the larger questions tackled in *jalīl al-kalām*, but also the subtleties of the constituents of creation and the wide range of inquires about human behaviour covered in *daqīq al-kalām*.[1]

Whereas *jalīl al-kalām* is a branch of theology of immense importance that relates to the intellectual investigation of the relationship between the metaphysical and the physical worlds, *daqīq al-kalām* concerns inquiry into how God's creation operates. It was the later theologians who developed the *daqīq* branch of the subject. According to contemporary physicist M. B. Altaie, historically, *daqīq al-kalām* dealt with problems of natural philosophy, the most prominent of which were the questions of the creation, or eternity of the world, and of causality. However, later Muslim theologians did not stop there but continued to discuss the concepts of space, time, motion and many other aspects of the physical world.[2]

The questions tackled in *daqīq al-kalām* are now essential subjects that need to be at the forefront of contemporary Muslim scholarship, and perhaps should be recognised as the cornerstone of the numerous contemporary sciences that Muslims need to master. For instance, Altaie argues that *daqīq al-kalām* could constitute a basis for a contemporary Islamic philosophy of science. To this end, he is in the process of searching through ideas from the past history of Islamic theology for ones that might serve as possible candidates for integration with contemporary philosophies of natural science.[3]

There is a need to acknowledge that the modern sciences must be incorporated into the framework of Muslim thought. Such modern sciences as sociology, anthropology and psychology are highly developed intellectual tools but they have failed to be successful

1 Florentin Smarandache and Salah Osman, *Neutrosophy in Arabic Philosophy*, Ann Arbour, MI: Renaissance High Press, 2007, p. 129.

2 Altaie, '*Daqīq al-Kalām*: The Islamic Approach to Natural Philosophy.'

3 M. B. Altaie, M. B., 'Daqīq al-Kalām: A Basis for an Islamic Philosophy of Science', *Cambridge Muslim College Papers*, no. 4.

in Muslims societies because without a faith-based structure such sciences cannot have any real impact on believing Muslims whose world view is based upon the Islamic creed. Throughout history, there have been numerous examples of Muslim scholars conducting scientific investigations that recognised the context of the societies that were being studied. The most well known is the work begun by Ibn Khaldūn in his *Muqaddima*, where he developed theories to explain contemporary human society and its social history. This was the commencement of the science now known as sociology. Today, there is a need for Muslims to utilise sociology and anthropology to study Muslim and non-Muslim societies alike in order to understand the nation state, urbanisation and social movement, the global financial system, neo-liberal capitalism, etc. However, without a theologically oriented form of thinking, the void that exists in the Muslim world when it comes to scientific thinking will continue. Furthermore, even if a theologically oriented form of thinking becomes a cornerstone for these sciences, there is still an urgent need to develop and uphold a rigorous, systematic methodology that is not governed by rigid religious, political or social ideologies.

Another modern science that shares much in common with classical Muslim scholarship is psychology, whose historical counterpart was *ʿilm al-nafs* (science of the self). In the past, *ʿilm al-nafs* was considered a spiritual rather than a clinical science and was considered part of theology, Sufism or even philosophy, but it covered numerous aspects that would today be recognised as belonging to the science of psychology.[1] In Islamic history, it was initially the philosophers who adapted ideas about the self from Greek thought and combined them with the Islamic concept of *nafs*. From there, theologians, Sufis and other philosophers developed these ideas into a refined subject. *ʿIlm al-nafs* was used by Muslim scholars to discuss the inner work-

1 See Ali Ayten, *Din Psikolojisi* [Psychology of Religion], Istanbul: İz Yayıncılık, 2010.

ings of the soul, relationships with others and with God. They also dealt with conditions like anxiety, melancholy and distress, and pioneered a practical approach to the treatment of mental conditions. However, past scholars did not approach their subject in the same way as in modern psychology; instead, they focused on the self (*nafs*) and evaluated its powers. In so doing, they studied human attitudes, motivations and behaviour within the context of Islamic theology and devised classifications combining the spiritual and physical sides of the human being.

The contemporary psychologist of religion Ali Ayten rightly argues that Muslims in the modern world need psychology to better understand the motives behind human behaviour and emotions, and to help them cultivate virtuousness in our ever more materialistic world. People must be mentally as well as physically healthy; as psychology supports mental health, it can be an aid to making people more balanced and virtuous and in protecting them from mental strains that can develop into clinical problems. Yet without connecting their physical and psychological health to their spiritual well-being, Muslims today are in danger of becoming divorced from their faith due to the increasingly stressful modern materialistic lives they lead.[1] Thus, the case of psychology serves to illustrate that there is not only a need for Muslims to adopt modern sciences and services but to also do so within a framework of belief which theology is well-placed to provide.

But what would such a faith-based implementation of psychology look like? Ayten suggests that the answer to this question may be found by looking at examples from the past, especially to *ʿilm al-nafs*. He argues that there is an urgent need to adapt and combine modern psychology with knowledge derived from Islamic civilization so as to apply it to modern Muslim society, just as Muslim scholars in the past successfully adapted and combined ideas of the self from other civilisations with the Islamic concept of *nafs*.

1 Ibid.

Through this development the theologians, Sufis and philosophers developed the subject of *ʿilm al-nafs*. Given the overlap in the subject matter of psychology and the classical science of *ʿilm al-nafs*, perhaps the two could be combined and integrated with both being subjected to rigorous critical analysis. Ayten also stresses that localised knowledge about *ʿilm al-nafs* in the Muslim world cannot be neglected either and that empirical studies need to be conducted so as to understand the current situation of the Muslim world. Moreover, these developments are only possible if social scientists respect people's beliefs rather than dismissing them as irrelevant, or worse as mere superstitions. He concludes that these initiatives can lead to an acceptable solution.[1] But the present study indicates that, due to a lack of resources or a robust theological discourse, it has not yet been possible for psychology or any of the other modern sciences to be incorporated into a Muslim framework. Thus, one of the first steps in rectifying this situation is to revive Islamic theology. This case illustrates how a revived discipline of *ʿilm al-kalām* that is fully engaged with the modern social sciences would bring many benefits (both material and spiritual) to Muslim societies.

The last example of *daqīq al-kalām*'s role in advancing contemporary Muslim societies relates to the natural sciences, particularly the interesting research being done on *kalām* atomism in connection with quantum physics. In a recent article entitled, 'Continuous Re-creation: From Kalam Atomism to Contemporary Cosmology', the contemporary Turkish theologian Mehmet Bulgen observes that theories which have been developing in the West since the last century, such as relativity and quantum mechanics, have given rise to contemporary scientific cosmology.[2] However, he criticises this new cosmology for not offering a complete and consistent picture of the universe due to the incompatibility of quantum mechanics

1 See Ali Ayten, *Erdeme Dönüş* [Returning to Virtues], Istanbul: İz Yayıncılık, 2014.

2 Mehmet Bulgen, 'Continuous Re-creation: From Kalam Atomism to Contemporary Cosmology', *Kalam: Journal of Islamic Theology*, vol. 1, 2015, pp. 57–64.

and general relativity.[1] The main reason for this incompatibility is the fact that whereas quantum mechanics is based on discontinuity and probability, the theory of general relativity mainly assumes continuity and determinism, resulting in a clear contradiction and conflict in scientific cosmology today.[2] The foremost goal of western cosmologists has been to solve this conflict by introducing a unified theory called 'the theory of everything', which includes the quantisation of space-time (also known as quantum gravity). Bulgen argues that the most important theories developed with the aim of merging these two in modern cosmology are the string theory, known as M-theory, and the Loop Quantum Gravity theory. They both very strongly suggest that space-time must be a discrete and discontinuous construction. In his recent book *Kalām Atomism and Modern Cosmology*, Bulgen contends that these contemporary unified theories can be successfully used to revive and explore Ashʿarī theological doctrines such as occasionalism, which posits the continuous re-creation of all things by God and rejects causality.[3] Thus, not only can Islamic theology advance modern science in the Muslim world, but modern science can also reinvigorate traditional *kalām*.

This book has presented an overview of the intellectual history of Islamic theology taking the six articles of faith as its starting point. As the preceding chapters demonstrate, studying the intellectual history of Islamic theology and that of the Sunni schools of thought is imperative for anyone who wants to understand the discourse and debates concerning the creed and its development over time. However, the metaphysics of Islamic theology covers

1 Quantum mechanics concerns the universe at the smallest scale while general relativity relates to space-time at the largest scale.

2 See Mehmet Bulgen, 'The Relevance of Quantum Physics to Kalam Atomism', in Cemaleddin Erdemci and Fadil Aygan, eds., *International Imam al-Ashʿari and Ashʿarites Symposium (21–23 September 2014)*, Istanbul: Beyan Press, 2015, pp. 381–94.

3 See Mehmet Bulgen, *Kalām Atomism and Modern Cosmology*, Dubai: Kelam Research Media, forthcoming.

much more than these six articles of faith; it also encompasses many topics such as the oneness of God (*tawḥīd*), free will, transcendence, immanence, trust, faith, knowledge and the theories of causality and occasionalism, all of which have been written about at length over the last fifteen centuries of Islamic intellectual history. Moreover, the branch of *jalīl al-kalām* in the theological tradition was not simply a form of literalist piety that only rephrased the scriptures but rather, as noted, developed and refined an internally coherent metaphysical framework, especially within the two major Sunni schools of theology.

BIBLIOGRAPHY

Aasi, Ghulam Haider, *Muslim Understanding of Other Religions: A Study of Ibn Hazm's* Kitāb al-Faṣl fi al-Milal wa al-Ahwā' wa al-Niḥal, New Delhi: Adam Publishers, 2007.

Abū Ḥanifa, al-Nuᶜmān b. Thābit, *al-Fiqh al-akbar*, comments and trans. by Muhammad bin Yahya Ninowy, http://www.central-mosque.com/aqeedah/fiqakbar.pdf, accessed April 1, 2014.

Abu-Rabiᶜ, Ibrahim M., *The Blackwell Companion to Islamic Contemporary Thought*, Oxford: Blackwell Publishing, 2006.

Adang, Camilla, *Muslim Writers on Judaism and the Hebrew Bible: From Ibn Rabban to Ibn Hazm*, Leiden: E. J. Brill, 1996.

Ahmed, Akbar S., *Postmodernism and Islam: Predicament and Promise*, London: Routledge, 1992.

Ahmed, Habibuddin, *The Nature of Time and Consciousness in Islam*, Hyderabad: Islamic Thought and Science Institute, 2000.

Akgunduz, Ahmed, 'Bediuzzaman's View of Divine Determination (*al-Qadar*) and Free Will (*al-Irādah al-Juz'iyyah*)', Nursi Studies Database, İstanbul İlim ve Kültür Vakfi, http://www.iikv.org/academy/index.php/articles/article/view/1716/3387, accessed July 30, 2013.

Albayrak, İsmail, 'Qur'anic Narrative and Isra'iliyyat in Western Scholarship and in Classical Exegesis', Ph.D. thesis, University of Leeds, 2000.

———, 'Re-Evaluating the Notion of Isra'iliyyat', *D. E. Ü. İlahiyat Fakültesi Dergisi*, vol. XIII–XIV, 2001, pp. 69–88.

Aldosari, Ayedh Saad, 'A Critical Edition of al-Hādī in Māturīdī Doctrine of the Ḥanifite-Māturīdī Imām ᶜUmar al-Khabbāzī', Ph.D. thesis, University of Wales Trinity Saint David, 2012.

Alfarabius [Abū Naṣr Muḥammad al-Fārābī], *Compendium Legum Platonis*, ed. F. Gabrieli, London: Warburg Institute, 1952.

Ali, AbdullahYusuf, tr., *The Meaning of the Holy Qur'ān*, Beltsville, MD: Amana Publications, 2001.

Allen, Ronald J., *A Faith of Your Own: Naming What You Really Believe*, London: Westminster John Knox Press, 2010.

Altaie, M. B., 'Daqīq al-Kalām: A Basis for an Islamic Philosophy of Science', *Cambridge Muslim College Papers*, no. 4.

———, '*Daqīq al-Kalām*: The Islamic Approach to Natural Philosophy', Islamic Philosophy Online, http://www.muslimphilosophy.com/ip/Altaie-Lecture2.pdf, accessed February 15, 2015.

Asad, Muhammad, *The Message of the Qur'an*, Gibraltar: Dar al-Andalus, 1964.

Ashʿarī, Abū al-Ḥasan al-, *Kitāb al-lumaʿ fī al-radd ʿalā Ahl al-Zaygh wa'l-Bidaʿ*, ed. and trans. Richard Joseph McCarthy, Beirut: al-Maktaba al-Kāthūlīkiyya, 1952.

Ayten, Ali, *Din Psikolojisi* [Psychology of Religion], Istanbul: İz Yayıncılık, 2010.

———, *Erdeme Dönüş* [Returning to Virtues], Istanbul: İz Yayıncılık, 2014.

Azami, M. M. al-, *The History of the Qur'anic Text from Revelation to Compilation*, Leicester: Islamic Academy, 2003.

Badham, Paul and Linda Badham, eds., *Death and Immortality in the Religions of the World*, New York: Paragon House, 1987.

Barker, Gregory A. and Stephen E. Gregg, eds., *Jesus beyond Christianity*, Oxford: Oxford University Press, 2010.

Başaran, Yasin Ramazan, 'The Idea of Subjective Faith in al-Maturidi's Theology', *Journal of Islamic Research*, vol. IV, no. 2, December 2011, pp. 167–70.

Basit, Abdul, *The Global Muslim Community at a Crossroads*, Santa Barbara, CA: Praeger, 2012.

Berenbaum, Michael and Fred Skolnik, eds., *Encyclopaedia Judaica*, Detroit: Macmillan Reference USA, 2007.

Berkey, Jonathan P., *Popular Preaching and Religious Authority in the Medieval Islamic Near East*, Seattle: University of Washington Press, 2001.

Berzin, Alexander, 'Historical Sketch of Buddhism and Islam in Afghanistan', Berzin Archives, November 2001 (revised December 2006), http://www.berzinarchives.com/web/en/archives/study/history_buddhism/buddhism_central_asia/history_afghanistan_buddhism.html, accessed August 15, 2014.

———, 'Historical Survey of the Buddhist and Muslim Worlds' Knowledge of Each Other's Customs and Teachings', Berzin Archives, August 2009, http://www.berzinarchives.com/web/en/archives/study/islam/general/historical_survey_knowledge.html, accessed 22 February 2016.

Bhat, Abdur Rashid, 'Free Will and Determinism: An Overview of Muslim Scholars' Perspective', *Journal of Islamic Philosophy*, vol. II, no. 1, 2006, pp. 7–24.

Bīrūnī, Muḥammad b. Aḥmad al-, *Tārīkh al-Hind*, trans. Edward C. Sachau as *Alberuni's India*, 2 vols., Delhi: Low Price Publications, 2003.

Böwering, Gerhard, ed., *The Princeton Encyclopedia of Islamic Political Thought*, Princeton: Princeton University Press, 2013.

Braude, William G., *The Midrash on Psalms*, New Haven, CT: Yale University Press, 1959.

Brockopp, Jonathan E., *Islamic Ethics of Life: Abortion, War, and Euthanasia*, Columbia: University of South Carolina Press, 2003.

Brown, Norman O., 'The Apocalypse of Islam', *Social Text*, vol. VIII, Winter 1983–84, pp. 155–71.

Bucaille, Maurice, *The Bible, the Qur'an, and Science: The Holy Scripture Examined in the Light of Modern Science*, trans. Alistair D. Pannell, Indianapolis, IN: American Trust, 1979.

Bulgen, Mehmet, 'Continuous Re-creation: From Kalam Atomism to Contemporary Cosmology', *Kalam: Journal of Islamic Theology*, vol. I, 2015, pp. 57—64.

———, *Kelam Atomculuğu ve Modern Kozmoloji*, Ankara: TDV, 2005.

———, *Kalām Atomism and Modern Cosmology*, Dubai: Kelam Research Media, forthcoming.

———, 'The Relevance of Quantum Physics to Kalam Atomism', in Cemaleddin Erdemci and Fadil Aygan, eds., *International Imam al-Ashʿari and Ashʿarites Symposium (21–23 September 2014)*, Istanbul: Beyan Press, 2015, pp. 381–94.

Burge, S. R., 'Angels in Islam: A Commentary with Selected Translations of Jalāl al-Dīn al-Suyūṭī's *Al-Ḥabā'ik fī akhbār al-malā'ik* (The Arrangement of the Traditions about Angels)', Ph.D. thesis, University of Edinburgh, 2009.

Burkett, Delbert Royce, *An Introduction to the New Testament and the Origins of Christianity*, Cambridge: Cambridge University Press, 2002.

Calder, Norman, Jawid Mojaddedi and Andrew Rippin, eds., *Classical Islam: A Sourcebook of Religious Literature,* London: Routledge, 2012.

Calverley, Edwin E. and James P. Pollock, eds., *Nature, Man and God in Medieval Islam*, Leiden: E. J. Brill, 2002.

Campanini, Massimo, *An Introduction to Islamic Philosophy*, Rome: Eulama Literary Agency, 2008.

Campbell, Joseph Keim, Michael O'Rourke and David Shier, eds., *Free Will and Determinism*, Cambridge, MA: MIT Press, 2004.
Ceric, Mustafa, *Roots of Synthetic Theology in Islam: A Study of the Theology of Abu Mansur Al-Maturidi (d. 333/944)*, Kuala Lumpur: International Institute of Islamic Thought and Civilization, 1995.
Ceylan, Yasin, *Theology and Tafsīr in the Major Works of Fakhr al-Dīn al-Rāzī*, Kuala Lumpur: International Institute of Islamic Thought and Civilization, 1996.
Cohn-Sherbok, Dan and Christopher Lewis, *Beyond Death: Theological and Philosophical Reflections of Life after Death*, Basingstoke: Palgrave Macmillan, 1995.
Cornell, Vincent J., ed., *Voices of Islam*, London: Praeger Publishers, 2006.
Cragg, K., *The Call of the Minaret*, New York: Oxford University Press, 1956.
Danner, Victor, *The Islamic Tradition: An Introduction*, New York: Amity House, 1988.
Davies, Noel and Martin Conway, *World Christianity in the 20th Century*, London: SCM Press, 2008.
D'Costa, Gavin, *Christianity and World Religions: Disputed Questions in the Theology of Religions*, Chichester: John Wiley and Sons, 2009.
Eaton, Gai, *Islam and the Destiny of Man*, Cambridge: The Islamic Texts Society, 1994.
———, *Remembering God*, Cambridge: The Islamic Texts Society, 2000.
Elder, Earl E., ed. and tr., *A Commentary on the Creed of Islam: Saʿd al-Dīn al-Taftāzānī on the Creed of Najm al-Dīn al-Nasafī*, New York: Columbia University Press, 1950.
Emerick, Yahiya, *The Complete Idiot's Guide to Understanding Islam*, ALPHA: A Pearson Education Company, 2002.
Encyclopaedia of Islam, 2nd ed. (*EI²*), 12 vols., Leiden: E. J. Brill, 1960–2005.
Esposito, John L., *Islam: The Straight Path*, New York/Oxford: Oxford University Press, 1998.
———, *The Oxford Dictionary of Islam*, Oxford: Oxford University Press, 2003.
Fakhry, Majid, *A History of Islamic Philosophy*, 3rd ed., New York: Columbia University Press, 2004.
Faruqi, Ismail Raji al-, *Al Tawḥīd: Its Implications for Thought and Life*, Herndon, VA: International Institute of Islamic Thought, 1986.
Fischel, Walter Joseph, *Ibn Khaldūn in Egypt*, Berkeley: University of California Press, 1967.

Flew, Anthony, *The Question of God: An Introduction and Sourcebook*, London: Routledge, 2001.

Friedmann, Yohanan, 'Medieval Muslim Views of Indian Religions', *Journal of the American Oriental Society*, vol. xcv (1975), pp. 214–21.

Gardner, W. R. W., *The Qur'anic Doctrine of God*, Colombo: Christian Literature Society of India, 1916.

Ghazālī, Abū Ḥāmid al-, *al-Maqṣad al-asnā fī sharḥ asmā' Allāh al-ḥusnā*, trans. David B. Burrell and Nazih Daher as *The Ninety-Nine Beautiful Names of God*, Cambridge: The Islamic Text Society, 1992.

———, *Kitāb dhikr al-mawt wa-mā baʿdahu*, trans. T. J. Winter as *The Remembrance of Death and the Afterlife: Book* XL *of The Revival of the Religious Sciences*, Cambridge: The Islamic Texts Society, 1989.

———, *Kitāb al-tawḥīd wa'l-tawakkul*, trans. David B. Burrell as *Faith in Divine Unity and Trust in Divine Providence*, *The Revival of the Religious Sciences*, Book xxxv, Louisville, KY: Fons Vitae, 2001.

———, *A Return to Purity in Creed*, Philadelphia: Lamp Post Productions, 2008.

———, *The Alchemy of Happiness*, trans. Claud Field, London: M. E. Sharpe, 1991.

Guénon, René, *The Reigns of Quantity and the Signs of the Times*, Hillsdale, NY: Sophia Perennial, 2004.

Hacınebioğlu, İsmail L., *Does God Exist? Logical Foundations of the Cosmological Argument*, Istanbul: İnsan Publications, 2008.

Ḥaddad, ʿAbdallāh b. ʿAlawī al-, *The Lives of Man*, trans. Mostafa al-Badawi and ed. T. J. Winter, Lousiville, KY: Fons Vitae and Quilliam Press, 1991.

Halverson, Jeffry R., *Theology and Creed in Sunni Islam: The Muslim Brotherhood, Ashʿarism and Political Sunnism*, New York: Palgrave Macmillan, 2010.

Hamidullah, Muhammad, *Introduction to Islam*, London: MWH Publishers, 1979.

Hancock, Angela Dienhart, *Karl Barth's Emergency Homiletic, 1932–1933: A Summons to Prophetic Witness at the Dawn of the Third Reich*, Cambridge: Wm. B. Eerdmans Publishing, 2013.

Haneef, Suzanne, *What Everyone Should Know About Islam and Muslims*, Lahore: Kazi Publications, 1979.

Harries, Richard, Norman Solomon and Timothy Winter, eds., *Abraham's Children: Jews, Christians and Muslims in Conversation*, London: T & T Clark International, 2006.

Harrison, Victoria S., *Religion and Modern Thought*, London: SCM Press, 2012.

Haykal, Muhammad Husayn, *The Life of Muhammad*, Kuala Lumpur: Islamic Book Trust, 1994.

Hergenhahn, B. R., *An Introduction to the History of Psychology*, London: Cengage Learning, 2009.

Hussain, Amjad M., *A Social History of Muslim Education: From the Prophet's Period to Ottoman Times*, London: Ta-Ha Publishers, 2013.

———, 'Jesus in Islam: The Classic Texts', in Gregory A. Barker and Stephen E. Gregg, eds., *Jesus Beyond Christianity*, Oxford: Oxford University Press, 2010.

Ibn al-ʿArabī, Muḥyī al-Dīn, *Fuṣūṣ al-ḥikam*, trans. R. J. Austin as *Ibn al'Arabi: The Bezels of Wisdom*, London: SPCK, 1980.

Ibn al-Jawzī, *Kitāb al-quṣṣāṣ wa'l-mudhakkirīn*, ed. and trans. Merlin S. Swartz, Beirut: Dār al-Mashriq, 1986.

Ibn Fūrak, Abū Bakr Muḥammad b. al-Ḥasan, *Mujarrad maqālāt al-Shaykh Abī al-Ḥasan al-Ashʿarī*, ed. Daniel Gimaret, Beirut: Dār al-Mashriq, 1987.

Ibn Kamāl Pāshā, Shams al-Dīn Aḥmad b. Sulaymān, 'The Disagreements between the Ashʿarīs and Māturīdīs', http://marifah.net/articles/disagreementsbetweenasharisandmaturidis-ibnkamalbasha.PDF accessed 15 August 2014.

Ibn Khaldūn, *The Muqaddimah: An Introduction to History*, ed. and trans. Franz Rosenthal, Princeton, NJ: Princeton University Press, 1967.

Ibn al-Nafīs, *Theologus Autodidactus*, ed. M. Meyerhof and Joseph Schacht, Oxford: Oxford University Press, 1968.

Ibn al-Naqīb al-Miṣrī, Aḥmad, ʿUmdat al-sālik wa-ʿuddat al-nāsik, trans. Nuh Ha Mim Keller as *Reliance of the Traveller: A Classic Manual of Islamic Sacred Law*, Beltsville, MD: Amana Publications, 1991.

Ibn Qayyim al-Jawziyya, *Kitāb al-rūḥ*, ed. and trans. Layla Mabrouk as *The Soul's Journey after Death*, http://ia600409.us.archive.org/6/items/KitabAlRuhSummary-IbnAlQayyim/23713846-The-Souls-Journey-After-Death.pdf.

Ibn Ṭufayl, *Ibn Tufayl's Hayy Ibn Yaqzan: A Philosophical Tale*, trans. Lenn Evan Goodman, Chicago: University of Chicago Press, 2009.

Inglis, John, *Medieval Philosophy and the Classical Tradition: In Islam, Judaism and Christianity*, London: Routledge Curzon, 2005.

Izutsu, Toshihiko, *The Concept of Belief in Islamic Theology*, New York: Arno Press, 1980.

Jazā'irī, ʿAbd al-Qādir al-, 'Chess and the Divine Decree', trans. Hamza

Yusuf, *Seasons: The Journal of the Zaytuna Institute*, vol. III, no. 1, spring 2006, pp. 16–17, http://www.scribd.com/doc/24300197/Chess-and-the-Divine-Decree-Jaza-Iri, accessed August 1, 2013.

Jeffery, A., 'Al-Biruni's Contribution to Comparative Religion', in *Al-Biruni: Commemoration Volume*, Calcutta: Iran Society, 1951, pp. 125–60.

Jones, Lindsay, ed., *Encyclopedia of Religion*, 2nd ed., Detroit: Macmillan Reference USA, 2005.

Judd, Steven, 'Were the Umayyad-Era Qadarites Kāfirs?', in Camilla Adang et al., eds., *Accusations of Unbelief in Islam: A Diachronic Perspective on Takfīr*, Leiden: Brill, 2016, pp. 42–55.

Juwaynī, Imām al-Ḥaramayn al-, *A Guide to Conclusive Proofs for the Principles of Belief*, trans. Paul E. Walker, Qatar: Garnet Publishing, 2000.

Kamali, Mohammad Hashim, 'Causality and Divine Action: The Islamic Perspective', http://www.ghazali.org/articles/kamali.htm, accessed July 10, 2013.

Kapic, Kelly M. and Bruce L. Mccormack, *Mapping Modern Theology: A Thematic and Historical Introduction*, Grand Rapids, MI: Baker Books, 2012.

Keller, Nuh, 'Ashari and Maturidi School of Islamic Belief', Reflections of a Traveler [blog], February 3, 2007, https://baraka.wordpress.com/2007/02/03/ashari-and-maturidi-school-of-islamic-belief/, accessed August 15, 2014.

———, 'Kalam and Islam: Traditional Theology and the Future of Islam', lecture, Aal al-Bayt Institute of Islamic Thought, Amman, Jordan, January 4, 2005; text archived at http://masud.co.uk/kalam-and-islam/, accessed January 5, 2016.

Kelly, Henry A., *Satan: A Biography*, Cambridge: Cambridge University Press, 2006.

Khalidi, Tarif, *Images of Muhammad*, New York: Doubleday, 2009.

Khalil, Mohammad Hassan, *Between Heaven and Hell: Islam, Salvation, and the Fate of Others*, Oxford: Oxford University Press, 2013.

Khan, Arshad, *Islam, Muslims and America*, New York: Algora Publishing, 2003.

Khan, M. S., 'A Twelfth Century Arab Account of Indian Religions and Sects', *Arabica*, vol. XXX, no. 2, Jun. 1983, pp. 199–208.

Kishk, Abdu'l-Hamid, *The World of the Angels*, London: Dār al-Taqwa, 1994.

Latief, Hilman, 'Comparative Religion in Medieval Muslim Literature', *American Journal of Islamic Social Sciences*, vol. XXIII, no. 4, Fall 2006, pp. 28–62.

Lawrence, Bruce B., 'Shahrastānī on Indian Idol Worship', *Studia Islamica*, vol. XXXVIII, 1973, pp. 61–73.

———, *Shahrastānī on the Indian Religions*, The Hague: Mouton, 1976.

Leaman, Oliver, ed., *The Qur'an: An Encyclopedia*, London: Routledge, 2006.

Legenhausen, Muhammad, *Contemporary Topics of Islamic Thought*, Tehran: Alhoda Publishers, 2000.

Lings, Martin, *Muhammad: His Life Based on the Earliest Sources*, Cambridge: The Islamic Texts Society, 1991.

MacDonald, Duncan Black, *Development of Muslim Theology, Jurisprudence, and Constitutional Theory*, New York: Charles Scribner, 1903.

Madelung, W., *Religious Schools and Sects in Medieval Islam*, London: Variorum Reprints, 1985.

Maqsood, Ruqaiyyah Waris, *Teach Yourself Islam*, 3rd ed., Chicago: McGraw-Hill, 2006.

Martin, Richard C., ed., *Encyclopedia of Islam and the Muslim World*, New York: Macmillan Reference USA, 2004.

Mattson, Ingrid, *The Story of the Qur'an: Its History and Place in Muslim Life*, Oxford: Blackwell Publishing, 2008.

Māturīdī, Abū Manṣūr Muḥammad b. Muḥammad, *Kitāb al-tawḥīd*, ed. Fatḥ Allāh Khulayf, Beirut: Dār al-Mashriq, 1970.

Māwardī, ʿAlī b. Muḥammad b. Ḥabīb al-, *al-Aḥkām al-sulṭāniyya wa'l-wilāyāt al-dīniyya*, trans. Wafaa H. Wahba as *The Ordinances of Government*, London: Garnet Publishing, 2000.

Mayer, Toby, 'Ibn Sīnā's "Burhān al-Ṣiddīqīn"', *Journal of Islamic Studies*, vol. XII, no. 1, 2001, pp. 18–39.

McCloud, Aminah Beverly, Scott W. Hibbard and Laith Saud, *An Introduction to Islam in the 21st Century*, Oxford: Blackwell Publishing, 2013.

McGrath, Alister E., *Christian Theology: An Introduction*, 2nd ed., Oxford: Blackwell Publishing, 1997.

———, *Theology: The Basics*, Oxford: Wiley-Blackwell, 2012.

Meijer, Roel, *Global Salafism: Islam's New Religious Movement*, Oxford: Oxford University Press, 2009.

Metzger, Bruce M., and Michael Coogan, *The Oxford Companion to the Bible*, New York: Oxford University Press, 1993.

Minorsky, V., 'Gardīzī on India', *Bulletin of the School of Oriental and African Studies*, vol. XII, no. 3–4, 1948, pp. 625–40.

Morewedge, Parwiz, ed., *Islamic Philosophical Theology*, Albany: State University of New York Press, 1979.

Murata, Sachiko, *The Tao of Islam*, Albany: State University of New York Press, 1992.

Murata, Sachiko and William C. Chittick, *The Vision of Islam*, London: I. B. Tauris, 1996.

Nadvī, Sulaymān, *Sirat ul Nabi*, trans. Mohammad Saeed Siddiqui, New Delhi: Kitab Bhavan India, 2004.

Nasafī, Najm al-Dīn Abū Ḥafṣ ʿUmar b. Muḥammad b. Aḥmad al-, 'The Nasafī Creed', trans. Tahir Mahmood Kiani, http://marifah.net/articles/matnalnasafiyya.pdf, accessed 29 March 2013.

Nasr, Seyyed Hossein, *A Young Muslim's Guide to the Modern World*, Cambridge: Islamic Texts Society, 1993.

———, ed., *Islamic Spirituality: Foundations*, London: Routledge and Kegan Paul, 1987.

———, ed., *Islamic Spirituality: Manifestations*, New York: SCM Press, 1991.

———, *Traditional Islam in the Modern World*, London: Kegan Paul International, 1987.

———, *Ideals and Realities of Islam*, Cambridge: The Islamic Texts Society, 2001.

Nasution, Harun, 'The Place of Reason in ʿAbduh's Theology: Its Impact on His Theological System and Views', Ph.D. thesis, McGill University, 1968.

Nelson, K., *The Art of Reciting the Qur'an*, Cairo: American University in Cairo Press, 2001.

Nesbitt, Eleanor, and Gopinder Kaur, *Guru Nanak*, Calgary: Bayeux Arts, 1999.

New World Encyclopedia contributors, *New World Encyclopedia*, http://www.newworldencyclopedia.org/, accessed 8 March 2016.

Nicholi, Armand M., *C. S. Lewis and Sigmund Freud Debate God, Love, Sex, and the Meaning of Life*, New York: Free Press, 2003.

Noegel, S. B. and B. M. Wheeler, *The A to Z of Prophets in Islam and Judaism*, Lanham: Scarecrow Press, 2010.

Nuʿmānī, Shiblī and Sulaymān Nadvī, *Sīrat al-Nabī* [in Urdu], Lahore: Maktaba Tamir-i-Insaniat, 1975.

Nursi, Bediüzzaman Said, *The Words: Risale-i Nur*, Ankara: İhlâs Nur Neşriyat, 2001.

Nyazee, Imran, *Theories of Islamic Law*, Islamabad: Islamic Research Institute, 1991.

Obayashi, Hiroshi, ed., *Death and Afterlife: Perspectives of World Religions*, New York: Greenwood Press, 1992.

Obuse, Kieko, 'The Muslim Doctrine of Prophethood in the Context of Buddhist-Muslim Relations in Japan: Is the Buddha a Prophet?', *Muslim World*, vol. C, no. 2–3, April/July 2010, pp. 215–32.

O'Neill, Maura, *Women Speaking, Women Listening: Women in Interreligious Dialogue*, Maryknoll, NY: Orbis Books, 1990.

Pessagno, J. Meric, '*Irāda, Ikhtiyār, Qudra, Kasb*: The View of Abū Manṣūr al-Māturīdī', *Journal of the American Oriental Society*, vol. CIV, no. 1, January–March 1984, pp. 177–91.

———, 'The Uses of Evil in Maturidian Thought', *Studia Islamica,* vol. LX, 1984, pp. 59–82.

Pew Research Center, 'The World's Muslims: Unity and Diversity', report by Pew Forum on Religion and Public Life, August 9, 2012, http://www.pewforum.org/2012/08/09/the-worlds-muslims-unity-and-diversity-executive-summary/ accessed 17 May 2014.

Qadiri, K. H., *The Prophets of India*, Patna: Khuda Bakhsh Oriental Public Library, 1992.

Rahman, F., *Prophecy in Islam*, London: George Allen and Unwin, 1958.

Rahman, H. U., *A Chronology of Islamic History*, London: Mansell Publishing, 1989.

Ramadan, Tariq, *Western Muslims and the Future of Islam*, Oxford: Oxford University Press, 2005.

Ramli, Wan Adli Wan, 'A Critical Study of Liberal Interpretations of the Qur'an on the Concept of "Religious Pluralism"', Ph.D. thesis, University of Wales, Lampeter, 2011.

Rapaport, Samuel, ed., *Tales and Maxims from the Midrash*, London: Routledge, 1907, available online, http://www.sacred-texts.com/jud/tmm/index.htm, accessed February 20, 2016.

Rāzī, Fakhr al-Dīn al-, *al-Tafsīr al-kabīr*, [Cairo:] al-Maṭbaʿa al-Bahiyya al-Miṣriyya, [1357/1938].

———, *Tafsīr mafātiḥ al-ghayb / al-Tafsīr al-kabīr*, http://www.altafsir.com/Tafasir.asp?tMadhNo=0&tTafsirNo=4&tSoraNo=6&tAyahNo=102&tDisplay=yes&UserProfile=0&LanguageId=1, accessed: July 1, 2013.

Rippin, Andrew, *Muslims: Their Religious Beliefs and Practices*, New York: Routledge, 1990.

Roberts, J. M., *The Penguin History of the Twentieth Century: The History of the World, 1901 to the Present*, London: Penguin Books, 1999.

Robinson, Neil, *Islam: A Concise Introduction*, Richmond, Surrey: Curzon Press, 1999.

Rodwell, J., *The Koran*, [no place]: Everyman Library, 1994.
Rubin, Uri, *Between Bible and Qur'an: The Children of Israel and the Islamic Self-Image*, Princeton, NJ: Darwin Press, 1999.
Russell, Bertrand, 'Is There a God?' [1952] in *The Collected Papers of Bertrand Russell*, vol. XI: *Last Philosophical Testament, 1943–68*, ed. John C. Slater and Peter Köllner, London: Routledge, 1997, pp. 543–48.
Rustom, Mohammed, *The Triumph of Mercy: Philosophy and Scripture in Mulla Sadra*, Albany: State University of New York Press, 2012.
Sachedina, Abdulaziz Abdulhussein, *Islamic Messianism: The Idea of Mahdi in Twelver Shiʿism*, Albany: State University of New York Press, 1981.
Saeed, Abdullah, *Islamic Thought: An Introduction*, London: Routledge, 2010.
———, 'The Charge of Distortion of Jewish and Christian Scriptures', *Muslim World*, vol. XCII, Fall 2002, pp. 419–36.
———, *The Qur'an: An Introduction*, London: Routledge, 2008.
Schimmel, Annemarie, *And Muhammad Is His Messenger: The Veneration of the Prophet in Islamic Piety*, Chapel Hill: University of North Carolina Press, 1985.
———, *Deciphering the Signs of God*, Edinburgh: Edinburgh University Press, 1994.
———, *Islam: An Introduction*, Albany: State University of New York Press, 1992.
Schmidt, W., *The Origin and Growth of Religion: Facts and Theories*, New York: Cooper Square Publishers, 1972.
Schmidtke, Sabine, 'Theological Rationalism in the Medieval World of Islam', *al-ʿUṣūr al-Wusṭā*, vol. XX, no. 1, April 2008, pp.17–31.
Schultz, Walter J., and Lisanne D'Andrea Winslow, 'Divine Compositionalism: A Form of Occasionalism or a Preferable Alternative View of Divine Action?', paper presented at the Occasionalism East and West conference, Harvard University, May 4–5, 2013, http://occasionalism.org/wp-content/uploads/2012/11/SCHULTZ-WINSLOW-PAPER.pdf.
Segal, Eliezer, *Introducing Judaism*, London: Routledge, 2009.
Sell, Edward, *The Faith of Islam*, 2nd ed., London: Routledge, 2000.
Shah, Mustafa, 'Trajectories in the Development of Islamic Theological Thought: The Synthesis of Kalam', *Religion Compass*, vol. 1, no. 4, 2007, pp. 430–54.
Shah-Kazemi, Reza, *Common Ground between Islam and Buddhism*, Louisville, KY: Fons Vitae, 2010.

Shahrastānī, Muḥammad b. ʿAbd al-Karīm al-, *Muslims Sects and Divisions: The Section on Muslim Sects in* Kitāb al-milal wa'l-niḥal, trans. J. G. Flynn and A. K. Kazi, London: Kegan Paul International, 1984.

Shaked, Haim, *The Life of the Sudanese Mahdi*, London: Transaction Publishers, 2008.

Sharpe, Eric J., *Understanding Religion*, London: Bloomsbury Academic, 1997.

Shepard, William, *Introducing Islam*, 2nd ed., London and New York: Routledge, 2014.

Shepherd, John J., *Ninian Smart on World Religions*, Farnham, Surrey: Ashgate, 2009

Shibli, Nomani and Suleman, *Nadvi, Seerat-un-Nabi*, Lahore: Tamir-i-Insaniat, 1975.

Shihadeh, Ayman, *The Teleological Ethics of Fakhr al-Dīn al-Rāzī*, Leiden: Brill, 2006.

Shoshan, Boaz, *Popular Culture in Medieval Cairo*, Cambridge: Cambridge University Press, 1993.

Singer, Isidore, ed., *The Jewish Encyclopedia*, New York: Funk and Wagnalls, 1901–1906, available online, http://www.jewishencyclopedia.com/, accessed 20 February 2016.

Smarandache, Florentin and Salah Osman, *Neutrosophy in Arabic Philosophy*, Ann Arbor, MI: Renaissance High Press, 2007.

Smart, Ninian, *Dimensions of the Sacred: An Anatomy of the World's Beliefs*, Berkeley: University of California Press, 1999.

Smith Jane I., and Yvonne Y. Haddad, *The Islamic Understanding of Death and Resurrection*, Albany: State University of New York Press, 1981.

Smith, Wilfred Cantwell, *Islam in Modern History*, Princeton, NJ: Princeton University Press, 1957.

———, *On Understanding Islam: Selected Studies*, Berlin: Walter de Gruyter, 1981.

Stowasser, Barbara Freyer, *Women in the Qur'an, Traditions, and Interpretation*, Oxford: Oxford University Press, 1996.

Sweetman, J. Windrow, *Islam and Christian Theology*, London: Lutterworth Press, 1945.

Ṭabarī, Abū Jaʿfar Muḥammad b. Jarīr al-, *Tārīkh*, trans. Franz Rosenthal as *The History of al-Ṭabarī*, Albany: State University of New York Press, 1989.

Ṭaḥāwī, Abū Jaʿfar Aḥmad b. Muḥammad al-, *al-ʿAqīda al-Ṭaḥāwiyya*, trans. Hamza Yusuf as *The Creed of Imam al-Ṭaḥāwī*, New York: Zaytuna Institute, 2007.

Terzić, Faruk, 'The Problematic of Prophethood and Miracles: Mustafa Sabri's Response', *Islamic Studies,* vol. XLVIII, no. 1, Spring 2009, pp. 5–35.

Tymieniecka, Anna-Teresa and Nazif Muhtaroglu, eds., *Classic Issues in Islamic Philosophy and Theology Today*, London: Springer, 2010.

Ulrich, Rudolph, *Al-Māturīdī and the Development of Sunnī Theology in Samarqand*, Leiden: Brill, 2005.

Ünal, Ali, *The Resurrection and the Afterlife*, Istanbul: Tughra Books, 2000.

Usmani, Shabbir Aḥmad, tr., *The Noble Qur'an: Tafseer-e-Usmani*, New Delhi: Idara Isha'at-e-Diniyat, 1992.

Vasalou, Sophia, *Ibn Taymiyya's Theological Ethics*, Oxford: Oxford University Press, 2016.

Waardenburg, Jacques, *Muslim Perceptions of Other Religions*, New York: Oxford University Press, 1999.

Watt, William Montgomery, *Islamic Philosophy and Theology*, London: Aldine, 1962.

Wensinck, A. J., *The Muslim Creed*, Cambridge: Cambridge University Press, 1932.

Wheeler, Brannon, ed., *Teaching Islam*, Oxford: Oxford University Press, 2002.

Williams, Elaine, 'It's the Way He Tells Them', *Times Higher Education*, December 19, 1997, http://www.timeshighereducation.co.uk/story.asp?storyCode=105068&sectioncode=26, accessed 2 December 2008.

Winter, T. J., 'Islam, Irigaray, and the Retrieval of Gender', April 1999, http://www.masud.co.uk/ISLAM/ahm/gender.htm.

———, 'Jesus and Muḥammad: New Convergences', *Muslim World*, vol. XCIX, no. 1, January 2009, pp. 21–39.

———, ed., *The Cambridge Companion to Classical Islamic Theology*, Cambridge: Cambridge University Press, 2008.

Ya'ocov, Yehoiakin Ben, *Concepts of Messiah: A Study of the Messianic Concepts of Islam, Judaism, Messianic Judaism and Christianity*, Bloomington, IN: West Bow Press, 2012.

Yaran, Cafer S., *Islamic Thought on the Existence of God*, Washington, DC: Council for Research in Values and Philosophy, 2003.

———, *Understanding Islam*, Edinburgh: Dunedin Academic Press, 2007.

Yusuf, Hamza, *Purification of the Heart: Translation and Commentary of Imam al-Mawlud's* Matharat al-Qulub, [no place]: Starlatch Books, 2004.

Yusuf, Imtiyaz, 'Islam and Buddhism Relations from Balkh to Bangkok and Tokyo', *Muslim World*, vol. C, no. 2–3, April/July 2010, pp. 177–86.

INDEX

Aaron, 92, 110, 127, 134–5, 144, 164, 168
Aasi, Ghulam Haider, 162, 165
Abbasid period, 19, 20, 149, 150, 153, 178, 182; theological debate, 29
ʿAbd Allāh b. al-ʿAbbās, 187
ʿAbd Allāh b. ʿAmr b. al-ʿĀṣ, 189
ʿAbd Allāh b. Salam, 189, 190
ʿAbd Allāh b. ʿUmar, 189
ʿAbd al-Jabbār, Abū al-Ḥasan, 184
ʿAbd al-Malik, Caliph, 248
Abdel Haleem, Muḥammad, 199, 210
Abduh, Muḥammad, 192, 270–1
Abraham, 62, 90, 92; Feast of Sacrifice, 132–3; *Ḥadīth*, 131, 132; Hebrew Bible, 131, 132; prophet and messenger, 110, 125–6, 127, 131–4; Qur'ān, 131, 132, 133–4; *Ṣuḥuf Ibrāhīm*, 164
Abrahamic religions, 6, 125–6, 127; different concept of God in, 44–50; see Christianity; Islam; Judaism
Abū Bakr al-Ṣiddīq, 16, 92, 176–7
Abū Ḥanīfa, 28, 32–3, 124; *al-Fiqh al-akbar*, 1n, 124; Murji'ism, 21–2; see also Ḥanafī school of law
Abū Hurayra, 119–20, 189
Abū Rayya, Maḥmūd, 192
Abū Yūsuf, 28, 33
ʿadāla, see divine justice
Adam, 3, 92; angels and, 102; creation of, 89, 98, 202, 203, 206; exile from the Garden, 130, 202, 203–204; *ḥadīth*, 98; Iblīs, 98, 99, 100; the primordial prophet, 109, 110, 111, 112, 130; prophet and messenger, 110, 112; Qur'ān, 130
al-Afghānī, Jamāl al-Dīn, 267–8, 270, 271
Afterlife, see Hereafter
Aga Khan, 20
agnosticism, 58, 193, 281, 292
Ahl al-dhimma, see 'protected people'
Ahl al-Kitāb, see People of the Book
Ahl al-Sunna wa'l-Jamāʿa, see Sunni Islam
Aḥmad b. ʿAbd Allāh, Muḥammad, 226
Aḥmad Khan, Sir Seyyed, 97, 271
Aḥmad, Mīrzā Ghulām, 227
the Aḥmadiyya, 127, 227
ʿĀ'isha bint Abī Bakr, 17, 22, 98, 161
Ākhira, see Hereafter
ʿAlawīs, 77n
ʿAlī b. Abī Ṭālib, 16–18, 21, 22, 53, 76, 226; death, 19
ʿAlī, Amīr, 271
Ali, Yusuf, 51
al-ʿAllāf, Abū Hudhayl Muḥammad, 71, 251–2
Altaie, Mohammed Basil, 294
ʿAmr b. ʿUbaid, 25
Angel of Death (ʿAzrā'īl/ʿIzrā'īl), 86, 87, 203, 214, 230
angels, 86–8, 102, 107, 235; Adam, 102; Battle of Badr, 93; belief in (article of faith), 2, 5, 6, 9, 35–6, 84–5 (*risāla*, *nubuwwa*, 6, 199–200); belief in angels as outdated, 83–4; cosmos, 89; creation of, 87, 89, 98, 101; al-Ghazālī, Abū Ḥāmid, 88, 103; *ḥadīth*, 85, 87, 88, 90, 98, 103; human beings/angels differ-